EVERYDAY FORMS OF PEASANT RESISTANCE

Written under the auspices of the
Center of International Studies, Princeton University

EVERYDAY FORMS OF PEASANT RESISTANCE

Edited by

FORREST D. COLBURN

M. E. Sharpe, Inc.
ARMONK, NEW YORK
LONDON, ENGLAND

Available in the United Kingdom and Europe from M. E. Sharpe,
Publishers, 3 Henrietta Street, London WC2E 8LU.

Library of Congress Cataloging-in-Publication Data

Everyday forms of peasant resistance / edited by Forrest D. Colburn.
      p.   cm.
  Bibliography: p.
  Includes index.
  ISBN 0-87332-575-3—ISBN 0-87332-622-9 (pbk.)
  1. Opposition (Political science)—Case studies. 2. Peasantry—Case
studies. 3. Rural poor—Case studies. I. Colburn, Forrest D.
JC328.3.E94   1989   89-10143
305.5′633—dc20   CIP

Printed in the United States of America

BB 10 9 8 7 6 5 4 3 2 1

CONTENTS

List of Contributors   vii

Introduction   ix
Forrest D. Colburn

1. Everyday Forms of Resistance
James C. Scott   3

**2. Between Submission and Violence: Peasant Resistance in
the Polish Manorial Economy of the Eighteenth Century**
Jacek Kochanowicz   34

**3. Saboteurs in the Forest: Colonialism and Peasant
Resistance in the Indian Himalaya**
Ramachandra Guha   64

**4. The Conspiracy of Silence and the Atomistic Political
Activity of the Egyptian Peasantry, 1882–1952**
Nathan Brown   93

**5. Class, Gender, and Peasant Resistance
in Central Colombia, 1900–1930**
Michael F. Jiménez   122

**6. Struggling Over Land in China: Peasant Resistance
after Collectivization, 1966–1986**
David Zweig   151

7. Foot Dragging and Other Peasant Responses to the Nicaraguan Revolution
    Forrest D. Colburn   175

8. How the Weak Succeed: Tactics, Political Goods, and Institutions in the Struggle over Land in Zimbabwe
    Jeffrey Herbst   198

Commentary
    Milton J. Esman   221

Index   229

LIST OF CONTRIBUTORS

Nathan Brown, Department of Political Science,
George Washington University

Forrest D. Colburn, Department of Politics,
Princeton University

Milton J. Esman, Department of Government,
Cornell University

Ramachandra Guha, Center for Ecological Science,
Indian Institute of Science

Jeffrey Herbst, Department of Politics,
Princeton University

Michael F. Jiménez, Department of History,
Princeton University

Jacek Kochanowicz, Department of Economics,
Warsaw University

James C. Scott, Department of Political Science,
Yale University

David Zweig, Fletcher School of Law and Diplomacy,
Tufts University

Introduction

Forrest D. Colburn

This volume inquires into how the rural poor, still the majority in the world, defend themselves against the predations of politics.

For the sake of convenience the rural poor are described as peasants. Numerous discussions about what constitutes a peasant remain inconclusive. At times it is important to acknowledge the heterogeneity of the rural poor. Not so here. Thus the definition adopted is broad, with only two easily satisfied characteristics: (1) the peasant works in agriculture, and (2) he or she has a subordinate position in a hierarchical economic and political order.

The central argument advanced about peasant political behavior appears in the opening chapter by James Scott. He summarizes and extends the thesis of *Weapons of the Weak*,[1] his book about the peasantry in a small corner of Malaysia. Scott argues that peasant rebellions are few and far between. Instead, it is more enlightening to understand what can be called everyday forms of peasant resistance: foot dragging, dissimulation, feigned ignorance, false compliance, manipulation, flight, slander, theft, arson, sabotage, and isolated incidents of violence, including murder, passed off as crime. These forms of struggle stop well short of outright collective defiance, a strategy usually suicidal for the weak. While these kinds of resistance are often a form of individual protection or self-help, they are not trivial. They limit the imperial aspirations of lords, monarchs, colonialists, nationalist parties, and dictatorships of the proletariat.

The clever and finely tuned employment of everyday forms of resis-

Helpful comments on earlier drafts were provided by Henry Bienen, Michael Jiménez, James Scott, and Norman Uphoff.

tance is made possible by peasants challenging the dominant ideology. The poor refuse to accept the proffered rationalization for their subordination. Implicit in this challenge is the development of the peasants' own view of their social, political, and economic setting, a view as likely as not reinforced by their slang, symbols, and analogies. Peasants' interpretation of their condition, and their "private transcript," facilitates the minimum cooperation necessary to succeed in everyday forms of resistance. Most important is simply a conspiracy of silence. For Scott the absence of revolt stems not from the hegemony of a dominant ideology (or its obverse, the "false consciousness" of the poor), but from what Marx called the "dull compulsion of economic relations." Given their precarious situation, peasants find the public challenge of the dominant ideology and those who stand behind it imprudent. But they do work the system to their maximum advantage (or minimum disadvantage, per Hobsbawm), ever testing the limits of the possible.

Everyday forms of peasant resistance have three general consequences. First, advantages secured by peasants enhance their welfare. Whether it be a poached rabbit that provides a hearty stew or desertion from an ill-fated army that saves a life, commonplace resistance assists those who all too often live close to the margin of survival. Second, the cumulation of peasants' evasionary tactics can erode away unpopular customs, laws, government policies, or, in the extreme, a regime itself. Third, practices of resistance and off-stage discourse can lay the groundwork for more overt political activity once the constellation of forces moves to the previously weak peasants' favor.

Scott's portrait of everyday forms of peasant resistance is followed by specific studies of the phenomenon in seven countries. By design, the cases vary not only geographically but also temporally. Some are historical analyses while others are contemporary treatments. The universe of cases is also distinguished by discussions of both capitalist and socialist regimes. All too often these regimes are discussed in isolation from one another, a separation resulting in ideological parochialism and, more generally, a failure to distinguish what is peculiar to a given type of political regime and what prevails commonly across the political spectrum.

The opening case study is by Jacek Kochanowicz, an economic historian at the University of Warsaw. He explores the evolution of Poland's manorial economy in the eighteenth century. A variety of modes of peasant resistance is exposed, including cunning ways by which losses are passed on to lords. Kochanowicz's lengthy time frame enables him to suggest propositions about how the viability of different kinds of peasant responses are determined by geographic, demographic, and institutional variables. The chapter shows the persuasiveness and richness of Scott's theory in a setting distinct from contemporary Malaysia and suggests that far-reaching changes in the strength and configuration of peasant resistance are likely to be determined by powerful structural variables neither of the peasants' nor lords' making.

Ramachandra Guha draws on archival sources to document peasant resistance to British colonialism in the forest zone of northern India. His essay views the weapons of the weak as a dynamic sequence of peasants' responses to perceived injustice. Guha's essay is of special interest because he gives serious attention to the relationship between everyday forms of protest and a range of "avoidance" protest tactics, including techniques like arson, that shade into a more confrontational mode of response. It is shown convincingly that what the authorities regarded as criminal activities were genuine expressions of social protest. Finally, Guha underscores Scott's conviction that unorganized and anonymous incidents of peasants' resistance have a historical impact—longstanding forms of peasants' resistance prove to be linked to Indian nationalist agitation.

Nathan Brown takes on, even more boldly, the difficult issue of the boundary between protest and criminal activity. His gripping account of the murder of Egyptian landlords by peasants suggests that Scott's repertoire of the weak's weapons can be extended, even if doing so raises definitional questions. Individual incidents of violence can be called protest if there is limited self-aggrandizement, if the motives include "sending a message," and, most importantly, if escape is possible through a local conspiracy of silence. In such instances atomistic behavior appears collective. The assertion that violent crime can be judged an everyday form of resistance is enhanced by the response it evokes. The official pronouncement may be that murder is wanton violence, with the ruling employing the police rather than the army. Yet if members of the elite judge differently and calibrate their exactions accordingly, then the effect of crime is political.

Michael Jiménez's analysis of Colombia teases out the community and household dynamics of the predations of rural politics. Divisions among peasants, including prominently differences of sex, are exploited, and used to camouflage exactions and discourage protest. In more successful instances, wittingly or not, hostility engendered by exactions is simply deflated upon the family in general and upon women in particular. But, likewise, when peasant resistance is forthcoming it is subtly differentiated: members of the same household can have assorted antagonists and various resources to employ in the contest.

David Zweig's essay on China has a different but complementary agenda. Instead of exploring peasants' arsenal, or the household repercussions of domination and resistance, Zweig is concerned with how variations in the ruling order—which in China is simply the state—affect peasant response. He asserts that peasant resistance is shaped by the state's: (1) ideological cohesion, (2) organizational unity, and (3) coercive capacity. Peasants exploit any possible cracks in the hegemony that seeks to capture them. Understanding peasant resistance is thus only possible through a knowledge of what peasants confront. Both sides of the equation must be studied. Zweig's analysis suggests that outcomes are tempered by the behavior of local officials who, caught between "the upper and lower jaws," make compromises to ensure their own survival. Local corruption or collusion further complicates the silent battle between the dominant and the dominated.

The final two case studies, of Nicaragua and Zimbabwe, further explore the issue introduced by Zweig—the importance of state cohesion and strength in delineating the range and audacity of peasant resistance and, equally important, the effectiveness of resistance. Nicaragua's peasants have been able to gain considerable advantages from a weak state, unintentionally contributing to its further weakness. It is an ironic outcome because the Sandinista regime is nominally committed to the peasantry and has undertaken certain policies (agrarian reform in particular) to aid the peasantry at considerable political and economic cost. Yet the peasantry has interpreted its interests narrowly, taking whatever the state has to offer, gleaning whatever other advantages that can be had, and avoiding contributing to the state. The initial years of post-revolutionary Nicaragua suggest that peasant modes of everyday resistance are not just employed against opprobrious regimes. Instead, they are continuously employed to garner any possible benefit, seemingly regardless of the ideology or benevolence of the local government. This predilection poses vexatious problems for any revolutionary or reformist group expecting to check an erstwhile elite's backlash with a "worker-peasant alliance."

In Zimbabwe the state is weak not so much because it is overextended and besieged, but because it is riddled with cleavages. Peasants exploit the cleavages and, indeed, are encouraged to do so by opportunist politicians. State weakness becomes peasant strength. Jeffrey Herbst's analysis serves as a reminder that peasants are far from united or conscious of themselves as a class: groups gain not only at a cost to the state but also at each others' expense. The discussion closes with Herbst highlighting an easily overlooked determinant of the success of everyday forms of resistance—the properties of the contested benefit. In Zimbabwe, for example, peasants succeed in their struggle for access to land, in large measure, because it has a relatively low cost to the government, less so than goods which entail expenditures.

Together the case studies illuminate the variety of protest forms employed by seemingly mute and helpless peasants. And the consequences of prosaic resistance are explored. Scott's conceptualization of everyday forms of resistance is endorsed at the same time that nuances are teased out and propositions are advanced suggesting how the theory should be tempered or extended.

Contributors to the collection are bound not only by an adherence to Scott's thesis as a point of departure, but also by a commitment to empirical research rather than deductive theorizing. Rich and colorful detail is offered without apology. Theory is not eschewed, but propositions are advanced only when prompted by empirical observation. Most important and most controversial, the contributors share a skepticism of state-centric approaches to the study of the rural poor, regardless of the regime in question. Peasants' prosaic resistance and the *mentalités* that justify their behavior are most easily studied by adopting peasants—individually and collectively—as the unit of analysis. One can otherwise hardly enter a world so densely camouflaged. In articulating peasants' political behavior, however, it is difficult to present peasants as other than the protagonist. Conversely, lord and state assume the role of the antagonist. The contributors are writing as scholars, but they invariably present a normative position: they side with peasants.

For those in authority, everyday forms of peasant resistance are at best a nuisance and at worst a threat. For those sympathetic to the authorities, this collection is likely to be perceived as, to quote an Ethiopian scholar invited to participate in the endeavor, "a celebration of disgraceful peasant behavior."

Regimes do differ. Some have more legitimacy than others. Likewise, some are more committed to aiding the rural poor. Still, all regimes, but perhaps those most committed to reform, do confront difficult choices including, for example, the relative weight of investment versus consumption. The last two case studies in the volume, Nicaragua and Zimbabwe, discuss newly established regimes more committed to aiding the rural poor than their predecessors—the Somoza dynasty and the Rhodesian colonial state. Yet here too the peasantry quietly pursues its own interests regardless of the consequences to the incipient states.

If the notion of "false consciousness" is dismissed, it is difficult to criticize peasant attempts at self-protection as misguided or illegitimate. Elites, whether traditional, capitalist, or socialist, often set goals (or at least strategies to achieve goals) different than peasants. If peasants are conscious and rational decision makers, clear-cut benefits must be provided when they are asked to change their behavior—be it involvement in cooperatives, the adoption of agricultural innovations, or political mobilization. Benefits must of course be perceived as such; among other things, that involves consideration of the time horizon and the risk involved. Without any perceived individual benefits—economic or noneconomic—peasants are unlikely to hearken to appeals of traditional culture, nationalistic aspirations, or class revolution. A well-intentioned regime is not enough.

The advantages of eschewing a state-centered perspective are not limited to greater ease in studying peasants and appreciating their differences with the state. Such a tack also encourages an awareness of the multiple dimensions of political domination and resistance. The state is not the only counterpart to peasants. In certain instances and locales it may not even be the major counterpart. Peasants typically are besieged by representatives of numerous domains: ethnic, religious, economic, social, and cultural. For example, the Catholic priest can be as meddlesome as the Communist cadre. And the moneylender can be as ruinous as the tax collector. The treatment of Colombia in this volume emphasizes the importance of an issue that seems especially far afield from the state—gender. Peasants often have a lengthy and disparate list of adversaries, whom they confront with an equally disparate arsenal of weapons of the weak.

Just as care must be taken not to romanticize "peasant rebellions," so care must be taken not to exaggerate what everyday forms of resistance can accomplish. As persistent as peasants' prosaic resistance is, the case studies suggest that while the accomplishments of their resistance are not insignificant, it is hardly capable of changing peasants' impoverished and subordinate status. Equally disheartening is peasants' dismal evaluation of states scattered across the continuum of political systems. The variety of tactics obscures a basic continuity. Stubborn and irreducible forms of peasant resistance are seemingly the truly durable weapons of the weak, both before and after the revolution. The implicit pessimism about political change was aptly posed by Barrington Moore: "Just what does modernization mean for the peasant beyond the simple and brutal fact that sooner or later they are its victims?"[2]

While Moore's pessimism is understandable for a historian looking at peasants from afar, the rich evidence presented in this collection of essays serves as a reminder of the inexhaustible will to live, to prosper, and to multiply. The vagaries of life are appreciated. Peasants are anything but indifferent to the details of their harvests, communities, and government. Precisely because of this, peasants, by definition of a subordinate status, engage in persistent everyday forms of resistance. In the process of defending themselves as best they can, peasants also have an impact—unwitting, slow, and quiet as it may be—on elites and their endeavors. Peasants too are agents of historical change.

Notes

1. James Scott, *Weapons of the Weak: Everyday Forms of Peasant Resistance* (New Haven: Yale University Press, 1986).
2. Barrington Moore, Jr., *Social Origins of Dictatorship and Democracy* (Boston: Beacon Press, 1966), p. 467.

EVERYDAY FORMS OF PEASANT RESISTANCE

1

Everyday Forms
of Resistance

James C. Scott

A pestilent pernicious people . . . such as take the oaths
to the Government, but underhand . . . labor its subversion.
—Bishop Trelawny, 1717

Introduction

In the ordinary use of the term, "development" is an activity organized
from above by governments and international agencies. It aims at
enlightening, benefitting, and making more productive the citizens/
subjects for whom it is intended, although the definition of what is a
benefit, what is enlightening, and so on, is made also from above.
Liberal democrats have, for a long time, been active in promoting a
view of development that incorporates the values and goals of its intended beneficiaries. Hence, we hear terms like "participatory development," and "grass-roots initiatives," "decentralization." The
purpose of such efforts is to humanize development and to provide the
feedback that might prevent tragic and costly mistakes.

More radical observers, generally from the intelligentsia, find such
initiatives hopelessly compromised and reformist. At best, they argue,
"participatory development" in the context of structural inequalities
and authoritarian regimes leads to trivial gains: at worst it only im-
proves marginally the efficiency of a fundamentally repressive system.
Up to this point, I believe, there is something to be said for the radical
critique of development. The radical solution to this dilemma, however, raises as many problems as it solves. Only a revolutionary victory

and the structural change it brings, they argue, can engender true participation and economic justice. Here the history of socialist revolutions is not encouraging. In most cases such revolutions have brought to power regimes that are, if anything, more successful in extracting resources from their subjects and regimenting their lives. The tragedies of the Great Leap Forward in China, collectivization in the U.S.S.R., and state-directed agriculture in Vietnam are hardly encouraging examples of participatory development.

The problem with both the liberal-democratic and the radical view of development is, I believe, that neither is sufficiently radical. Both views concentrate on formal, open, political activity and on the role of elites—whether conservative officialdom or a revolutionary vanguard party. What they miss is the nearly continuous, informal, undeclared, disguised forms of autonomous resistance by lower classes: forms of politics that I call "everyday resistance." In the analysis that follows I attempt to describe and analyze this generally ignored form of political action.

The Hidden Realm of Political Conflict

Descriptions and analyses of open political action dominate accounts of political conflict. This is the case whether those accounts are presented by historians, political scientists, journalists, statesmen, or leaders of popular movements. Some of the most telling analyses of conflict are in fact designed precisely to explain under what circumstances groups in conflict resort to one or another kind of open political action. Thus why some groups under certain conditions are likely to employ violent forms of political action—e.g., riots, rebellion, and revolutionary movements—rather than less violent forms—e.g., petitions, rallies, peaceful marches, protest voting, strikes, and boycotts—has occupied center stage. As a result of careful historical comparisons, social scientists have begun to grasp how certain social structures, state systems, cultural values, and historical practices help shape political action.

The undeniable advances made along these lines, however, are fatally compromised by a damagingly narrow and poverty stricken view of political action. There is a vast realm of political action, described below, that is almost habitually overlooked. It is ignored for at least two reasons. First, it is neither declared openly in the usually understood sense of "politics." Second, nor is it group action in the way collective action is usually understood. The argument developed here is that much of the politics of subordinate groups falls into the category of everyday forms of resistance, that these activities should most definitely be considered political, that they do constitute a form of collective action, and that any account that ignores them is often ignoring the most vital means by which subordinate classes manifest their political interests. The balance of this essay is devoted to sustaining and elaborating this claim.

The Brechtian or Schweikian forms of resistance I have in mind are an integral part of the small arsenal of relatively powerless groups. They include such acts as foot dragging, dissimulation, false compliance, feigned ignorance, desertion, pilfering, smuggling, poaching, arson, slander, sabotage, surreptitious assault and murder, anonymous threats, and so on. These techniques, for the most part quite prosaic, are the ordinary means of class struggle. They are the techniques of "first resort" in those common historical circumstances where open defiance is impossible or entails mortal danger. When they are practiced widely by members of an entire class against elites or the state, they may have aggregate consequences out of all proportion to their banality when considered singly. No adequate account of class relations is possible without assessing their importance. That they have been absent or marginal to most accounts of class relations is all too understandable. The purpose of many such techniques, after all, is to avoid notice and detection. Resistance of this kind is, ironically, abetted by both elites and social scientists whose attention is largely concentrated on those forms of resistance that pose a declared threat to power-holders: social movements, dissident sects, revolutionary groups, and other forms of publicly organized political opposition. Such groups, of course, are also far more likely to leave the written records—manifestos, minutes, membership lists, journalists' descriptions, and police reports—that help ensure them a firm place in the historical record.

Here it may be useful to distinguish "everyday" forms of class resistance from the more typical forms of political conflict that dominate the historiography of the peasantry and other subordinate groups. The easiest way to highlight the distinction is to contrast paired forms of resistance. The first in each pair is everyday resistance in my definition of the term while the second is a more direct, open confrontation having the same objective. Thus in one sphere lies the quiet, piecemeal process by which peasant squatters or poachers have often encroached on plantation and state forest lands; in the other a public invasion of property that openly challenges property relations. Each action aims at a redistribution of control over property; the former aims at tacit, de facto gains while the latter aims at formal, de jure recognition of those gains. In one sphere lies a process of cascading military desertion; in the other an open mutiny aiming at eliminating or replacing officers. In one sphere lies the pilfering of public and private grain stores; in the other an open attack on markets or granaries aiming at the redistribution of the food supply. The contrasts illustrate that those who employ everyday forms of resistance avoid calling attention to themselves. Such techniques are relatively safe, they often promise vital material gains, and they require little or no *formal* coordination let alone formal organization—although they typically rely on a venerable popular culture of resistance to accomplish their ends.

In each of these paired comparisons, the presumed objective is similar. Both squatters and land invaders hope to acquire the use of property; both deserters and mutineers may wish to end a costly battle or war. The relative safety—and it is *only* a relative safety—of everyday forms of resistance has much to do with the small scale of the action. Squatters virtually seep onto the land in small groups, often at night, to avoid calling attention to themselves; deserters are likely to slip away unnoticed when the opportunity arises. Each of these small events may be beneath notice and, from the perpetrator's point of view, they are often designed to be beneath notice. Collectively, however, these small events may add up almost surreptitiously to a large event: an army too short of conscripts to fight, a workforce whose foot dragging bankrupts the enterprise, a landholding gentry driven from the countryside to the towns by arson and assault, tracts of state land fully occupied by squatters, a tax claim of the state gradually transformed into a dead letter by evasion.

It is not far-fetched to suggest that the difference between everyday forms of resistance and more open forms of political conflict may often boil down to tactical wisdom. Peasants who consider themselves entitled to land claimed by the state may choose to squat rather than to invade openly in force because they know that an invasion will probably be met with armed force and bloodshed. When, on the other hand, the political climate makes a more open occupation of land comparatively safe, as in the Zimbabwe case described in this volume, something closer to a land invasion becomes plausible. Certainly, peasants and subordinate groups generally may find large-scale collective action inherently difficult owing to their geographical dispersion, ethnic and linguistic differences, a lack of organizational skills and experience, and so forth. It is no less likely, however, that their preferences in techniques of resistance may arise from the knowledge of surveillance, a realistic fear of coercion, and a past experience that encourages caution. If, as is sometimes the case, the same results may be achieved by everyday resistance, albeit more slowly, at a vastly reduced risk, then it is surely the more rational course. The invariably fatal results of slave uprisings in the antebellum U.S. South suggest that the long-term slave preference for flight, pilfering, foot dragging, and false compliance was largely a matter of tactical wisdom.

A skeptic might grant the argument made thus far and nevertheless claim that everyday forms of resistance do not belong in an account of class struggle because they are individual, not class, strategies and because they benefit individuals not classes. The first claim is largely untenable. It can be shown that most forms of everyday resistance cannot be sustained without a fairly high level of tacit cooperation among the class of resisters. This will become more apparent in examples described later. The second claim is true, but the personal benefit arising from everyday forms of resistance—providing it does not come at the expense of other members of the class[1]—can hardly disqualify them from consideration as a form of class conflict. Most forms of everyday resistance are, after all, deployed precisely to thwart some appropriation by superior classes and/or the state. If the resistance succeeds at all, it of course confers a material benefit on the resister. The disposition of scarce resources is surely what is at stake in any conflict between classes. When it is a question of a few poachers, arsonists, or deserters, their actions are of little moment for class conflict. When, however, such activities become sufficiently generalized to become a *pattern* of resistance, their relevance to class conflict is clear.

Consider the following definition that focuses on the process of appropriation:

> Lower class resistance among peasants is any act(s) by member(s) of the class that is (are) intended either to mitigate or to deny claims (e.g. rents, taxes, deference) made on that class by superordinate classes (e.g. landlords, the state, owners of machinery, moneylenders) or to advance its own claims (e.g. to work, land, charity, respect) vis-a-vis these superordinate classes.[2]

Three aspects of the definition merit brief comment. First, there is no requirement that resistance take the form of collective action. And yet *some* level of cooperation is generally evident in everyday forms of resistance since even the slave who pilfers or shirks depends on the complicitous silence of other slaves to escape detection. The same is, of course, true for the poacher who believes he and others like him have a right to the fish, game, and fuel of the nearby forest. Each depends for his success on a minimal level of group cohesion. Second—and this is a nettlesome issue—intentions are built into the definition. This formulation allows for the fact that many intended acts of resistance may backfire and produce consequences that were entirely unanticipated. Finally, the definition recognizes what we might call symbolic or ideological resistance (for example, gossip, slander, the rejection of demeaning labels, the withdrawal of deference) as an integral part of class-based resistance. From a broader perspective this definition recognizes, as I believe any convincing definition must, the role that self-interested acts must play in any realistic definition of peasant resistance. To do so affirms the fact that class conflict is, first and foremost, a struggle over the appropriation of work, property, production, and taxes. Consumption, from this perspective, is both the goal and the outcome of resistance and counter-resistance.[3] Petty thefts of grain or pilfering on the threshing floor may seem like trivial "coping" mechanisms from one vantage point, but from a broader view of class relations, how the harvest is actually divided belongs at the center.

Varieties of Practice, Unity of Purpose

The various practices that might plausibly be claimed to represent everyday forms of resistance are legion. To an outside observer it might appear quixotic to assemble them under the same heading. Their variety is nothing more than a mirror image of the variety of forms of appropriation; for every form of appropriation there is likely to be one—or many—forms of everyday resistance devised to thwart that appropriation. What gives these techniques a certain unity is that they are invariably quiet, disguised, anonymous, often undeclared forms of resisting claims imposed by claimants who have superior access to force and to public power. A brief analysis of four forms of everyday resistance will help illustrate this unity as well as delineate more sharply the circumstances that favor such resistance, the results it may achieve, the disguises it wears, the complicity it requires, and its limits.

The examples are selected both for their representative diversity and for the complementary analytical light they shed on the phenomenon of everyday resistance.

Poaching

For roughly three centuries, from 1650 to 1850, the most popular crime in England was almost certainly poaching. Although poaching is usually understood to refer to the "theft" of someone else's property in wild game, fish, and perhaps firewood, it comprises a vastly greater range of practices. Cottagers, laborers, and yeomen might encroach on gentry or crown property to take turf, peat, heath, rushes for thatching and lighting, brushwood, clay, stone, chalk, coal, to graze their own livestock, to pick medicinal herbs, or to till land. Both the objects and volume of poaching varied over time in keeping with the proximity of "poachable" resources, how hard-pressed the rural population was, the need for certain commodities, the risks of being apprehended, the likely punishment if apprehended, and the traditions animating the local community.[4] The issue came to be of such concern to large landowners and the crown that in the eighteenth century, draconian laws were passed specifying capital punishment for poachers. More precisely, it became a capital offense merely to be caught in disguise (hence the name, the "Black" Act) in the woods, the assumption being that anyone so attired was a poacher.

For our purposes, the most important fact about poaching is that the activity itself was part of the traditional subsistence routine of the rural population, an activity embedded in customary rights. Poaching as a crime, therefore, entails less a change of behavior than a shift in the law of property relations. It is the state and its law which suddenly transforms these subsistence routines into everyday forms of resistance. The process has, of course, been repeated for most colonial societies in which the state redefined the forest as government property and then imposed a whole series of regulations and officials to enforce them. It was unlikely that the surrounding population would accept the logic by which unimproved, natural environments and their resources might suddenly be declared state property and willingly relinquish their traditional practices. Michel Foucault has, in the context of post-revolutionary French history called attention to such state-created "crime."

> It was against the new regime of landed property—set up by a bourgeoisie that profited from the Revolution—that a whole peas-

ant illegality developed . . . ; it was against the new system of the legal exploitation of labor that workers' illegalities developed; from the most violent such as machine breaking . . . to the most everyday such as absenteeism, abandoning work, vagabondage, pilfering raw materials.[5]

In a comprehensive history of everyday forms of resistance, the section on poaching would no doubt be substantial. The nature of the forest (in other cases wastelands, commons, and so on) as a resource subject to competing claims is part of the explanation. Compare, for example, the relative ease of spiriting away firewood from a vast forest to the pilfering of grain from a well-guarded central granary. Any resource or good so geographically dispersed poses nearly insurmountable problems of enforcement. Forest guards, gamekeepers, are unlikely to make much of a dent on poaching when the possible sites of poaching and the potential poachers are legion. This means, in turn, that when a forest guard or gamekeeper does encounter a poacher, he is likely to be outnumbered. As E. P. Thompson describes it, the threats, beatings, torchings of cottages, and occasional murders of gamekeepers frequently intimidated them into inactivity.

The problems of enforcement, however, are not entirely attributable to geography and demography; they are due at least as much to tacit complicity, and occasionally active cooperation, among the population from which the poachers come. Consider the difficulties that poachers would face if local residents were actively hostile to them and willing to give evidence in court. Poaching as a systematic pattern of reappropriation is simply unimaginable without a normative consensus that encourages it or, at a minimum, tolerates it. Otherwise it would be a simple matter to apprehend offenders. The forms such coordination and cooperation might take are extremely difficult to bring to light. As Thompson notes, "There *might*, indeed, have been something in the nature of a direct tradition, stretching across centuries, of secret poaching fraternities or associations in forest areas."[6] What is significant is that such coordination can typically be achieved through informal, rural social networks and that when an "association" is formed its adherents have every reason—and often the means—to conceal its existence from the authorities and the historians.

Peasant Tax Resistance

If everyday resistance via poaching is the attempt to assert traditional claims to resources in the face of new property relations, tax resistance is a more defensive effort to defeat or minimize a direct appropriation. The successful resistance of the Malaysian peasantry to the state-collected Islamic tithe (*zakat*) can provide a closer look at the importance of normative complicity, deception, the nature of the state, and the importance of long-run analysis.[7]

The Islamic tithe itself, like its Christian and Judaic predecessors, is a tax of one-tenth of the gross harvest, collected in kind, intended to promote Islamic charity and education. Until 1960 tithe contributions were entirely local and voluntary; since then the provincial authorities have centralized its administration and mandated the registration of acreage and yields in order to enforce its collection. Opposition to the new tithe was so unanimous and vehement in the villages where I conducted research that it was a comparatively simple matter to learn about the techniques of evasion. They take essentially four forms. Some cultivators, particularly small holders and tenants, simply refuse to register their cultivated acreage with the tithe agent. Others underreport their acreage and/or crop and may take the bolder step of delivering less rice than even their false declarations would require. Finally, the grain handed over is of the very poorest quality—it may be spoiled by moisture, have sprouted, or be mixed with straw and stones so that the recoverable milled grain is far less than its nominal weight would suggest.

The unannounced achievements of this resistance have been impressive. A local, but probably representative sample, revealed that the grain actually delivered to the state averaged less than one-fifth of the 10 percent mandated by the law. Most notable, however, is the public silence maintained by the protagonists in this struggle. There have been no tithe riots, no tithe demonstrations, no petitions, no violent confrontations, no protests of any kind. Why protest, indeed, when quieter stratagems have achieved the same results at minimal risk? Unless one compared actual yields with tithe receipts, the resistance itself would remain *publicly* invisible, for it is the safer course for resisters to leave the tithe system standing in name while they dismantle it in practice. This activity may not qualify as a form of collective action or a social movement but it has nevertheless achieved comparable results without affording the state an easily discernible target. There is no organization to be banned, no conspiratorial leaders to round up or buy off, no rioters to haul before the courts—only the generalized noncompliance by thousands of peasants.

The tacit coordination that abets this resistance depends on a palpable "climate of opinion," a shared knowledge of the available techniques of evasion and economic interest. A *purely* economic interest account of such resistance, however, is inadequate. For one thing, the peasantry has a host of principled reasons for evading the tithe. There are gross inequities in its assessment (cultivators of crops other than rice, noncultivating landlords, businesspeople, officials, and wealthy Chinese all escape the tithe), its collection (irregularities in weighing and crediting), and, above all, in its distribution (not a single sack of grain has ever come back to the village for poor relief). A skeptic might regard such arguments as rationalizations designed to put a principled facade on crass calculations of advantage. If this were the case it would be hard to explain why most villagers still voluntarily give "private" tithe gifts to poor relatives, neighbors, religious teachers, and harvest laborers. In other words, there is convincing evidence that it is not as much parting with the grain alone that is resented so much as the unjust manner in which it is appropriated. The same consensus about fairness that sustains resistance to the official tithe simultaneously impels most peasants to make tithe gifts within the village and extended family.

The success of tithe resistance, or any resistance for that matter, is contingent on relationships of power. In this context, there is little doubt that the authorities could extract more of the tithe if they were determined to prosecute thousands of cases, raise the penalties for noncompliance, and appoint more enforcement personnel. It might not be cost effective as a revenue measure, but it could be done. It is, however, not done because the ruling party faces electoral competition for the Muslim vote and it judges that the political costs of alienating many of their rural electoral allies would be prohibitive. Two aspects of the dilemma faced by the government are worth emphasizing. First, the effective resistance of the official tithe was initially made possible by the peasantry's tacit use of its political weight, in the knowledge that the government would hesitate before proceeding against them. It is for similar reasons that peasants avoid taxes and default on agricultural loans under regimes that depend on their active support in one fashion or another. The second, and ironic, aspect of the resistance is that once it has become a customary practice it generates its own expectations about what is permissible. Once this happens it raises the political and administrative costs for any regime that subsequently decides it will enforce the rules in earnest. For everyday resisters there is safety in numbers and successful resistance builds its own momentum.

Resistance of the kind described here may be pursued for centuries over a terrain of power that favors now the authorities and now the peasantry. Thus, for example, peasant resistance in France to the Catholic tithe, abolished only after the French Revolution, provides an account of varying techniques of resistance over more than three centuries.[8] Those who have examined this record have been struck by the techniques, persistence, and long-run success of resistance. Although there were indeed occasionally tithe strikes, riots, and petitions, it is clear that the less visible forms of evasion were of greatest significance in reducing the actual tithe collection to manageable proportions. LeRoy Ladurie and Gay, surveying the evidence, advise historians to "study the ingenuity of peasants faced with disaster and explain why for centuries the tithe remained at a level which was just tolerable."[9]

Marc Bloch has taken the case for the significance of everyday forms of resistance and expanded it to the history of agrarian class relations generally. Bloch would direct our attention *away* from the rebellions that hold pride of place in the archival record and toward the nonspectacular forms of class struggle. As he wrote, "Almost invariably doomed to defeat and eventual massacre, the great insurrections were altogether too disorganized to achieve any lasting result. The patient, silent struggles stubbornly carried out by rural communities over the years would accomplish more than these flashes in the pan."[10]

Desertion

Accounts of poaching and tithe evasion inevitably suggest that everyday forms of resistance are a matter of nibbling, of minute advantages and opportunities that can have little effect on overall relationships of power. Acts that, taken individually may appear trivial, may not have trivial consequences when considered cumulatively. From a state-centric, historical view, many regime crises may be precipitated by the cumulative impact of everyday forms of resistance that reach critical thresholds. This is perhaps most strikingly evident in the case of desertion from armies.

As Armstead Robinson has carefully documented, everyday forms of resistance played a key role in the collapse of the Confederacy during the United States Civil War.[11] Incensed by laws that exempted many sons of plantation owners from conscription, impelled to save their families from the subsistence crisis of 1862 and, in any case, having little stake in defending slavery, the poor, hill country white yeomanry deserted the Confederate Army in great numbers. Robinson estimates that as many as 250,000 hill country whites deserted or avoided conscription altogether—a figure that is five times higher than the number of whites from the Confederate States who actually switched sides and served in the Union Armies. Their refusal to participate in what they termed "a rich man's war and a poor man's fight" was decisive in Lee's defeat at Antietam and in eastern Tennessee. As a Southern clergyman noted, "our army has melted like a snow wreath, and chiefly by desertion."[12] Defections from the ranks were compounded by massive shirking, insubordination, and flight among the slave population, which deprived the Confederacy of the food supplies and revenues it needed to prosecute the war successfully. Neither the defections nor the shirking and flight could have been sustained unless there had been a consensus that sustained it and prevented the authorities from bringing it to a halt. These "mutinous" activities were not part of a rebellion; they were not organized or coordinated by anyone—and yet their aggregate impact was as deadly, if not more so, as any large open movement of sedition might have been.

Comparable cases abound. How is it possible, for example, to explain the collapse of the Czarist army and the subsequent victory of the Bolsheviks without giving due weight to the massive desertions from the front in the summer of 1917 and the accompanying, unorganized, land seizures in the countryside? Few, if any, of the rank-and-file participants intended a revolution, but that is precisely what they helped precipitate.[13] R. C. Cobb's account of draft resistance and desertion in both post-revolutionary France and under the early Empire are, in the same vein, compelling evidence for the role of everyday resistance in bringing down regimes.[14]

Quite apart from military desertion, the social historian could examine profitably the role of petty tax resistance in producing, over time, the "fiscal crisis of the state" that frequently presages radical political change. Here too, without intending it, the small self-serving acts of thousands of petty producers may deprive a regime of the wherewithal to maintain its ruling coalition and prevail against its enemies. Short of revolution, there is little doubt that massive peasant noncompliance has often been responsible for major shifts in agrarian policy in the Third World.

Agrarian Resistance to State Socialism

The property relations prevailing in a society closely determine the political shape the struggle over appropriation will take. In a liberal regime of private property in land, the struggle will typically pit the direct producers, whether small holders, laborers, or tenants, against the owners of the other factors of production (landowners, money-lenders, banks, and so on). Conflict with the state, when it occurs, is likely to focus on its fiscal and monetary policy or, at more radical moments, on the distribution of property in land. Under state social-ism, by contrast, all the vital decisions about commodity prices, the prices of agricultural inputs, credit, cropping patterns, and—under collectivization—the working day and the wage, are direct matters of state policy. Conflicts that might have been seen as private sector matters, with the state not directly implicated, become, under state socialism, direct clashes with the state. The peasant meets the state as employer, buyer, supplier, moneylender, foreman, paymaster, and tax collector.

Given the state-centric orientation of political studies, it is hardly surprising that everyday forms of resistance should seem so rife under such regimes. Part of this is simply an optical illusion created by the state having assumed the role of direct owner of the means of produc-tion and direct appropriator. Part is not illusion at all. Though it may occasionally improve his or her welfare, the aim of state socialism is invariably to reduce the autonomy of a strata previously classifiable as *petite bourgeoisie*. The loss of autonomy by itself has been a source of ferocious resistance. State farms and collectives often break the direct link between production and consumption typical of petty bourgeois producers and this in turn creates a new terrain of resistance. For the small peasant, a reduction of labor in production is likely to be reflected on the dinner table whereas, for the laborer of the state farm, a with-drawal of labor effort is not necessarily reflected directly in consump-tion. Finally, a major reason why everyday forms of resistance are so common in state-socialist forms of agriculture is because such systems allow little else in the way of opposition. Controlling directly the means of coercion, the state typically forecloses open protest, except in utter desperation, and the formal bodies that purport to represent the interests of agriculturists are, as often as not, transmission belts for instructions from the authorities.[15]

Over the long run, and frequently at tragic costs to themselves, people involved in everyday forms of resistance can provoke a fiscal crisis that leads to a change in policy. The massive economic reforms implemented in the People's Republic of China beginning in 1978 and associated with the rise to power of Deng Xiaoping are a case in point. From one perspective, the dismantling of the collectives, the inauguration of the "family responsibility system," the encouragement of petty trade and markets, may be viewed as a rational, centrally made decision to encourage growth by far-reaching reforms. While such a view is not precisely wrong, it entirely misses the fact that everyday forms of peasant resistance over nearly two decades were instrumental in forcing this massive policy change.[16] Following the policy-induced famine of the Great Leap Forward, which, by current estimates, claimed between 10 and 20 million lives, it appears that the desperate peasantry, assisted often by local cadres, redoubled its resistance against fearful odds. A host of strategies emerged, which included the underreporting of land, misreporting of cropping patterns and yields, making exaggerated claims about thefts and spoilage of grain, illegal procurements, hoarding of grain for local welfare funds, and so on. In addition, since one's working day belonged to the collective and since this work was heavily taxed (through pricing and delivery regulations), the reappropriation of time from the collective for private economic activities became a significant means of resistance and survival. The goal of most of these stratagems was to minimize the grain that the local brigade or commune would have to hand over to higher authorities. Underreporting and other techniques were frequently encouraged by local team leaders and cadres who had learned the bitter lessons of compliance with planned targets.

> If he [team leader] reported too honestly on our income to the brigade, then the orders that would come down each year would be for us to turn over more to the brigade. And that would mean less income for the team members. So the team leader would just tell them what he had to; he wouldn't let them know the real situation.[17]

The aim of China's peasantry in denying grain to the authorities was subsistence and survival. When all these petty acts were aggregated, however, their consequence was, by 1978, a procurement stalemate between the state and rural producers. Population growth and sluggish yields owing to low procurement prices meant that per-capita consumption was steady or declining. Unless production was reorganized, the state could only invest more in industry and administration by risking serious disorders. Local and occasionally provincial authorities were tacitly encouraging the resistance both to revive local production and to protect local consumption needs.

Many of the "reforms" instituted in 1978 were nothing more than the ex-post facto legalization of practices that peasants and local cadres had been quietly pursuing. Although their objectives were seldom more than "working the system to their minimum disadvantage" their persistence contributed greatly to an abrupt reversal of economic policy, the historical significance of which is still being played out.[18]

Such tacit conspiracies of a good part of the countryside against the encroaching socialist state are by no means confined to China. Thus when Hungarian peasants defended their interests in the late 1940s and early 1950s against subsistence-threatening crop deliveries to the state, they avoided any direct confrontations.[19] Although they farmed their own small holdings (or in cooperatives that were formally independent) the system of forced deliveries imposed a de facto serfdom upon them, determining what they might plant, how much they had to deliver, and the price they would receive. One stratagem that might lessen their burden was the underreporting of cultivated acreage. Whenever land came under a new jurisdiction (e.g., inheritance, transfer to cooperatives, confiscation from "kulaks") a fraction of the land mysteriously disappeared; by 1954 it was estimated that 1.3 million acres of arable—equivalent to the cultivated surface of one of the nation's largest counties—had evaporated in this fashion.[20] It was *impossible* to recover. Black markets for production concealed from the state grew apace. Birth certificates were forged so that more of the local population was above age 65 and thus eligible for quota reductions. Local authorities abetted these evasions since any reduction in the local quota made it that much easier for them to fulfill the plan targets. Livestock was, administratively speaking, spirited away as well.

> The kulaks transferred their animals to the small peasants, small peasants to their relatives in the cities. They had special techniques for hiding sheep in the well, for slaughtering pigs at night by the light of a floating wick, for milking the cows secretly, for keeping chickens and even pigs under the bed.[21]

The net result of these defensive strategies from below was declining procurements. By 1954, the least successful procurement year, there appeared no way to extract more from an increasingly bold and recalcitrant peasantry. As Rev notes, it may not quite be correct to say that the peasantry overthrew the government in 1956, but it is reasonable to claim that the liberalization after 1954 came about primarily as a result of peasant resistance. The subsequent economic and social reforms enacted in Hungary and, for that matter, in Central Europe generally, he claims, are little more than the legalization of the practices of resistance given a new policy guise by professional reformers.[22] The parallels with China are striking. This achievement, once again, was not won by open political opposition but rather through the aggregated acts of millions of agriculturalists. Although there was no secret conspiracy among them, they knew they were not alone. Like other Central European peasantries, they shared a tradition of centuries of resistance, and they knew that a generalized resistance reduces the risk to which every single resister is exposed. Even so, the cost was not negligible; by 1953 the proportion of peasants who had been imprisoned and sent to internment camps exceeded 20 percent of the total village population.[23]

There is no assurance, however, that everyday forms of resistance and the procurement crises they can provoke will lead to concessions by the state. Nowhere is this so apparent as in the history of the Soviet Union. In 1921, the peasantry had fought the Leninist state to a bitter and costly standstill, which was followed by the liberalization of the New Economic Policy period. By 1929–30 cultivators had, by hiding, privately selling (e.g., grain requisitioned for delivery), or destroying their produce and livestock, brought the Stalinist state to a similar procurement impasse. They themselves were on the brink of starvation. This time the response was Stalin's decision to fully collectivize. The deportations, executions, and famine which followed cost, at a conservative estimate, 10 million lives.[24] When the prize-winning author Sholokhov wrote reporting impending famine and complaining about the brutalities of collectivization, Stalin replied caustically about the forms of ''quiet'' resistance practiced by the peasantry.

> And the other side is that the esteemed graingrowers of your district (and not only of your district alone) carried on an 'Italian strike' (sabotage!) and were not loath to leave the workers and the Red Army without bread. That the sabotage was quiet and outwardly harmless (without bloodshed) does not change the fact that the esteemed grain growers waged what was virtually a 'quiet' war against Soviet power. A war of starvation, dear Comrade Sholokhov.[25]

By using the full might of the Soviet state, by sending urban party cadres to supervise collectivization (many being replaced when they championed peasant interests), executing or deporting to labor camps those who resisted collectivization, and seizing grain regardless of the consequences for local subsistence, the authorities prevailed. The results for production were ruinous, but the Soviet state now controlled more of that production as well as the life of the producers. Although public use of the term "famine" was strictly forbidden in this period, one candid official made it clear what kind of war was being fought.

> A ruthless struggle is going on between the peasantry and our regime. It's a struggle to the death. *This year was a test of our strength and their endurance*. It took a famine to show them who is master here. It has cost millions of lives but the collective farm system is here to stay. We've won the war.[26]

This official declaration of victory serves to emphasize that direct confrontations of power nearly always favor the state whose coercive power can be more easily mobilized and focused. A far longer historical view of this war of attrition in state appropriation might, however, yield a less straightforward assessment. Contemporary collective farm workers, reacting to near subsistence wages in the state sector, respond by shirking, by the concealing of production, by sideline activities— often using state property—by diverting labor to the personal plot. Once again, the producers pay a high cost for this resistance. They work a second workday on their private plots for a marginal return that is nearly zero and which is "a colossal exploiter of children, the aged, and the invalid."[27] To an outside observer it appears that a petty bourgeoisie is attempting to reconstitute itself, but in such cramped conditions that the results look like the self-exploitation described by the Hammonds for English weavers or by Chayanov for Russian artisan/flax-growing peasants of an earlier date. The effects of this resistance reach Gorbachev in the form of aggregate production statistics from a perennially weak state farm sector. It could not occur, however, without the tacit or active complicity of petty officials all the way down to clerks, drivers, agronomists, foremen, and technicians who seldom resist the temptation to treat their small corner of state power as private property. Noncooperation by the producers is something of a daily plebescite on the confiscation of their labor in the state sector but it cannot, by itself, *force* a reorganization of agriculture along less exploitive lines. What the producers can do, though, is to determine what will not elicit their active cooperation and productive effort.

Evading the Written Record

The perspective urged here suggests that the historiography of class struggle has been enormously distorted in a state-centric direction. The events that claim attention are the events to which the state, the ruling classes, and the intelligentsia accord most attention. Thus, for example, a small and futile rebellion claims attention out of all proportion to its impact on class relations while unheralded acts of flight, sabotage, or theft, which may have far greater impact, are rarely noticed. The small rebellion, such as the doomed slave uprising, may have a symbolic importance for its violence and its revolutionary aims, but for most subordinate classes historically such rare episodes were of less moment than the quiet unremitting guerrilla warfare that took place day in and day out.

Everyday forms of resistance rarely make headlines. But just as millions of anthozoan polyps create, willy-nilly, a coral reef, thousands upon thousands of petty acts of insubordination and evasion create a political and economic barrier reef of their own. And whenever, to pursue the simile, the ship of state runs aground on such a reef, attention is typically directed to the shipwreck itself and not the vast aggregation of actions which make it possible.[28] The perpetrators of these petty acts very rarely seek to call attention to themselves. Their safety lies in their anonymity. Peasants succeed in their small stratagems to the extent that they do not appear in the archives. This is not to say that their resistance leaves no traces; it is rather that the traces must be teased out of the record by the historian who knows what he or she is looking for. Changes in the volume of grain deliveries from certain districts, mysterious declines in livestock holdings, failures to realize conscription quotas, demographic shifts that may indicate flight, or complaints by authorities and landowners about an increase in shirking and/or pilfering may point to a key area of political activity in which vital territory is being gained or lost by antagonistic classes. Even here the evidence is most likely to signal significant changes in the level of resistance, not the slower, grinding, background resistance, which is likely to go unnoticed.

It is also comparatively rare that officials of the state wish to publicize the insubordination behind everyday resistance. To so do would be to admit that their policy is unpopular and, above all, would expose the tenuousness of their authority in the countryside—neither of which most sovereign states find in their interest. The nature of the acts themselves and the self-interested muteness of the antagonists thus conspire to create a kind of complicitous silence which may all but expunge everyday forms of resistance from the official record.

This anonymity contributed to an earlier view of the peasantry as a class that vacillated between abject passivity and brief, violent, and futile explosions of rage. It is, of course, true that the "on-stage" behavior of peasants during periods of quiescence yields a picture of submission, fear, and caution. By contrast peasant insurrections seem like visceral reactions of blind fury. What is missing from the account of "normal" passivity is the slow, silent struggle over crops, rents, labor, and taxes in which submission and stupidity are often no more than a pose—a necessary tactic. The public record of compliance and deference is often only half of the double life that W. E. B. DuBois understood all subordinate groups were obliged to lead. "Such a double life with double thoughts, double duties . . . must give rise to double works and double ideals, and tempt the mind to pretense or revolt, to hypocrisy or radicalism."[29] The "explosions" of open conflict that typically dominate the official record are frequently a sign that normal and largely covert forms of class struggle are failing—or, alternatively, have succeeded so well that they have produced a political crisis. Such declarations of open war, with their mortal risks, generally come only after a protracted struggle on different terrain.

What Counts as Resistance

It can be and has been objected that the activities grouped under the term everyday resistance hardly merit attention. From this point of view they represent trivial coping mechanisms that are either nonpolitical forms of self-help or, at best, prepolitical. I take this to be basically the position of Eric Hobsbawm, Eugene Genovese, and others.[30]

The case against moving everyday forms of resistance closer to the center of the analysis of class relations rests on the claim that these activities are marginal because they are (1) unorganized, unsystematic, and individual, (2) opportunistic and self-indulgent, (3) have no revolutionary consequences, and/or (4) imply in their intention or logic an accommodation with the structure of domination. An argument along these lines necessarily implies that "real resistance" is organized, principled, and has revolutionary implications.

The questions of opportunism and self-indulgence were treated earlier. It is sufficient to recall that if class domination is a process of systematic appropriation, then the measures devised to thwart that appropriation constitute a form of resistance. All class struggle must necessarily join self-interested material needs with conflict.

Turning to the consequences and intentions of everyday forms of resistance, it is certainly true that the "resisters" rarely intend to make a revolution and their actions do not openly challenge existing power arrangements. It can also be demonstrated convincingly, however, that the motives of peasants and even proletarians who are part of revolutionary movements are rarely, if ever, aiming at revolutionary objectives.[31] Revolutionary action, in other words, is typically undertaken by rank-and-file actors who do not have revolutionary aims. Beyond this, however, actions such as pilfering, desertion, poaching, and foot dragging do imply, by the very fact that they avoid open confrontations, a certain accommodation with existing power relations. This position has some merit. It is rather like the claim that the poacher, by his secretiveness, recognizes the norm of law-and-order. The poacher in this case might be contrasted with, say, a revolutionary appropriation in which property is openly seized in the name of justice. To dismiss poaching with this argument, however, is to overlook entirely the vital role of power relations in constraining forms of resistance open to subordinate groups. The mortal risks involved in an open confrontation may virtually preclude many forms of resistance. If only open, declared forms of struggle are called "resistance," then all that is being measured may be the level of repression that structures the available options. More than one peasantry has been reduced brutally from open, organized, radical activity at one moment to sporadic acts of petty resistance at the next. What has changed in such cases is typically *not* the aims of the peasantry but the effectiveness of domination.

There is, however, an additional problem deriving from a restricted conception of what constitutes organized activity. While much of everyday resistance is comprised of individual actions, this is not to say that these actions lack coordination. A concept of cooperative activity, derived largely from formal, bureaucratic settings, is of little assistance in understanding actions in small communities with dense informal social networks and rich, historically deep, subcultures of resistance to outside claims. It is, for example, no exaggeration to assert that much of the folk culture of the peasant "little tradition" amounts to a legitimization, or even a celebration, of precisely the kinds of evasive forms of resistance described earlier. In this and other ways (e.g., tales of bandits, tricksters, peasant heroes, religious myths, carnivalesque parodies of authorities) the peasant subculture helps to underwrite dissimulation, poaching, theft, tax evasion, evasion of conscription and so on. While folk culture is not coordination in any formal sense, it often achieves a "climate of opinion" that, in other more institutionalized societies, might require a public relations campaign. One of the striking things about peasant society is the extent to which a whole range of complex activities from labor exchange to wedding preparations to rituals are coordinated by networks of understanding and practice. It is the same with boycotts, with techniques for evading taxes and forced crop deliveries, and with the conspiracy of silence surrounding thefts from landlords. No formal organizations are created because none are required; and yet a form of coordination is achieved that alerts us to the fact that what is happening is by no means merely random individual action. Nor is it too much to suggest that the historical experience of the peasantry has favored such forms of social action because they are opaque to outside surveillance and control.[32]

Everyday forms of resistance are, it should be clear, not a peasants' monopoly. Anyone who has analyzed the measures taken by landowners in the face of an announced land reform, to evade its application to their holdings by dispersing titles, bribing officials, or changing cropping patterns will recognize the pattern. Here it is worth noticing that, as in the case of peasants, everyday resistance is being used against a party of greater formal power: in this case the state. Generally, then, *such resistance is virtually always a stratagem deployed by a weaker party in thwarting the claims of an institutional or class opponent who dominates the public exercise of power.*

Several objections could be made against so inclusive a definition. The term, it might be claimed, ought only to be applied to classes at the bottom of the social stratification. By itself, this objection carries little weight since such an analytical concept should, in principle, be applied to any behavior that meets its definitional criteria. Two more serious and related objections remain. The first is that classes higher in the social stratification typically have a variety of other political resources that allow them to influence elites and officials. Thus the middle and upper classes in a liberal democracy have a variety of channels, including political campaigns, lobbying, and legal assistance by which they can influence power. For the peasantry and other subordinate groups, throughout much of history, everyday forms of resistance have been the only resort short of rebellion. A second issue is the question of the intention behind the resistance. Implicitly, the definition presupposes a situation in which those who use everyday resistance find the claim or exaction they are resisting *unjust* and yet are intimidated by the fear of retaliation from any open, public protest of that injustice. It is this sense of injustice that is responsible for the tacit cooperation that develops among the resisters. Evidence of intention is, naturally, hard to come by when there are strong incentives to conceal one's intentions. But when both a systematic, established pattern of resistance occurs, undergirded by a popular culture that encodes notions of justice and anger encouraging that resistance *and* a relation of domination that seems to preclude most other strategies, then, it almost certainly satisfies the definition.[33]

Subordination and Political Dissimulation

The control of anger and aggression is, for quite obvious reasons, a prominent part of the socialization of those who grow up in subordinate groups. Much of the ordinary politics of subordinate groups historically has been a politics of dissimulation in which both the symbols and practices of resistance have been veiled. In place of the open insult, the use of gossip, nicknames, and character assassination; in place of direct physical assault, the use of sabotage, arson, and nocturnal threats by masked men (e.g., Captain Swing, the Rebecca Riots, Les Demoiselles); in place of labor defiance, shirking, slowdowns, and spoilage; in place of the tax riot or rebellion, evasion, and concealment.

All of these forms of political struggle can be conducted just beneath the surface of a public realm of deference, compliance, and loyalty. No public challenge is ventured; no field of direct confrontation is volunteered. To be sure, such forms of struggle are best suited to those realms of conflict where the problems of control and supervision by authorities are greatest. The state finds it far simpler to collect an excise tax on imported luxury vehicles coming to the major port than to patrol its borders against smuggling grain or to collect an income tax from its peasantry.

The advantages of everyday forms of resistance lie not merely in the smaller probability of apprehension. Their advantage lies at least as much in the fact that they are generally creeping incremental strategies that can be finely tuned to the opposition they encounter and that, since they make no formal claims, offer a ready line of retreat through disavowal. Tenant farmers who are in arrears on their rents to a landlord are in a different position from tenant farmers in arrears to the same extent who have also declared that they are not paying because the land is theirs by right. State authorities and dominant elites will naturally respond with greater alacrity and force to open defiance that seems to jeopardize their position. For this reason, subordinate groups have attempted, when possible, to assert their resistance on the safer terrain of undeclared appropriation. Their stratagems minimize the maximum loss. Squatters, for example, unless they have political support, will typically move off private or state lands when faced with force, only to return quietly at a later date. What everyday resistance lacks in terms of gestures and structured claims, it compensates for by its capacity for relentless pressure and the safety and anonymity it typically provides its users.

Perhaps the most striking characteristic of normal resistance by subordinate groups—both symbolic and material, is the pervasive use of disguise. The disguise is of two main types, with many intermediate possibilities. First and most common is the concealment or anonymity of the resister. The poacher, the pilferer, the deserter, and the tax evader hope their acts will be undetected or passed over. Similarly, the propagators of rumor and gossip are, by definition, anonymous; there is no apparent producer but scores of eager retailers. The use of disguises is often not just metaphorical but literal. Peasant and early working class protest in Europe provides innumerable examples of collective action where the message was clear but the messengers were disguised. In the Captain Swing "disturbances" in the 1830s it was common for farm laborers to come in disguise at night with torches and insist on the destruction of threshing machines. Everything about the protest was quite specific except for the *personal* (not the class) identity of the protesters. The tradition of lower classes wearing disguises in order to speak bitter truths to their superiors is, of course, firmly institutionalized in the carnival and a variety of other rituals of folk culture.

By contrast, a great deal of symbolic resistance by peasants and other subordinate groups reverses this arrangement. Instead of a clear message delivered by a disguised messenger, an ambiguous message is delivered by clearly identified messengers. Many of the folktales of peasant and slave culture fall into this category. The enormously popular trickster figures among such groups (e.g., Til Eulenspiegel, Brer

Rabbit, the mouse-deer of Malaysian culture) are taken both as disguised forms of aggression and implicit strategic advice. Because they are veiled, however, they do not offer the authorities a clear-cut occasion for retaliation. Slave spirituals stressing Old Testament themes of liberation and justice or what have been called the "World Upside Down" broadsheets (e.g., woodcuts depicting a serf being led on horseback by his lord) might be seen in the same light. And it has always been common for peasants, when making threats against elites or authorities, to deliver those threats in the form of euphemisms. Thus, for example, arsonists threatening wealthy farmers or aristocratic landholders in early eighteenth-century France would use known formulas for their threats: "I will have you awakened by a red cock!" "I will light your pipe," "I will send a man dressed in red who will pull everything down."[34] The meaning of the message was, of course, perfectly transparent, but the use of euphemism offered an avenue of retreat.

Many forms of resistance in dangerous circumstances are intended to be ambiguous, to have a double meaning, to be garbled so that they cannot be treated as a direct, open challenge and, hence, invite an equally direct, open retaliation. For this reason it would be instructive to devise a theory of political masking by subordinate groups. An analysis of the pattern of disguises and the forms of domination under which they occur could contribute to our understanding of what happens to "voice," in Albert Hirschman's meaning of that term, under domination. Open declarations of defiance are replaced by euphemisms and metaphors; clear speech by muttering and grumbling: open confrontation by concealed noncompliance or defiance. This brief exposition of everyday forms of resistance is hardly the place to develop a theory of political disguises, but Table 1 is intended to suggest one possible line of inquiry.

Gestures, Resistance, and Rebellion

To understand better the context and function of everyday forms of resistance it may be helpful to contrast them to political gestures. The poacher, who hopes to escape notice, may further his aim by making a public show of deference and devotion to those on whose property claims he is secretly encroaching. A practical act of resistance is thus often accompanied by a public discursive affirmation of the very arrangements being resisted—the better to undermine them in practice.

Table 1

Domination and Disguised Resistance

Form of Domination	Forms of Disguised Resistance
1. Material domination: appropriation of grain, taxes, labor, etc.	Everyday forms of resistance e.g., poaching, squatting, desertion, evasion, foot dragging Direct opposition by disguised resisters e.g., masked appropriations, carnival
2. Denial of status: humiliation, disprivilege, assaults on dignity	Hidden transcript of anger, aggression, and a discourse of dignity e.g., rituals of aggression, tales of revenge, creation of autonomous social space for assertion of dignity
3. Ideological domination: justification by ruling groups for slavery, serfdom, caste, privilege	Development of dissident subculture e.g., millennial religion, slave "hush arbors," folk religion, myths of social banditry, and class heroes.

When the act of everyday resistance is *meant* to be noticed—meant to send a signal—as in the case of arson or sabotage, then the resisters take special care to conceal themselves, often behind a facade of public conformity.

We may contrast this pattern with acts of resistance in which the emphasis is reversed. If everyday resistance is "heavy" on the instrumental side and "light" on the symbolic confrontation side, then the contrasting acts would be "light" on the instrumental side and "heavy" on the symbolic side.[35] A few examples may help sharpen the contrast. During the Spanish Civil War anti-clerical supporters of the Republic invaded churches and cathedrals in order to disinter the remains of priests, bishops, cardinals, and nuns who were buried in the crypts.[36] Their exhumed remains were then spilled onto the steps of the churches by the crowds to be publicly seen by the population—most particularly by the enemies of the Republic. It would be hard to imagine a more powerful act of anti-clerical symbolism, a more extreme act of public desecration and contempt. To this day the episode is remembered and invoked publicly by the right in Spain as an example of left-wing barbarism. What is notable about the revolutionary exhumations in Spain is that they approached the limit of pure symbolic action. No property was redistributed, no one was murdered,[37] nor was the balance of military force altered in any apparent way. The objective was rather to publicly exhibit the utmost contempt for the Spanish church, its symbols, and its heroes. As a declaration of war, symbolically speaking, revolutionary exhumations belong at the opposite end of a continuum of forms of resistance from the low profile poacher.

A huge realm of political conflict belongs to the san.e genus of public, symbolic confrontations. The wearing of black armbands to commemorate a political martyr, hunger strikes, not to mention the cultural confrontations invited by various counterculture groups are precisely intended as discursive negations of the existing symbolic order. As such, they fail unless they gain attention. If everyday resistance represents disguised forms of struggle over appropriation, then revolutionary exhumations represent public, open forms of confrontation over the symbols of dominant discourse. Both forms of action are integral to political conflict.

Most "everyday resisters" are rather like opponents of a law who estimate that it is more convenient to evade it or bribe their way around it rather than to change it. In the case of the peasantry, of course, the state and its laws are typically inaccessible, arbitrary, and alien. The notion of collective public action to change the structure of, say, property law or civil rights is confined largely to the literate middle class and the intelligentsia.

Directing attention to the strategic reasons for the symbolic low profile of everyday resistance may cast some light on how changes in the forms of political action occur. First, it is undeniable that everyday resistance is less threatening to public domination precisely because it avoids an engagement at that level. If squatters invaded private or state land publicly, and declared their *right* to use it as they saw fit, they would, in effect, be declaring that they were not squatters and, instead, directly challenging property arrangements. This is more menacing to political authority and it is exactly what the Diggers did during the English Revolution when the balance of power temporarily freed them to act openly. Everyday resistance, then, *by not openly* contesting the dominant norms of law, custom, politeness, deference, loyalty, and so on, leaves the dominant in command of the public stage. Inasmuch as every act of compliance with a normative order discursively affirms that order, while every public act of repudiation (e.g., failure to stand during national anthems in the United States) represents a threat to that norm, everyday resistance leaves dominant symbolic structures intact.[38]

If, however, the perceived relationship of power shifts in favor of subordinate groups, everyday resistance may well become a direct and open political challenge and surreptitious or disguised symbolic dissent may become a public renunciation of domination. Aesopian language may give way to direct vituperation, and everyday forms of resistance to overt, collective defiance.

The prehistory of many large rebellions and revolutions might be retrospectively recast along these lines. A pattern of quiet resistance both symbolically and materially suddenly becomes generalized, massive, and open as the political situation presents new possibilities that previously seemed utopian. The French peasantry who burned chateaux and abbeys in 1789 were presumably not perfectly allegiant retainers to their kings and lords in 1788. The shifts in power that make possible new forms of resistance may often originate outside the immediate domain we are considering, as in cases of world-wide trade slumps, defeat in war, and so on. They may also originate in the very process of resistance and counterresistance. Balzac, though his disapproval is apparent, captures the process with respect to poaching and gleaning.

> Do not imagine that Tonsard, or his old mother or his wife and children ever said in so many words, we steal for a living and do our stealing cleverly. These habits had grown slowly. The family began by mixing a few green boughs with the dead wood, then, emboldened by habit and by a calculated impunity . . . after twenty years the family had gotten to the point of taking wood as if it were *their own* and making a living almost entirely by theft. The rights of pasturing their cows, the abuse of gleaning grain, of gleaning grapes, had gotten established little by little in this fashion. By the time the Tonsards and the other lazy peasants of the valley had tasted the benefits of these four rights acquired by the poor in the countryside, rights pushed to the point of pillage, one can imagine that they were unlikely to renounce them unless compelled by a force stronger than their audacity.[39]

Balzac, it should be added, observes that many of these new ''rights'' were entrenched by peasants taking advantage of the revolution and the political vacuum that followed it.

Everyday forms of resistance may be thought of as exerting a constant pressure, probing for weak points in the defenses of antagonists and testing the limits of resistance. In the case of poaching, for example, there may be a fairly stable tension over time between poachers and gamekeepers. But when, say, it turns out that over the past few months taking rabbits is punished or prevented much less frequently, the volume of poaching and the number of participants are likely to swell to a point where a custom or even a right to take rabbits threatens to become established.[40] Alternatively, any number of events might impel poachers to run more risks—e.g., a crop failure, an increase in meat prices, higher taxes—so that their boldness and numbers overwhelm the existing capacity of those who enforce game laws. There is strength in numbers, and poaching that becomes generalized to whole communities may, as Balzac notes, require new levels of coercion to reestablish the old balance.[41] The hydraulic metaphor implicit here of water of variable pressure, straining against a (movable!) retaining wall having certain strengths and weaknesses is necessarily crude but, perhaps, suggestive.

Much the same approach might be applied to symbolic defiance. Slaves, serfs, tenant farmers, and workers, in public, say pretty much what their masters, lords, landlords, and bosses expect them to say. Yet, there are likely to be hidden transcripts of what subordinates actually think that can be recovered in off-stage conversation in slave quarters, veiled cultural performances (e.g., folktales, carnival). This hidden transcript may be pictured as continually testing the line of what is permissible on-stage. One particularly intrepid, risk-taking, angry, unguarded subordinate says something that just touches or crosses the line. If it is not rebuked or punished, others, profiting from the example, will venture across the line as well, and a new de facto line is created, governing what may be said or gestured. In revolutions, one is likely to see unbridled anger—the entire hidden transcript—spoken openly and acted openly. It is unlikely that we can account for the *content* of this action by reference to outside agitators, their ideology, or even the aspirations engendered by a revolutionary process. The revolutionary actions might well have been prefigured in their practices of resistance and in their off-stage discourse. What had changed was above all the conditions that had previously confined the public expression of these actions and sentiments.

Notes

1. From whom the appropriation is extracted makes all the difference in the world. A poor peasant who extends his field by ploughing furrows into another poor peasant's land or secretly harvests some of his neighbor's grain is surviving at his neighbor's expense. So is the sharecropper who obtains his share-tenancy by outbid-

ding other would-be sharecroppers and agreeing to hand over more of the harvest. Everyday forms of class resistance must, by definition, have at least the intention of improving the balance of appropriation for members of the subordinate group.

2. James C. Scott, *Weapons of the Weak: Everyday Forms of Peasant Resistance* (New Haven: Yale University Press, 1985), p. 290.

3. See Utsa Patnaik, "Neo-Populism and Marxism: The Cayanovian View of the Agrarian Question and Its Fundamental Fallacy," *Journal of Peasant Studies* 6 (1979): 398–99.

4. See E. P. Thompson, *Whigs and Hunters: The Origin of the Black Act* (New York: Pantheon, 1975) *passim* and Thompson, "Poaching and the Game Laws in Cannock Chase," in Douglas Hay et al., *Albion's Fatal Tree: Crime and Society in Eighteenth Century England* (London: Allen Lane, 1975), pp. 189–253. See also John Brewer and John Styles, eds., *An Ungovernable People: The English and their Law in the 17th and 18th Centuries* (New Brunswick: Rutgers University Press, 1980).

5. Michel Foucault, *Discipline and Punish: The Birth of the Prison*, translated by Alan Sheridan, (New York: Vintage, 1979), p. 274.

6. Thompson, *Whigs and Hunters*, p. 58.

7. For a far more detailed analysis see my "Resistance Without Protest and Without Organization: Peasant Opposition to the Islamic Zakat and the Christian Tithe," *Comparative Studies in Society and History* 29 (July 1987): 412–36.

8. *Ibid.*

9. Emmanuel LeRoy Ladurie, *Tithe and Agrarian History from the 14th Century to the 19th Century: An Essay in Comparative History*, translated by Susan Burke (Cambridge: Cambridge University Press, 1982), p. 27.

10. Marc Bloch, *French Rural History: An Essay on its Basic Characteristics*, translated by Janet Sondheimer (Berkeley: University of California Press, 1970), p. 170. Note Bloch's implicit characterization of the "patient, silent struggles" as in some sense *more organized* than the great insurrections.

11. Armstead L. Robinson, *Bitter Fruits of Bondage: Slavery's Demise and the Collapse of the Confederacy: 1861–65*, forthcoming (New Haven: Yale University Press), ch. 5.

12. *Ibid.*, ch. 8.

13. Marc Ferro, "The Russian Soldier in 1917: Undisciplined, Patriotic, and Revolutionary," *Slavic Review* 30 (September 1971): 483–512.

14. Richard Cobb, *The Police and the People: French Popular Protest, 1789–1820* (Oxford: Clarenden Press, 1970), pp. 96–97.

15. In the cases considered below we are also dealing with Marxist parties that have a decided view of the role of the peasantry in the revolutionary alliance with the proletariat. As Lenin observed, "Petty bourgeois proprietors are willing to help us, the proletariat, to throw out the landed gentry and the capitalists. But after that our roads part."

16. See Daniel Kelliher, *Peasant-State Relations in China During Rural Reforms: 1978–1984* (Ph.D. dissertation, Yale University, 1985) on whose argument I rely heavily here. For other parallels see Goran Hyden, *Beyond Ujamaa in Tanzania* (London: Heineman, 1980) and Christine Pelzer White, *The Role of Collective Agriculture in Rural Development: The Vietnamese Case*, Research Report 3592, (Institute of Development Studies, University of Sussex, 1984, mimeographed).

17. From an interview with an ex-team leader reported by Vivienne Shue in *The Reach of the State: Sketches of the Chinese Body Politic* (Stanford: Stanford University Press, 1988), p. 111.

18. The phrase comes from Eric Hobsbawm, "Peasants and Politics," *Journal of Peasant Studies* 1 (1973): 7.

19. Istvan Rev, "The Advantages of Being Atomized: How Hungarian Peasants Coped with Collectivization," *Dissent* (Summer 1987): 335–49

20. *Ibid.*, p. 338.

21. *Ibid.*, p. 342.

22. *Ibid.*, pp. 344–45.

23. *Ibid.*, p. 342.

24. See, particularly, the analysis of the human toll in the Ukraine in Robert Conquest, *The Harvest of Sorrow: Soviet Collectivization and the Terror-Famine* (New York: Oxford University Press, 1986).

25. Quoted in *ibid.*, p. 232. For more on the patterns of peasant resistance to "dekulakization," forced requisitions, and collectivization see the careful judgments of Moshe Lewin, *The Making of the Soviet System* (New York: Pantheon, 1985).

26. M. M. Khateyevich, quoted in Conquest, *op. cit.*, p. 261. Emphasis added.

27. See the remarkable descriptions recently translated from the *samizdat* manuscript of Lev Timofeev (a pseudonym), *Soviet Peasants, or: The Peasants' Art of Starving*, translated by Jean Alexander and Alexander Zaslavsky; Armando Pitassio and Victor Zaslavsky, eds. (New York: Telos Press, 1985), p. 80.

28. The search for public scapegoats is, of course, quite common as a means of coping with such failures. But it is rare that the search for scapegoats touches large numbers of people as it did with the "wreckers" and "kulaks" in the U.S.S.R. in the late 1920s and early 1930s or the "kulaks" in Hungary during collectivization.

29. W. E. B. DuBois, "On the Faith of the Fathers," pp. 210–25 of DuBois, *The Souls of Black Folks* (New York: New American Library, 1969), pp. 221–22.

30. Inasmuch as I have made the case against this position in much more detail in *Weapons of the Weak: Everyday Forms of Peasant Resistance*, (New Haven: Yale University Press, 1985), ch. 7, I confine myself here to a few schematic comments.

31. The main exception, and it is undeniably an important one, is the case of millennial movements whose objectives are revolutionary. See ch. 8 of *Weapons of the Weak* for a more elaborate exposition of the case made in this paragraph.

32. And not just the peasantry. In this context see the fine article by William M. Reddy, "The Textile Trade and the Language of the Crowd of Rouen, 1725–1871," *Past and Present* 74 (February 1977): 62–89. Reddy argues that it was precisely the *lack* of organization in crowd behavior that was enabling and that the crowd came to value and use spontaneously in the knowledge that it was the most effective, least costly, means of protest. The cultural understandings were so well developed that any just grievance could, he claims, bring together a crowd without any planning or organization, let alone formal leadership.

33. It would be difficult, though perhaps not impossible, for middle-class tax resistance to satisfy the same conditions.

34. Andre Abbiateci, "Arsonists in 18th Century France: An Essay in the Typology of Crime," translated by Elborg Forster, in Robert Forster and Orest Ranum, eds., *Deviants and the Abandoned in French Society: Selections from the Annales: Economies, Societés, Civilizations* 4 (Baltimore: Johns Hopkins, 1978), p. 158.

35. It goes without saying that symbolic actions can have large instrumental consequences and vice versa.

36. Bruce Lincoln, "Revolutionary Exhumations in Spain, July 1936," *Comparative Studies in Society and History* 27 (April 1985): 241–60.

37. In the course of the Civil War in Republican-held areas many thousand clerics were, in fact, killed—either killed by angry crowds or executed for anti-Republic activities.

38. For moral norms, the importance of public confirmation or repudiation is

magnified. Take, for example, the common norm of a religiously sanctified marriage as the only legitimate basis for family life. Compare, then, a pattern of unsanctified, common law marriages that are widespread but unannounced and undeclared as public acts, to a social movement against sanctified marriage that openly repudiates the norm itself. The latter is, of course, a more immediate threat to the norm although the former pattern may well, by accretion, eventually bring the norm into question.

39. Honoré de Balzac, *Les Paysans* (Paris: Pleades, 1949).

40. In his account of poaching in the Hampshire forests, E. P. Thompson reports that when Bishop Peter Mews, who had had a particularly antagonistic relationship with his tenants over their rights, finally died, the tenants took full advantage of the brief vacancy before a new bishop was appointed. "The tenants," he writes, "appear to have made a vigorous assault on the timber and deer." Thompson, *Whigs and Hunters*, p. 123.

41. The process I am describing of cumulative noncompliance is a form of social action familiar to any motorist faced with speed limits. If the official speed limit is 55 miles per hour, no one is concerned about being fined for driving 56 m.p.h. Well, what about 57, 58, 60, 65? Let us imagine that, on the basis of experience, motorists know they can "get away with" 60 m.p.h. The flow of traffic is then likely to move at this speed; the police can't arrest everyone so they single out only the most egregious violators of these informal norms. Once a 60 m.p.h. practice is established, the process continues. A few (intrepid, rushed, wealthy?) drivers are always testing the limits and threatening to establish a new "tolerated" informal limit. Responses are of course possible; the state may choose to raise the speed limit lest its formal regulations become an object of derision or it may redouble its enforcement. Like all social action, such patterns to be more accurate would have to be thoroughly reflexive. Thus, one might ask, wouldn't a *clever* state, knowing all this, set the official speed at 55 m.p.h., planning on the fact that the actual traffic flow will be roughly 65 m.p.h. This is true but fails to be sufficiently reflexive, for the calculations of such a state are based on assumptions about noncompliance which have been inferred by actual patterns of past resistance.

2

Between Submission and Violence: Peasant Resistance in the Polish Manorial Economy of the Eighteenth Century

Jacek Kochanowicz

Poland in the second half of the eighteenth century is an example of a preindustrial agrarian society with a social order based on the dominance of nobility and the serfdom of peasants. Together with the rest of Eastern Europe, and in contrast to Western Europe, this society was characterized by the weakness of towns and the relatively insignificant political role of the burghers. Poland, however, differed from earlier agrarian societies in at least two important respects: first, the country was increasingly involved in the international division of labor, exporting crops and importing manufactured luxury products. It slowly drifted toward the status of a backward, peripheral economy. Second, it was surrounded by countries which, while possessing more or less similar economies, developed much more elaborate state machineries with centralized power, army, taxation, and bureaucracy.[1] In this respect Poland, ''the democracy of the nobles,'' differed from other absolutist Eastern countries. As a result, Poland is not only a good case of peasant resistance at the early stages of modernization, but also a good case for comparison with other, more ''modern'' societies. Here, the game was played by lord and peasant only. In neighboring countries, there was a triangle: the lord, the peasant, and the state. Broadening the field of comparison to include the West, it is necessary to take into consideration yet another segment of the society, namely the bourgeoisie.

Three points are advanced in this chapter. First, contrary to assumptions often made tacitly or even opinions expressed openly, peasants were not just puppets of lords or victims of their abuse, but, because of their resistance, had a certain measure of autonomy within the existing social order. Second, this resistance, against which lords were almost helpless, was itself an important element of the social and economic system, an element without which this system cannot be fully understood. Third, in the long run, the benefits of passive resistance for the peasants diminished as the peasant population grew.

There is another, more methodological dimension. Records for studying the Polish preindustrial peasantry are scarce and there are varying, even conflicting, interpretations, which to a certain degree are ideologically determined. These constraints stem from the fact that during the nineteenth and twentieth centuries, the peasant question was one of the most important social and political issues in Poland, as it was in all East European countries. The peasant problem was discussed and studied extensively by politicians and scholars. Curiously, however, the problem of peasant resistance emerged only slowly in those debates. During the 1930s it was examined by Marxist-oriented historians, but only in respect to the nineteenth century. These studies were polemical in examining the official historiography of the period, which concentrated mostly on the questions of national independence. Contemporaneous studies of eighteenth-century agrarian history left aside problems of class tensions and divisions.

In the 1950s and early 1960s, advances were made in agrarian and peasant history. As a result of the land reforms of 1944 and the disappearance of the landowning class, private archives were made public and important collections of sources were published. (It must be remembered, however, that many other records were destroyed during the war.)

Second, considerable progress was achieved in the previously nonexistent field "history of the material culture," i.e., studies of consumption and techniques of production.

Third, during the fifties, the history of peasantry became fashionable, not to say obligatory, because of a specific form of Marxism of the day—Stalinism. Marxism, which in the mid-war period was popular among tiny groups of antiestablishment historians and which in the forties was advocated still by a minority of young, leftist historians, now became the only official ideology, often with disastrous results. There were scholars who could not teach and publish. There were others who put on some sort of camouflage and pretended to adhere to the official doctrine. There were polemics that fell below the acceptable level of academic courtesy. There were fields of research that became taboo. For economic history, however, the period was not lost. The field attracted many gifted, young people, who could not engage in political history research. The Marxist perspective, despite its crude form, brought in the subject of the laboring masses and the problem of class tensions, which had been neglected before the war.

After 1956 Marxism was still quite popular among a large number of Polish intellectuals. The period 1968–70 was the end of the Prague Spring, the complicated and sad events of the Polish March 1968, and finally the shooting of workers on the Gdansk coast in 1970, which brought about a disillusionment with the official ideology. In the 1960s, however, Polish Marxism was probably at its best, open to Western thought, discovering Gramsci and structuralism, and trying to adapt itself to the rigors of U.S. empirical sociology. Peasant studies flourished as an area of rural sociology. Strangely, however, after 1956, these developments touched the study of the agrarian and peasant past only marginally. Interest in them began to diminish, and the main body of literature remained more traditional. The great wave of interest in peasant problems in the West, the discovery of Chayanov and the discussion of Third World peasantry, hardly affected Polish historical research on peasant problems. Many scholars moved toward other problems, and others stuck to descriptive monographs.

When in the 1950s the history of peasantry was approached by young scholars, they were looking, first of all, for class struggle.[2] The opening, tacit assumption was that class struggle should lead to rebellion, comparable to the French jacqueries, the German Peasant War, or the Russian and Ukrainian rebellions of the seventeenth and eighteenth centuries. The Marxist approach of that period posed the problem rather than attempting to solve it. The method of study usually consisted of simple, traditional descriptions of cases found in the records; the methodology was less rigorous than an analysis of the strictly economic aspects of peasant life. There was a tendency to paint a very dark picture of the conditions of peasantry and of the upper strata of Polish society.

There were numerous citations of cases of abuse and brutality. The language of description was full of adjectives condemning the "exploitation" and "reactionary attitudes" of the Polish nobility. There were oversimplifications, stemming from the Stalinist version of Marxism, which reduced all history to the history of class struggle. National history was rewritten according to the propaganda of the times. The stress was put on descriptions of the most radical and active forms of resistance. Researchers were looking mainly for evidence of rebellions, uprisings, and insurrections, often overestimating their actual significance. In fact, many cases of such rebellions were found, but they were mostly local ones. "Class consciousness" and "class solidarity" were often assumed to exist as dimensions of peasant thinking and behavior. Apart from class divisions between the peasantry and the nobility, researchers were looking for class stratification inside the peasantry itself and for signs of the beginnings of capitalism in the countryside. In this, they followed in Lenin's footsteps in his analysis of prerevolutionary Russia.

Despite these shortcomings, the studies are, in fact, invaluable. An enormous mass of material, difficult to analyze, was studied with painstaking effort. Knowledge of peasant social history was broadened, and new, important aspects were revealed. Aside from local rebellions, these studies show a variety of other forms of resistance. They were sometimes called "passive," but the classifications for "passive" and "active" forms were questioned. Instead it was proposed that one should speak rather about "open" and "hidden" or "concealed" forms of resistance.[3]

This discussion, which was started and somehow ended without a conclusion by Polish historians during the 1950s, is close to the perspective advanced by James Scott in his book, *Weapons of the Weak*, about Malaysian peasantry. But there are differences as well. First, the sophistication of present-day anthropology, social history, and Marxism were not possible for that generation of scholars. Second, they could not ask "their" peasants what they thought about the world they lived in. As a result, one of the issues that is central to Scott's hypothesis, namely, that of resistance at the level of symbols, is something which is almost impossible to study in respect to Polish preindustrial peasants. At the most, one can only hypothesize.

Combining autochthonous Marxist historiography with Scott's hypotheses about peasant behavior is useful in recounting the development of the Polish manorial economy. The trove of archival material unearthed by earlier, and more deterministic, Marxist scholars supports the central proposition advanced by Scott—that peasant behavior is best conceptualized as lying between submission and violence.

Serfdom and Estate Farming

The so-called "second serfdom" was established in Poland during the fifteenth and sixteenth centuries, when estates began to assume the main role in the agricultural economy, using compulsory, peasant labor for market production. Currently, there are two explanations for the establishment of Poland's feudal economy.[4] One line of interpretation stresses market forces that led to the profitability of large estates, geared toward export.[5] The other underscores the play of class or socio-political forces. A strong nobility versus a weak bourgeoisie and a weak state was able to obtain a series of royal privileges that limited the rights of the bourgeoisie and effectively tied peasants to the land. These two interpretations are not mutually exclusive; rather they are complementary. For example, exports were high despite decreasing productivity only because serfdom helped to suppress peasant consumption.

Estate farming gained importance during the sixteenth century, a golden era for the Polish economy, culture, and politics. In the eighteenth century the share of arable land under direct management of the manor reached roughly half of that available in an average village.[6] The rest was used by the peasants for their own needs. There were no technological differences between estate and peasant farming. Three field rotations and an open fields system were used, with estate fields dispersed among the peasants' plots. The work on estate land was performed by peasants, supervised by manorial officials or by the lord himself. Wheat, rye, oats, and barley were the main crops produced; rye and wheat for sale, barley for beer consumption, and oats for fodder.

The estate farm was market oriented. In those parts of Poland that had access to navigable rivers, the Vistula in particular, it was also export oriented. (Mazovia and Little Poland were most important from this point of view.) In other parts, especially in Great Poland, which was more densely urbanized, estate products were sold in local markets.[7]

The goal of the estate economy was to sell abroad as much grain as possible and avoid buying means of production for money. In general, everything could be provided by the estate itself. Labor was serf labor, draft animals were cared and provided for by the peasants, and seed,

building materials, and so on, were provided by the estate. The nobleman needed money if he wanted to buy more land. Land could be
bought only by the nobility—the bourgeoisie were excluded—and it was
a market for whole estates. Apart from the purchase of land, the
noble class needed money for consumption of imported, luxury goods
such as cloth, arms, wine, furniture, silver, and china. Economic
and social position depended not only on the efficiency of the economic performance of the estate, but on terms of trade of Polish grain
versus imported goods. In this respect, the situation favored the
Polish nobility in the sixteenth century when it had almost no competitors in the Western market. In the seventeenth century the economy was
devastated by wars, especially the war with Sweden, and it recovered
with great difficulty. Market possibilities were never as good as before
because of new competitors and because of the increase of Western
European production. After the first partition of Poland in 1772,
Prussian tolls on the Vistula River became a new obstacle to Polish
exports.

Motivated by his desire to sell as much as possible, the estate owner
faced limitations in managing his farm. The marketable surplus depended on the amount of land under manorial supervision. In order to
acquire more arable land, the lord could either organize land clearing,
if unused land was available, or take part of the land used by the
peasants. The second way was simpler. The rights of peasants to the
land were by custom only, and on private estates the lord could do what
he pleased. He usually, however, respected prevailing local customs
and at least pretended to adhere to them. Peasants were moved off their
land when they did not manage their own farms efficiently or when
their families were too small to provide labor for the work required, as
in the case of widows who did not remarry. Sometimes land was
claimed by a lord after land surveys were made, when the estate was
going to be sold or passed on to heirs. The lord could claim then that
particular peasants used more land than was allotted to them. Generally
speaking, the lord wanted the peasant allotment to be only as big as
necessary to support the peasant family and draft animals.[8] Any pretext
to reduce its size was good enough, especially when harvests were
good. In the long run, however, the tendency to reduce the size of the
peasant farm was self-destructive, since it reduced the possibilities of
peasant animal husbandry. It meant not only that there were not enough
draft animals to work estate lands, but that the land was not manured
well enough and yield ratios fell.

Peasant Economy[9]

There is no doubt that the peasant's situation deteriorated between the sixteenth and eighteenth centuries because of the economic system and war devastation.[10] Of course, it is impossible to calculate the level of peasant income or consumption, or their mortality rate. However, the average area of peasant holdings diminished substantially, as can be seen by comparing the size of holdings listed in records from the sixteenth century with those from the eighteenth century. Agricultural productivity, in terms of yield/seed ratio, also diminished. It can be safely assumed that both peasant consumption and their market surplus decreased. At the same time, labor obligations increased dramatically from the early sixteenth century to the eighteenth century.

The estate owner wanted peasant farms to be only big enough to allow for labor force reproduction. To a certain extent, he was interested in their differentiation because he needed some households to perform manual work only and others to work with draft animals. It would be a simplification, however, to regard peasant economic and social structures as mere reflections of the lord's wishes. There were other factors as well, although it is difficult to ascertain their relative roles. Most probably, there was a "Chayanovian" mechanism, correlating family size and structure with the area of land the family used.[11] Peasants with smaller families could "hire" additional labor. Servants worked not for money, but for "bed and board." They were treated like members of the family, except for the rights of inheritance. They came not so much from the class of the rural proletariat, as from other, probably poorer, peasant families, with "too many" children. Sometimes they were socially handicapped, orphans, cripples, mentally retarded, and so on. The line between help provided by the village "welfare system" and exploitation is not easily drawn.

Peasants with too little or too much land, relative to family needs and possibilities, could try to buy or sell land within the village.[12] Although the land was the property of the owner of the village, there was a small market for land among the villagers themselves, usually with the lord's approval.

Demography was another factor that influenced the social structure of the village. This has not been studied systematically for this period, especially on a small scale, and there is only indirect evidence. It may be assumed, however, that the decreasing size of peasant holdings was not only a consequence of the estate taking land, but also of demographic pressure. There was also a possibility of a capitalist-type social differentiation of the peasant class. The existence of such a possibility was argued in the fifties, although it is doubtful that it could have been significant. [13]

As a result of these factors the social structure of the villages, which were in the orbit of the feudal estates, may be presented as follows: (1) a tiny majority of a so-called "privileged" population, i.e., peasants who were not serfs; (2) the majority of the population were serfs, who were further divided into landed peasants, and these divided again into holders of larger or smaller plots, and landless peasants; (3) there was a marginal population as well.

Analytically speaking, a distinction can be made between "subsistence" and "profit-making" peasant farms. While there is the possibility that a certain number of the latter existed in eighteenth-century Poland, for the most part they were outside the estate system. For example, there were so-called "Dutch settlers," who were very experienced in cultivating new and difficult land. They usually payed rent in money instead of performing labor obligations. Technologically, they were above manorial serfs. In Royal Prussia, i.e., the territories around Gdansk, manors often used hired labor rather than serfs, and peasants payed rent in money. They engaged in commercial production for the markets of Gdansk, Torun, or Elblag, used hired labor, and made extensive use of credit.

Estate farming was not widespread in the submountain regions. The soils there were poor, and peasants could not produce enough even for subsistence. They often engaged in protoindustrial activities, such as textile production;[14] some of them were lucky enough to make small fortunes.[15] These peasant fortunes could be found even within the estate system, but they seem rare.[16]

On the whole, one would have to regard peasant agriculture as subsistence farming. But a closer look at the peasant economy suggests that the term "subsistence" is not an adequate one. First of all, peasants tried to establish a relationship with the internal market. This market was weak, but the peasants had some advantage over the nobles because their production was much more diversified; they produced not only grain, but animal products, vegetables, crafts, dairy products, and so on. However, a detailed analysis of this problem is impossible because of the lack of peasant household records. The assumption that peasants were selling goods is based on data from the manorial estates, which got substantial revenues from the forced sale of alcoholic drinks to peasants. Another basis for this assumption comes from the tentative calculation of market surpluses of peasant farms of different categories. The economic and social role of money in peasant economy is not well known. It was probably used for ceremonial purposes—weddings, purchases of land, savings, small acquisitions like salt and iron tools, and for drinks at the lord's inn.[17]

However, there is another reason for regarding peasant economy as something other than "subsistence." Most peasant families did not have enough land to support them exclusively. During a bad year, even a relatively large farm produced less food than required for consumption. It is difficult to say much about smaller farms and landless peasants, because the problem has not been studied systematically. They must have earned part of their income by working for richer neighbors, in the manor, or by engaging in some form of nonagricultural activity. When analyzing peasant economic behavior, it would be better to describe economic goals as "survival" rather than subsistence.

Peasant economic behavior seems perfectly rational[18] and explicable in terms of the neoclassical economic framework. That the Polish peasants of the eighteenth century were not "modernizing," or "income maximizing," but rather "risk-avoiding" stems from: (1) the very narrow constraints of serfdom, (2) restricted market possibilities, (3) their low level of income, and (4) their low level of knowledge. When some of these constraints were loosened, more enterprising behavior became apparent.

Institutional Context

Forms of peasant resistance should be regarded as attempts to either maintain or broaden autonomy within the existing socioeconomic system. Before starting to analyze them in a more detailed way, the institutional, legal, and ideological aspects of the prevailing social order must be reviewed.

Peasants were serfs. Serfdom was introduced gradually by a series of royal privileges for the nobility, expanding their rights over the village population and restricting the rights of the peasants. In practice, serfdom meant that peasants could not leave the village without the lord's consent and that they were subject to his administrative and judicial powers. They had no right to appeal to the royal courts.

There were different forms of manorial administration. Sometimes the everyday life of the village was controlled by the lord and his officials, but often the village community had a limited self-government.[19] Its highest authority was a meeting of all adult members of the community, with decisions reached by majority voting. This meeting could pass laws governing village affairs. Community members elected a jury and the village leader. These organs had judiciary and administrative powers. The jury tried small criminal matters and settled "civil" cases, like quarrels over inheritance, debts, and so on. Serious criminal cases were usually brought to the royal court in the nearest town by the lord and the community, but the community had to cover the expenses of keeping the prisoner. The village officers collected taxes, appointed minor functionaries, such as watchmen and shepherds, and controlled the fulfillment of labor obligations owed to the lord. Sometimes the village community had its own property, distinct from the property of individual families, such as forests, meadows, and, especially, communal funds. Village officers maintained a "box" containing official documents, especially those listing privileges granted to the village.

Of course, all the decisions of the village institutions had to be approved by the lord. He held the village officials responsible for obligations owed him and often suggested, or even chose, candidates for various functions. He selected them from among the village elite, counting on their authority, but, at the same time, making them responsible for village loyalty. Candidates tried to avoid this honor, since the institutions of the village community were used by lords to pass unpopular decisions.

The peasants in the royal domains, approximately 30 percent of the whole area of Crown Poland, i.e., Great Poland, Little Poland, Mazovia, Royal Prussia, were probably better off than those in private villages—"probably" because the royal domains are much better documented than the private estates, especially the smaller ones, and as a consequence are better known. The royal domains were usually given for life as a reward for services rendered to king and state. The holder of the domain had to pay part of his revenue, theoretically one-fourth, to the royal treasury. These estates are relatively well documented because of the periodic revisions by parliamentary commissions. Peasants in these domains were considered owners of their houses and hereditary rights to their allotments were to be respected. There existed a so-called Referendary Court to which the peasants could appeal the abuses of the holders.[20]

As far as private estates were concerned, organization differed between those belonging to one-village noblemen and those that were the property of magnates. Magnates sometimes owned tens of private towns and hundreds of villages, and, especially in the eastern part of the Commonwealth of Poland and Lithuania, were able to create administrative and police structures which constituted mini-states. The latter were either managed by huge bureaucracies or rented out to landless noblemen. Peasants were often allowed to lodge complaints against officials or noblemen-tenants and to a certain extent were protected against their abuses.

What made the Polish situation different from that of the neighboring countries, Prussia, Russia and the Hapsburg Empire, was the absence of an absolutist state.[21] This lack probably cost Poland its independence, but it had some positive effects for the peasants. They paid smaller taxes than peasants in neighboring countries. They were not conscripted into the army. A state and police apparatus that could help nobility enforce serfdom was almost nonexistent. On the other hand, the state did not protect peasants against lords, as it at least pretended to do in the Hapsburg Empire after the 1780s.

The ideological aspects of this social system are most difficult to reconstruct, and one can only pose questions for future research. Very little is known of what the nobility thought about the peasants. There are traces of biblical rationalization of serfdom. Did the village owners recognize an idea of "moral economy," a right to survive?[22] Did the nobility develop a paternalistic mentality, trying to rationalize their rule over the peasantry by their duties toward them?[23] Since they were not attacked, as the slaveholders in the United States were by abolitionists, they did not have to develop an ideology defending serfdom.[24] Only in the last years of independence, reformers among the nobility started to address the conditions of the peasantry, but programs of reforms were restricted to ideas of placing the peasants under the protection of the law.

It is much more difficult to imagine what the peasants thought about the world. It is not possible to know to what extent they regarded serfdom as something unavoidable, or how they imagined their utopia.

Land and Duties

In the feudal world, survival depended on land. Peasants had to fight to maintain and to enlarge their holdings against the lords of the manors, who were trying to expand estate territory.[25] Technically, attempts to expand the area of land under family control meant clearing small plots in forests or tilling parts of manorial fields belonging to their own lord or to neighboring estates. In the latter case, there were incursions into manorial as well as peasant fields, with peasant solidarity ending at the boundaries of the village. Tilling the land of other estates was easier, because the peasants' master was either indifferent to or supportive of such activities. Disputes between neighboring villages over land sometimes developed into small battles, where not only fists, but sticks and tools were used as weapons.[26] Complaints of peasants from one estate against peasants of another were quite frequent.[27] Villagers took advantage of unclear legal situations, when the right of property to a certain piece of land was claimed by more than one lord. In such cases, the dispute between the nobles could easily be exploited by the peasants. Peasants often targeted their activities against the property of small noblemen, or against Church property, dispersed within the fields of the landed estate to which they belonged. The fact that serfs had no legal status helped in this case because they could not be brought to court.

When such activities were directed against their own lord,[28] peasants made efforts not to be discovered. Land cleared in forests, for example, was more easily concealed from manorial officials. Small pieces of land were added to peasant strips little by little. One holder of a royal domain complained, for example, that villagers tilled into the manorial forest that bordered their fields, cut the trees and erected a new fence.[29] The scattering of peasant and manorial strips in a three-field rotation system made such practices relatively easy. Surveys of land in the royal domains were always being demanded by domain holders and almost always showed that the villagers had more land than they were entitled to.[30] These surveys led to disputes about the measuring techniques used to check the area of peasant holdings. (Of course, this was before the metric system was introduced, and only traditional measures were used to measure the long, narrow strips of land. The width of a strip was determined by tilling.) Despite the efforts of central authorities, there were no effective standardized measurements. Surveys of land led to accusations against owners, officials, and surveyors that they used measuring sticks that were too short to show that the peasants had too much land.[31]

Of course, peasants wanted to keep the newly cleared land without any obligations. When nobles or manorial officials discovered illegal clearings, they either burdened them with new obligations, or legalized them. At the same time, they took away other, better parts of the peasants' holdings, or simply attached the new land to the demesne. The typical decree of the Referendary Court ordered the peasant fields measured. If it was found that they used more land than was recorded in the survey, the land was placed under appropriate obligations.[32] Whenever possible, village communities resisted these newly established obligations.

Most of the cases put before the Referendary Court concerned disputes between the domain holders and the villagers over land.[33] Peasants usually complained that the holder did not honor old privileges given to the community by the king. Commissions were set up by the court to oversee the matter, and surveyors were ordered to measure the fields. Both the manor and the holder tried to make the surveyors sympathetic to their cause, and sometimes peasants were successful. The Referendary Court was not impartial, of course. Simply by their superior social position, domain holders had a better chance of having a sympathetic hearing than the peasants. It attempted to channel peasant grievances, to avoid uncontrolled forms of resistance, and to protect the physical and human capital of the domain against misuse by the tenant holder.

At the same time, the possibility of bringing cases to court raised peasant consciousness. Peasants had to organize, to meet several times in order to discuss their complaints, to find a scribe, to formulate their grievances, to elect the delegates—the Court was in Warsaw—to collect money to finance their trip, and to prepare themselves for the blackmail and abuse of the holder who tried to prevent them from using the legal system and often meted out cruel revenge after they decided to go ahead with their suits.

For peasants, the Referendary Court was a way of validating their rights to the land, since the Court's rulings were used as arguments in further disputes with the holders. In this respect peasants on the private estates, particularly the smaller ones, were in a worse situation. On large estates, where in particular the estate lands were sometimes rented out or managed by hired officials, peasants appealed to the owners with complaints about the holders or officials in the same way that peasants in the royal domains used the Referendary Courts.[34]

Peasants tried to use the legal system when it suited them. Otherwise, they challenged the feudal monopoly of land ownership silently. For example, they would enter into small land transactions with peasants of other estates and with small noblemen, or secure their debts on the land. The discovery of land transactions, unregistered in the village court records, gives examples of such practices. These transactions, allowed only within a given estate, were often further restricted to small units. It was obvious from the owner's point of view that the amount of land the family used should be in direct proportion to the labor services rendered.[35] With the sale of land, obligations were transferred from one family to another. Land sales occurred when changes in the size and structure of the family changed their consumption needs and production capacities.[36] Sometimes peasants sold land when they were in debt.[37] How much and which part they sold depended on their needs and on topographical conditions, but it introduced chaos into manorial policy.[38]

Not only land, but wood for fuel and for construction was necessary for peasant households. Manors and villages clashed over the use of forests. Owners went to considerable lengths to protect forests. The frequent mention of this matter in the instructions given to officials is a good indication that those regulations were bent. On many estates Friday and Saturday were the only days on which people were allowed to enter the forest. Only fallen wood could be removed. Cutting even a dead tree was forbidden. Draft animals and axes were to be confiscated. Wood for construction could be removed only by special permission.[39] Peasants were constantly abusing these rules by going to the woods at night and by destroying the bark of a tree below ground level in order to kill it.[40] Any manorial property that could be stolen was. Grain was taken from barns, and fish were taken from ponds. Fruit trees were cut down.[41]

Fights over feudal rent were another dimension of peasant resistance. In the feudal system, obligatory labor in manorial fields was the principal form of rent.[42] If a manor did not need labor, it often demanded money instead. If it did not have enough labor, it demanded so-called "compulsory hiring," which meant paid work, but at low rates.[43]

In order to secure enough peasant work of the proper kind, the lord not only had to prevent his peasants from leaving the estate, but also had to intervene in family matters.[44] An abandoned farm, from his point of view, was a waste since obligations were not performed. Consequently, widowers and widows were ordered to remarry or move from the land.[45] The lord tried to marry off each adult male and settle him on a farm, a large one if possible, since labor with draft animals was more important than manual labor. Often this was done against the wishes of the peasants because it meant that working hands were lost for the family farm. The preference of adult males for staying together was fought by the manor.[46] Peasants often resisted getting bigger farms and preferred staying on smaller ones.[47] There is no contradiction between such attitudes and the attempts, noted earlier, to expand the area of land under family control, since the latter incurred no additional duties. Lords tried to restrict the practice of dividing land among heirs, promoting instead the idea of paying off younger brothers.[48] In general, private owners were more successful in intervening than were the administrators of royal domains, where peasants took advantage of weak management.[49]

Owners, with a certain dose of self-serving paternalism, looked after the state of peasant huts, tools, and animals, afraid that they would have to assist the peasants in a moment of need. During bad harvests, work animals at manorial fields were slaughtered or sold. "Many serfs, caring only about eating, used to forsake their husbandry, to eat more and to sow less . . . before the harvest they used to feign hunger and ask the manor for help," complained an owner.[50] Hugo Kołłątaj, a famous political writer of the Polish Enlightenment and a landed nobleman himself, did not seem to understand this method of peasant self-defense when he wrote to his administrator that "a farmer ruins himself most when he looks to the manor for assistance."[51] But this very practice of passing on losses to the lord was one of the important means of peasant resistance.

The peasant had very great possibilities in this respect, observes Witold Kula. The peasant held in his hand the key elements in the reproduction of the estate and in a certain sense he himself was a key element in the estate's reproduction. Thus, in a poor year, he could keep his own consumption at its previous level by giving less to eat to the livestock, which was more valuable to the lord than to himself. The lord had to either help the peasant feed the livestock, or else, should the livestock die off, supply the peasant with other livestock so that the land did not go untilled. The peasant could even eat the grain that was set aside for sowing his plot; and if in the following year the peasant was unable to sow his piece of land, once again the lord could not remain indifferent because that would have lessened the production potential of the estate and created a danger of a devastation of his property.[52]

Since there were many different tasks to be performed on the estate and obligations were multiple and very specific, there was room for constant haggling between the owner, or his officials, and the peasants.

Are peasants' sons, for example, to be allowed to perform the labor on manorial fields?[53] Can a servant be sent to work instead of the peasant himself?[54] Is a particular demand in accordance with local custom? Was it so before? Is it in accordance with an inventory, written so and so many years ago? Is it in accordance with a privilege given to that particular village; if it was royal was it given by some past king? Officials sometimes despaired. Like any other managers, they had to react to changing conditions, such as weather, bad or good harvests, prices, the need to change the labor allocation among various tasks, etc. At all times, however, they faced a stonewall of resistance from peasants, who not only claimed that the managers' particular demands were not in accordance with what was granted to the peasants, but silently blackmailed the managers with the possibility of complaints to the estate owner.

The usual way to resist labor obligations was to perform them carelessly. "Peasants know ways to make work look finished in appearance only, when in reality it is not well done," complained an owner, instructing his officials about supervising labor.[55] Instructions for overseers are full of remarks concerning the need for constant supervision of peasants working on estate land. The mere fact that they are sometimes extremely detailed shows how much of a problem was created by foot dragging villagers. They showed up late for work, worked carelessly, and took prolonged lunch breaks. "Pay attention that serfs show up for work in the morning, and not at mid-day," an owner instructs his administrator.[56] Contemporary observers often noted that the labor intensity of peasants working estate fields was much lower than when they worked on their own fields.[57] They brought the worst tools and weakest animals to work. They resisted, often successfully, the introduction of more efficient, but more labor intensive tools, for example, scythes instead of sickles for harvest.[58]

Short of rebellion, the most radical form of resistance against feudal rent was the refusal to perform labor obligations. In royal domains, it was usually connected with long, protracted disputes between village communities and domain holders, usually with corresponding litigation in the Referendary Court.[59] Sometimes several villages joined the dispute. If it was not settled, and peasants did not work for a long time—some "strikes" lasted for more than a year—the estate could be ruined.

The fight over labor obligations was undoubtedly related to the increase in the amount of labor demanded by the estates. The usual peasant argument was that "in the past" obligations were smaller, although it seems that this "past" was not more than one generation. However, increased incidents of resistance were usually connected with an actual rise in duties.

Low productivity of labor forced lords into hiring additional workers, keeping manorial draft animals, or giving livestock to peasants who lost their own. Obligatory labor duties, measured in days, were changed into a sort of piecework system, where detailed tasks were assigned to a laborer. Peasants hated this system and engaged in haggling over measures used to measure the amount of land to be tilled or harvested, complaining that manorial officials used too long a measuring stick and assigned tasks that were too hard.[60]

Labor in manorial fields was the principal, but not the only, burden. Peasants were also required to work several days per year maintaining bridges and roads. They had to travel when the manor was in need of transport services, had to guard against fire and thieves, and so on. In addition, they had to pay relatively small sums of money to the manor, and they were obliged to deliver rent in kind. This was a relic of the agrarian system, which preceded the feudal phase of the Polish economy, and was more like the agrarian order in the West, where rent in money predominated. Monetary payment, due to inflation, went down in value over the centuries. Small, but differentiated rent in kind, such as yarn, poultry, eggs, oats for the manor horses, and butter helped to meet needs of manorial households and were sometimes sold. These forms of rent were resisted by peasants, just as labor duties were. Rent in money or in kind was not delivered on time or at all. A certain nobleman complained that the "peasant communities would not deliver even the smallest tribute without the execution"[61]—i.e., the assistance—of the private soldiers of the owner of the estate; the soldiers were stationed and fed by the village as long as the villagers met the required demand. Sometimes peasants refused to pay money that was required of them instead of labor. There was a constant fight over the types of measures used when rent in kind, especially grain, was delivered. Grain, a traditional measure of volume, was used instead of a scale. Both sides claimed that the other side used the wrong kind of measuring container. According to peasants, the manor used containers that were too big. Peasants demanded that the grain be shaken and wanted the container to be heaped, when according to custom it should be strickled.[62]

Other sources of the lord's income were his monopolies. Peasants were obliged to use manorial mills and inns and to buy salt and herring only from the lord. The obligation to buy alcoholic drinks from manorial inns only was the most important of these monopolies.[63] Alcohol revenues of large estates were a considerable part of their monetary income, especially when grain export prices were bad.[64] The size of these revenues shows that, despite poor conditions, Polish peasants had money in their pockets. They were somehow able to sell part of what they produced at local markets and have part of their income in money.[65]

The lord's idea was to reduce peasant holdings to such a size as to allow him to reproduce, but not to produce surpluses for the market. If he did not succeed in this, another idea was to prevent peasants from making contacts with markets outside the *dominium*, and to siphon off as much money as possible via the village inn. Kula writes: "The peasant fought forcibly to be able to produce a surplus that he could sell; the lord did everything to prevent him from establishing a relationship with the market. . . . And yet it was precisely his relationship with the market which determined to a great extent the peasant's standard of living. . . ."[66] Within the big estates there were small, private towns, and peasants were forbidden to go to markets elsewhere. "People . . . will not be going to fairs in foreign [i.e., not belonging to the given estate] towns."[67] If, however, the peasants did earn money somewhere, it was given back to the lord via the inn. Sometimes peasants were even searched when they returned from town in order to make sure that they did not bring in prohibited drinks, produced somewhere else.[68]

Limits of Enforcement, Limits of Resistance

It was not so easy, however, to execute these and other rules. Lords could not confiscate land for the obvious reason that they were interested in people as well as land. They could not punish their subjects too severely, because the lords risked loss of labor when a peasant fled or was maimed or killed. Of course, beatings were common, although owners tried to restrict their personnel in using them and did not tolerate beatings in anger. "You should govern the serfs with love, without any rancor . . . with gracious fairness; if they commit an insubordination or any other particular offense, they are to be punished with three or five lashes."[69] On another estate, the standard punishment was five lashes for minor offenses, twenty lashes for major ones.[70] There were similar rules in the royal domain.[71]

It was relatively easy to punish outright offenses and insubordina-
tions; it was much more difficult to crush the stubborn, hidden resistance that was apparent only in slow work, evasions, tardiness, feigned
stupidity, and so on. In a sense, lords were helpless in the face of
peasant resistance, as can be seen from the long list of grievances of a
certain holder of a royal domain. He complained that peasants did not
appear for work at the required time, that they did not follow his
orders, and that, when they delivered grain, as rent, they used measures that were too small and grain of low quality. The lord also
complained that peasants brewed their own beer instead of buying it at
the inn, sowed abandoned pieces of land without manorial consent,
pretended not to have good animals for work at the manorial fields, did
not repay their debts in time, and did not deliver the required amounts
of yarn.[72] Another nobleman complained that his serfs did not come to
work, shirked additional duties such as fire watching or transport
work, failed to deliver rents in kind on time, and did not bring the
proper kind of wood from the forest for manorial use.[73] This type of
complaint was very frequent. Though probably exaggerated, it illustrates well how difficult it was to extract the requisite quantity and
quality of obligations on time.

Peasant resistance lowered labor productivity. The large estate holder could exert pressure on peasants. For example, the method used on
the estates of Primate Poniatowski, the brother of the last Polish king,
Stanislaw August Poniatowski, was to call in his private army. A
soldier was stationed in the village as long as the peasants resisted the
particular demands of an official. Villagers had to feed him, put up
with his abuses, and pay his liquor bills.[74] At the same time, however,
the greater the estate, the higher was the cost of supervision, since
supervisory personnel had to be supervised themselves. Owners were
quite conscious of the fact that their administrators were often more
interested in their side businesses than in the proper management of the
estate.[75]

The ultimate form of peasant ''passive'' resistance was to run away.
Instructions to officials give ample evidence that peasants abandoned
farms. The same can be seen in the decrees of the Referendary Court or
in village court records.[76] Peasant desertion, often caused by heavy
obligations, debts, harsh treatment by officials, theft of their belong-
ings, poverty, hunger, and so on, was a very frequent form of defense.
Running away, however, was not an easy matter. To start a new, free
farm somewhere in the woods was out of the question. Even if a peasant

family could reach uninhabited territory, it required too much capital and the cooperation of the wider community. The most frequent method was to go to some other landed estate, not very far away. Usually the fugitives were offered a better situation than before. Landless peasants were sometimes even offered a farm. The peasants' ignorance of geography made long distance escapes difficult. Nonetheless, there were cases of Polish peasants who went as far as neighboring countries, or even further, to Saxony, for example. There is no recognizable pattern of the direction of peasant escapes.

Peasants also fled to the towns, but this possibility was restricted because of low urbanization. But there are cases of vagrants of peasant origins being tried by courts in towns.

There were laws against the flight of peasants, and injunctions issued against the lords who took them in. But, on the whole, authorities were indifferent and treated escapes as a private matter of village owners, who usually organized the search themselves.[77] If a fugitive peasant was found, his master either tried to settle the matter with the lord who granted refuge to his serf out of court or brought suit against him. If the case was won, either the lord returned the fugitive serf or paid compensation. The problem was often complicated by fugitive peasants marrying local women. Flight was more frequent in the case of poorer peasants than of richer ones, who were more attached to their farms.

Escape was a very effective form of resistance and very costly for the lord in a number of ways. First, the lord lost part of his labor force. Second, peasants often took their animals and their supplies of corn and tools with them. Finally, search and court proceedings were very costly, and not every noble had the means to engage in them. Methods for preventing escapes were not very effective, despite the fact that the lord found guilty of taking in a fugitive not only had to return him or pay compensation, but also had to pay a heavy fine. Fugitive peasants were punished as well, of course, by their "proper" masters. It was the competition for labor among the lords, combined with the vastness of territory and the lack of a police force, that limited the ability of the nobility to tie peasants to the soil.

The threat of desertion could operate as a check on the lord's behavior only as long as labor, not land, was scarce. The problem of demographic pressure and land/labor ratio has not been studied systematically for this early period, but it seems that with the increase of population, land, not labor, gradually became scarce. There is only indirect evidence for this. For example, peasants, during their flights, avoided densely populated Little Poland.[78] Lords ceased to look for escaped serfs in this area at the end of the century.[79] The author of a certain political pamphlet observed that, "peasants marry, settle in new places, and nobody prevents them from doing so because there are plenty of people. . . . If a lazy person leaves, there are two more asking for his land."[80] In the early nineteenth century, it was relatively easy to abolish serfdom in the Duchy of Warsaw,[81] but the nobles insisted that all the land, both estate and peasant holdings, belonged to them. It is estimated that in the Kingdom of Poland, in 1827, there were almost one million landless peasants,[82] more than one-third the total peasant population at the time.[83] Population growth weakened the bonds of serfdom. More important, at the same time, it weakened the bargaining position of the peasants vis-à-vis the lords. Tying people to the soil ceased to be necessary; they clung to it themselves.

There are only tentative answers to the question of the degree of organization of peasant resistance and peasant solidarity. Many forms of resistance, like the careless performance of labor obligations, were undoubtedly spontaneous in nature. Illegal land clearings, theft, and so on, could be organized within the family, but attempts to graze animals or to claim some part of estate land demanded the organized action of the village community. Similarly, for the labor strikes to be successful, collective action was a sine qua non condition. Community members who were cowardly, hesitant, or disloyal must have been forced into compliance, often with harsh measures.[84] Since strikes were most effective when they went beyond a single village to a group of villages belonging to the same landed estate, peasants had to maintain channels of communication between villages.[85]

The problem of organization is linked to the social structure of the village. The government of the village, set up as an instrument to enforce manorial policies, turned against the lord when tensions arose.[86] Community leaders became leaders of the resistance, despite the brutal pressure put upon them by the manor.[87] In moments of open conflict, the administrative and legal skills they had acquired were used to the advantage of the village community. In royal domains and in magnate or church estates, village scribes prepared written complaints against abuses. Delegations were formed to go to the Referendary Court, and funds to support them were collected. Instead of disciplining peasants to perform labor obligations, village elders helped organized resistance into performing more than the community considered appropriate. Even when village officials were accused of acting illegal-ly, they continued to perform these functions in secret.

Filing complaints, although within the law, was not without its costs.[88] Sometimes complaints were written in a supplicatory tone, but often they contained threats or demands for the punishment of abusive officials. Such action was costly because a delegation had to be sent, and because the noble tenant or official could easily retaliate, seeking revenge on village elders or members of the delegation. The writing of complaints itself can be seen as a form of resistance.[89] Bonds of solidar-ity among peasants are illustrated by the help given fugitive peasants, and it is difficult to find cases of peasants helping in the search for fugitives, despite the fact that they were required to do so.[90]

There is no question that the system was in constant disequilibrium, with both sides trying to bend it to their advantage. Abuses against peasants were frequent. Not only were excessive obligations demand-ed, but beatings and brutal forms of repression and punishment led to injuries, maiming, and even death.

There is scant evidence about the ideological aspects of the noble-man-peasant conflict. The mentality and ideology of the Polish peasant-ry of that time has not been studied systematically. It is hard to know to what extent they tried to work and interpret prevailing symbols to their advantage by giving them a meaning different from that which suited their lords. The complaints they filed suggest that peasants were say-ing, "We accept the system, but we criticize the abuses." Perhaps, half-consciously, they realized that "open insubordination in almost any context will provoke a more rapid and ferocious response than an insubordination that may be as pervasive, but never ventures to contest the formal definition of hierarchy and power."[91]

A thin line separates those legal or semilegal forms of resistance from overt rebellion against manorial authority. There were no peasant insurrections in Poland. The Cossack uprisings in the Ukraine are not included. Cossacks were not serfs and did not work for the feudal economy. They were a frontier people with a military tradition, and, apart from economics, there were ethnic and religious reasons for their uprisings. However, there were many cases of local rebellions, with forms ranging from the refusal to perform obligations through starting small fights with manorial officials to organized, armed struggle, re-quiring the aid of royal soldiers to suppress them. Cases of such rebel-lions are better documented for the royal domains than for private estates. They usually started with the refusal to work on estate lands, which then turned into open attacks on the manor and armed clashes. However, they were always local in character. Leading roles were usually played by local peasant leaders, but local people were sometimes also assisted by outsiders. Most of these rebellions took place during the seventeenth century, probably because of the unstable political situation caused by wars, by a deteriorating economy, and by the fact that the costs of reconstruction were placed on the shoulders of the peasant.

In general, the effects of such rebellions were different. Sometimes the leaders were severely punished. Sometimes a settlement was reached between peasants and their lord. Apparently, peasants always waited for fairness within the system, for example, for a fair verdict of the Referendary Court. It seems that they did not take seriously the possibility of living without lords and obligations. Apart from local effects, the most important consequence of these rebellions was the noble class's constant fear of peasant war. Certainly, the unrelenting fear of peasant movement was greater than their potential danger.[92] That fear was important. It was a check on the behavior of the nobility toward the peasants.

Conclusion

In preindustrial Poland, everyday peasant resistance had two important effects. First, it was a check on the behavior of the lords. Second, it gave the peasants a degree of economic and social autonomy within the feudal system. Lords tried to maximize their gains by increasing the amount of peasant labor. But due to foot dragging tactics, peasant labor became less efficient. Efforts to impose stricter controls in turn tied up more resources. Brutality and abuse did not pay beyond a certain point. As a consequence, the lord had to take the interests of the peasants into consideration, at least to some degree. He had to establish a modus vivendi with them.

For the peasants, their constant resistance was the key to autonomy, to being more than just a factotum of the manorial farm. Their goal was to survive and to reproduce. The possibility of at least partial economic independence was a way to achieve this goal. The balance between lords and peasants was a precarious one, shifting according to the relative strength of each group and requiring the peasants to fight constantly for their autonomy.

This game was played in a world very different from the peasantry of today, even in the most backward and subsistence-oriented regions. The difference lies not in the type of economy itself, but in the nature of the surrounding world. The world of the preindustrial, Polish peasant was a world without alternatives. Illiterate, isolated, without the possibility of a different kind of life, they could not imagine a system different from the existing one. They could not write, so they did not leave records of what they thought. Consequently, it is impossible to know whether their consciousness was "false" or not. There are occasional reflections of their system of values in their petitions and complaints, although it must be remembered that these documents were written by hired scribes according to strict conventions. In these complaints, they usually compared the present unfair, and unjust situation with the past, when obligations were lower and rights were respected. Most likely they accepted the general idea of a hierarchical social order in which lords and serfs had their respective places and mutual obligations. It may be that another world was simply unimaginable. At the same time, they were often able to pursue considerably sophisticated and organized actions, carefully planned and executed. Perhaps explaining them in terms of "class consciousness" and "class solidarity" would be stretching concepts devised to analyze and mobilize the nineteenth century industrial workers. Surely, however, individuals and groups behaved rationally, seeking not so much utopia as the protection of their own interests.

The absence of an absolutist state in Poland weakened the position of the nobility versus the peasants. In extreme cases of open rebellion, royal soldiers were sent in to restore law and order. But in cases of minor disobedience or flight, nobles had to maintain social order themselves. A few decades later, when Poland was partitioned, the Polish nobility did not have any inhibitions about calling in foreign troops to assist them in forcing peasants to perform labor duties. For the peasant, the absence of the state meant that he had only his lord at his back, his taxes were considerably less than in neighboring countries, and he was not faced with conscription. At the same time, it is by no means certain that the absence of the state played to the peasant's advantage. In the second half of the eighteenth century, the absolutist regimes in neighboring countries, in Austria in particular, although they exploited peasantry, took peasants under their protection, setting limits on their obligations and giving them access to state courts. On balance, however, it seems that the Polish situation was slightly better since the absence of an efficient state administration left peasants more room to maneuver, especially since it improved the chance for escape.

The lack of political strength of the bourgeoisie weakened the position of the peasants not only in Poland, but throughout the whole of eighteenth-century Eastern Europe. It may be one of the factors that explains the lack of large-scale peasant rebellions, since the peasants could find neither leaders nor allies in the towns. This is only a tentative speculation, and its test would call for a comparative analysis of peasant movements in preindustrial Western and Eastern Europe.

In the long run, especially in the nineteenth century, peasants, despite their resistance, were losers. This did not stem from the weakness of the resistance itself, but was a result of larger developments—demographic change and modernization, occurring in the context of increasing backwardness. It must be added that, although the peasants were losers, the lords were not necessarily winners. Some of them were, but others were victims of the processes of change that narrowed the room for the landed classes. At the same time, a weak capitalist development did not make new places for them in the ranks of the bourgeoisie. Loss of independence was, of course, an enormous shock for the Polish nobility.

Demographic pressure, the fact that there were too many peasants, changed their position toward their masters and their possible employers. The first signs of overpopulation appeared in Poland even before the end of the eighteenth century, harbingers of a problem which, at the end of the nineteenth century and especially in the first half of the twentieth, became the most dramatic issue of Polish social life, when the masses of marginalized peasants posed a problem nobody knew how to resolve.

Modernization, where it occurred, was often state induced. For peasants it meant, first of all, taxes, which compelled them to sell no matter what the prices. Up to the middle of the nineteenth century, forced onto smaller and smaller parcels of land, they were now facing both the lords and the state.

The change in conditions, although considerable, was not complete. Despite the legal emancipation of the Polish peasants, which occurred gradually up to 1864,[92] the agrarian order, based on the coexistence of small peasant farms and big landed estates, prevailed in Poland until the Communist land reform of 1944. Peasants were linked to landowners by many informal ties. Social structure and national culture were dominated by the landowning class at least up until the First World War, if not longer. There were quarrels between peasants and landowners over many issues, such as pasturing rights, forest entry, debts, conditions of pay. The tactics of resistance, learned under the "old order" and passed on from generation to generation, tactics of stubbornness, pretended stupidity and clever manipulation of the small details of life, the ability to take advantage of whatever institutions were at hand, such as courts and legal proceedings, helped peasants to survive. These everyday forms of resistance helped peasants to face not only old adversaries, the landowner and his staff or the village moneylender, but new ones as well, whether they came into the village as tax collectors, bank representatives, middlemen, officials, or police officers. In the first half of the nineteenth century, Polish peasants, when cornered, were capable of rare, but violent forms of open rebellion. In the last half of the nineteenth and during the twentieth century, they used more and more new possibilities such as peasant cooperatives, cultural and educational organizations, and finally peasant political parties. But the weapons of the weak, the everyday forms of passive, hidden resistance, were and are always present in Poland.

Notes

1. For summaries of research on agriculture and peasantry done in Poland, see Stefan Inglot, ed., *Historia chłopów polskich* [History of the Polish Peasants] 1 (Warsaw: Ludowa Spłódzielnia Wydawnicza, 1970); Janina Leskiewiczowa, ed., *Zarys dziejów gospodarstwa wiejskiego w Polsce* [An Outline of the History of the Rural Economy in Poland] 1 (Warsaw: Państwowe Wydawniczo Rolnicze i Leśne, 1964).

2. Some studies are devoted entirely to the problems of "class struggle," for example, Janina Bieniarzówna, *Walka chłopów w Kasztelanii krakowskiej* [The Struggle of Peasants in the Castellany of Cracow] (Warsaw: Ludowa Spłódzielnia Wydawnicza, 1953); Janina Bieniarzówna, *O chłopskie prawa* [For the Rights of the Peasants] (Cracow: Wydawnictwo Literackie, 1954); Bohdan Baranowski, *Położenie i walka klasowa chłopów w królewszczyznach województwa łęczyckiego w XVI–XVIII wieku* [The Situation and the Class Struggle of the Peasants in the Royal Domains in the Province of Łęczyca] (Warsaw: PWN, 1956); Bohdan Baranowski, *Z dziejów antyfeudalnych ruchów chłopskich na Podlasiu* [From the History of Anti-feudal Movements in Podlasie] (Warsaw: PWN, 1953); Mirosław Francić, "Powstanie chłopskie w starostwie libuszkim w pięćdziesiątych latach XVIII w" [The Peasant Insurrection in the Royal Domain of Libusza in the 1750s], in Celina Bobińska, ed., *Studia z dziejów wsi małopolskiej w drugiej połowie XVIII wieku* [Studies in the History of the Countryside of Little Poland during the Second Half of the 18th Century] (Warsaw: Książka i Wiedza, 1957); Anna Owsińska, "Masowe wystąpienia cłopów w królewszczyznach na terenie wojewódzwa krakowskiego," [Mass Peasant Uprisings in the Royal Domains of the Cracow Province] in *ibid.*; Irena Rychlikowa, "Sytuacja społeczno-ekonomiczna i walka klasowa chłopów w dobrach Wodzickich-Poręba Wielka" [The Socio-Economic Situation and Class Struggle of Peasants from the Landed Estates of the Wodzicki Family-Poręba Wielka] in *ibid.*; Jerzy Topolski, *Położenie i walka klasowa chłopow w dobrach anybiskupstwa gnieznieńskiego w XVIII w.* [The Situation and Class Struggle of Peasants in the Landed Estates of the Archbishops of Gniezno]

(Warsaw: PWN, 1956). In other works on peasantry, chapters on "class struggle" were almost obligatory. Józef Leszczyński, "Walka chłopow z uciskiem i wyzyskiem feudalnym" [The Peasant Struggle Against Feudal Oppression and Exploitation] in Stefan Inglot, ed., *Historia*; Celina Bobińska, "Propriété foncière et luttes paysannes en Pologne méridionale au XVIIIᵉ siècle," *Annales Historiques de la Révolution Française* 36 (1964); Celina Bobińska, "Les mouvements paysans en Pologne aux XVIIIᵉ–XIXᵉ siècles. Problèmes et méthodes," *Acta Poloniae Historica* 22 (1970).

3. Topolski, *Położenie*, p. 208. Instead of "passive" and "active," he proposes a distinction based on range, duration, aims, and effects of resistance.

4. Jerzy Topolski, "La réféodalisation dans l'économie des grands domaines en Europe Centrale et Orientale, XVIᵉ–XVIIIᵉ siècles," *Studia Historiae Oeconomica* 6 (1972); Jan Rutkowski, "La gènese du régime de la corvée dans l'Europe centrale depuis le fin du Moyen age," in *La Pologne au XI-e Congrès International des Sciences Historiques* (Warsaw, 1930).

5. The classical formulation of this position is Immanuel Wallerstein, *The Modern World System*, Vol. 1 (New York: Academic Press, 1974). A critique of this view is given by Robert Brenner, "Agrarian Class Structure and Economic Development in Pre-Industrial Europe," in T. H. Aston and C. H. E. Philpin, *The Brenner Debate* (Cambridge: Cambridge University Press, 1985).

6. For a description of the economics of estate farming see Witold Kula, *An Economic Theory of the Feudal System* (London: NLB, 1976), pp. 44–61. A bibliography of monographs on the subject can be found in Jacek Kochanowicz, "L'exploitation paysanne en Pologne à la charnière des XVIIIᵉ et XIXᵉ siècles; Théorie, historie, historiographie," *Acta Poloniae Historica* 57 (1988).

7. Jerzy Topolski, "Commerce des denrées agricoles et croissance economique de la zone baltique aux XVIᵉ et XVIIIᵉ siècles," *Annales. E.S.C.* 2 (1974).

8. This is a key element of Kula's analysis of the place of the peasant farm within the estate system. See *An Economic Theory of the Feudal System*, p. 62.

9. For an outline of the theoretical interpretation, see Kochanowicz, "L'exploitation paysanne."

10. Władysław Rusiński, "Straty i zniszczenia w czasie wojny szwedzkiej 1655–1660" [Losses and Devastations during the War with Sweden 1655–1660] in Kazimierz Lepszy, ed., *Polska we czasie drugiej wojny północnej* [Poland during the Second Northern War] (Warsaw: PWN, 1957).

11. Jacek Kochanowicz, "The Peasant Family as an Economic Unit in the Polish Feudal Economy of the Eighteenth Century," in Richard Wall et al., eds., *Family Forms in Historic Europe* (Cambridge: Cambridge University Press, 1983).

12. Even a cursory look at published village court records reveals an abundance of cases of land sales and purchases within the village. For southern Poland this was analyzed by Celina Bobinska, "Pewne kwestie chłopskiego użytkowania gruntow i walka o ziemię" [Some Questions of the Use of Land by Peasants and the Struggle for Land] in Bobińska, ed., *Studia*, pp. 291–302. See as well Kochanowicz, "Peasant Family," pp. 164–65.

13. Helena Madurowicz and Antoni Podraza, "Ekonomiczne przesłanki i elementy kapitalistycznego rozwarstwienia wsi malopolskiej w drugiej połowie XVIII wieku" [Economic Causes and Elements of Capitalist Differentiation of the Countryside of Little Poland in the Second Half of the 18th century], in Bobińska, ed., *Studia*.

14. For a summary of research see Mariusz Kulczykowski, "Les activités industrielles des paysans dans les régions submontagneueses," in Celina Bobińska and Joseph Goy, eds., *Les Pyrénées et les Carpates* (Warsaw: PWN, 1981).

15. Kazimierz Dobrowolski, *Włościańskie rozporządzenia ostatniej woli na Podhalu w XVII i XVIII w.* [Peasants' wills in the Podhale region during the 17th and 18th

centuries] (Warsaw: Gebethner i Wolf, 1933). Note, in particular, the cases of the families Tylka and Cipka.

16. Leonid Żytkowicz, "Uwagi o bogaceniu sie chłopow" [Some Remarks Concerning Rich Peasants], *Historyka* 13 (1983).

17. Witold Kula, "Money and Serfs in Eighteenth Century Poland," in Eric Hobsbawm et al., eds., *Peasants in History* (Calcutta: Oxford University Press, 1980).

18. I agree with James C. Scott's position in *The Moral Economy of the Peasant* (New Haven: Yale University Press, 1976), p. 14.

19. Józef Rafacz, *Ustrój wsi samorządnej małopolskiej w XVIII wieku* [The Legal System of the Self Governed Village in Little Poland in the 18th Century] (Lublin, 1922).

20. Antonina Keckowa and Wladyław Płucki, eds., *Księgi Referendarii Koronnej z drugiej połowy XVIII wieku* [Decrees of the Referendary Court from the Second Half of the 18th Century] (Warsaw: Książka i Wiedza, 1955–57).

21. For a discussion in English of the reasons for the lack of absolutism in Poland, see Perry Anderson, *Lineages of the Absolutist State* (London: Verso, 1979), pp. 279–98.

22. Scott, *Moral Economy*.

23. Cf. analysis of American slavery by Eugene G. Genovese, *Roll, Jordan, Roll* (New York: Vintage Books, 1976).

24. Cf. Duncan J. MacLeod, *Slavery, Race and the American Revolution* (Cambridge: Cambridge University Press, 1974).

25. For a systematic discussion of the peasants' fight for land, see Bobińska, "Pewne kwestie."

26. *Ibid.*, pp. 325–29 for many examples of lords' tacit approval of their serfs tilling into other nobles' property.

27. Alicja Falniowska-Gradowska and Irena Rychlikowa, eds., *Lustracja wojewódzwa krakowskiego 1789* [Revision of Royal Domains in the Province of Cracow, 1789], Part I, pp. 102–103, and other examples in the same volume.

28. Bobińska, "Pewne kwestie," pp. 353–58; Zbigniew Ćwiek, *Z dziejów wsi koronnej* [From the History of the Countryside in the Royal Domaines] (Warsaw: PWN, 1966), p. 174.

29. Falniowska-Gradowska and Rychlikowa, p. 114.

30. Ćwiek, p. 174.

31. Witold Kula, *Measures and Men* (Princeton: Princeton University Press, 1986), pp. 136–40.

32. Keckowa and Pałuci, I, p. 549. See as well p. 562 in the same volume and vol. II, pp. 213, 254, 282, 321, 416–17.

33. *Ibid.*, passim.

34. Janina Leskiewiczowa and Jerzy Michalski, eds., *Supliki chłopskie z XVIII wieku z archiwum prymasa Michała Poniatowskiego* [Supplications of Peasants from the 18th Century from the Archives of Primate Michal Poniatowski] (Warsaw: Książka i Wiedza, 1954).

35. Keckowa and Pałucki, II, p. 306.

36. Kochanowicz, "Peasant Family."

37. Keckowa and Pałucki, II, p. 459.

38. Antoni Mączak, *Gospodarstwo chłopskie na Żuławach Malborskich w początkach XVIII wieku* [Peasant Farm in Zławy of Malbork at the beginning of the 17th Century] (Warsaw: PWN, 1962), p. 212; Bobińska, "Pewne kwestie," p. 296.

39. Bohdan Baranowski et al., eds., *Instrukcje gospodarcze dla dóbr magnackich i szlacheckich z XVII–XIX wieku* [Economic Instructions for the Estates of Magnates and Nobility during the 17th–19th Centuries], vol. 1 (Wrocław: Ossolineum, 1958),

pp. 152–53, 106, 218; Stefan Cackowski, *Gospodarstwo wiejskie w dobrach biskupstwa i kapituły chełmińskiej w XVII–XVIII w.* [Rural Economy in the Estates of the Bishop and Chapter of Chełmno] (Toruń: PWN, 1961), Part I, p. 231.

40. Ćwiek.

41. Cackowski, p. 231.

42. The length of the working day ranged from 9–12 hours in winter to 14–15 hours in summer. Alicja Falniowska-Gradowska, *Świadczenia poddanych na rzecz dworu w królewszczyznach województwa krakowskiego w drugiej polowie XVIII wieku* [Peasants' Obligations in the Royal Domains in the Province of Cracow in the Second Half of the 18th Century] (Wrocław: Ossolineum, 1964), p. 102.

43. Bohdan Baranowski, *Podstawowa siła pociągowa dawnego rolnictwa w Polsce* [Basic Draft in Traditional Polish Agriculture] (Wrocław: Ossolineum, 1966), p. 25.

44. Witold Kula, "La seigneurie et la famille paysanne en Pobogne au XVIIIe-siècle," *Annales. E.S.C.*, 1972; Kochanowicz, "Peasant Family."

45. Baranowski, *Instrukcje*, I, p. 458; II, pp. 459, 664.

46. Baranowski, *Instrukcje*, Keckowa and Pałucki, I, p. 438.

47. Ibid., I, p. 461 gives an example of regulations prohibiting peasants from having too small holdings.

48. Adam Vetulani, ed., *Księga sadowa Uszwi dla Wsi Zawada* [Records of the Village Court of Uszew and Zawada] (Wrocław: Ossolineum, 1957), pp. 216–18.

49. Dobrowolski, p. 62.

50. Baranowski, *Instrukcje*, I, p. 104.

51. *Ibid.*, p. 168.

52. Kula, *Economic Theory*, p. 64.

53. Keckowa and Pałucki, I, p. 225.

54. Madurowicz and Podraza, "Ekonomiczne przesłanki," pp. 239–40.

55. Baranowski, *Instrukcje*, II, p. 431.

56. *Ibid.*, p. 12.

57. Bohdan Baranowski, *Gospodarstwo chłopskie i folwarczne we wschodnieji Wielkopolsce w XVIII wieku* [Peasant and Manorial Economy in Eastern Great Poland in the 18th Century] (Warsaw: PWN, 1958), p. 142.

58. *Ibid.*, p. 140.

59. Owsińska, pp. 417–20 and passim; Bieniarzówna, *Walka*, p. 102; Ćwiek, pp. 243–56.

60. Kula, *Measures*, p. 136.

61. Leskiewiczowa and Michalski, p. 474.

62. Kula, *Measures*, pp. 129–35.

63. Baranowski, *Instrukcje*, I, p. 159.

64. M. Szczepaniak, *Karczma, wies i dwór. Rola propinacji na wsi wielkopolskiej od połowy XVII do schyłku XVIII wieku* [The Inn, the Village, and the Manor. The Role of *Propinacja* in the Countryside of Great Poland during the 17th–18th Centuries] (Warsaw, 1977), p. 144; Irena Rychlikowa, *Studia nad towarową produkcją wielkiej własnosci w Małoposce w latach 1764–1805* [Studies on the Commercial Production of Landed Estates, 1764–1805] (Wrockaw: Ossolineum, 1966), pp. 202–204.

65. Peasants' contacts with the market were not studied systematically. Cf. Kula, "Money."

66. Kula, *Economic Theory*, p. 73.

67. Baranowski, *Instrukcje*, I, p. 360. Cf. pp. 403, 407, where there are threats of punishment.

68. *Ibid.*, I, 154; Falniowska-Gradowska and Rychlikowa, p. 256.

69. *Ibid.*, p. 131.

70. *Ibid.*, II, p. 46.

71. Falniowska-Gradowska, Świadczenia, p. 115.

72. Keckowa and Patucki, I, p. 122.

73. Ibid., p. 129.

74. Leokiewiczowa and Michalski, pp. 174, 474, 508.

75. For examples of rules to restrict peasant labor for the administrator's own uses, or to protect the lord's forest against officials, see Baranowski, Instrukcje, I, p. 218; II, p. 342.

76. Apart from a major monograph, Staniław Sreniowski, Zbiegostwo chłopow w dawnej Polsce jako zagadnienie ustroju społecznego [The Flights of Peasants in Poland Before the Partitions as a Problem of the Social System] (Warsaw: Książka, 1948); the problem is only touched on by a number of studies. Even a cursory look at published records shows numerous cases of farms abandoned by fugitive peasants.

77. Baranowski, Instrukcje, I, p. 409 for an example of rules for searching for escaped peasants.

78. Śreniowski, p. 55.

79. Miroław Francić, Ludzie luźni w osiemnastowiecznym Krakowie [Vagrants in 18th Century Cracow] (Wrocław: Ossolineum, 1967), p. 45–56.

80. Quoted by Stefan Inglot, Proby reform włosciaonskich w Polsce XVIII wieku [Attempts at Peasant Reforms in Poland in the 18th Century] (Wrocław: Ossolineum, 1952), p. 21.

81. The Duchy of Warsaw was a small remnant of the Polish state created by Napoleon after his victory over Prussia in 1807 out of the territories taken by Prussia from Poland in 1772 and 1795.

82. Created by the Congress of Vienna out of part of the Duchy of Warsaw, united with Russia with the tsar as its head.

83. Zofia Kirkor-Kiedroniowa, Włoscianie i ich sprawa w dobie organizacyjnej i konstytucyjnej Królestwa Polskiego [Peasants and Peasant Question during the Organizational and Constitutional Period of the Kingdom of Poland] (Cracow: Akademia Umiejetnósci, 1912), pp. 110–11.

84. Owsińska, p. 429.

85. Bobińska, "Pewne kwestie," pp. 206–16; Owsińska, p. 431.

86. Bobińska, "Les mouvements."

87. Emanuel Rostworowski, "Rola urzędu wiejskiego w wlace klasowej wsi małopolskiej" [The Role of Village Self-Government in the Class Struggle of the Peasant Village in Little Poland], in Bobińska, ed., Studia.

88. For landed estates of magnates, see Baranowski, Instrukcje, passim.

89. Topolski, Położenie, pp. 221–40.

90. Cackowski, p. 232.

91. James C. Scott, Weapons of the Weak: Everyday Forms of Peasant Resistance (New Haven: Yale University Press, 1985), p. 33.

92. Emancipation meant two things: 1) the abolition of serfdom, i.e., granting personal freedom, and 2) granting rights of property to peasant holdings. The specific rules were different in the three countries that partitioned the former Polish state, and freedom and property rights were not always granted together. However, when granted property rights, peasants consistently got only their former holdings, while former manorial land was kept in the hands of landowners. In all three parts, there was a substantial group of landless peasants that gained only their freedom.

3

Saboteurs in the Forest: Colonialism and Peasant Resistance in the Indian Himalaya

Ramachandra Guha

Since 1973, the foothills of the Central Himalaya have been the epicenter of the Chipko (Tree Hugging) movement, a peasant-based initiative to stop commercial logging. The spectacular act of hugging the tree, by which the movement is identified, its setting in the ecologically fragile Himalaya—an area rich with religious and cultural significance—the participation of women, and the invocation of a Gandhian ethic have all helped to attract wide attention to the movement and marshall support for its program of ecological reconstruction.[1] However, Chipko is only one—though undoubtedly the most organized—in a series of protests against state intervention in the management of the forests. As the only source of softwoods in the Indian subcontinent, the Himalayan forests have been under intensive commercial exploitation (under the aegis of the state) since the closing decades of the nineteenth century. At the same time, systematic forest management has met with a remarkably sustained and uniform opposition by the village communities adversely affected by its workings.

An earlier version of this essay was published in Ranajit Guha, editor, *Subaltern Studies* IV (New Delhi: Oxford University Press, 1985). I am grateful to Kamini Adhikari, Anjan Ghosh, David Hardiman, Dharma Kumar, and K. Sivaramakrishnan for their critical comments on earlier drafts. I would also like to acknowledge the debt this chapter owes to Shekhar Pathak's pioneering research on social protest in Kumaun.

This chapter examines the trajectory of social protest against state forestry during the early decades of the twentieth century. It is set in British Kumaun, a territory bordering Tibet and Nepal, which was under colonial domination from 1815 to 1947. Here, the absence of popular protest in the first few decades of British rule had given rise to the stereotype of the "simple and law abiding hillman."[2] The state reservation of the Kumaun forests between 1911 and 1917, however, "met with violent and sustained opposition,"[3] culminating in 1921 when within the space of a few months the administration was paralyzed, first by a strike against statutory labor and then through an organized campaign in which the Himalayan pine forests "were swept by incendiary fires almost from end to end."[4]

Such a transformation in peasant consciousness and peasant revolt was closely related to an equally major change in the structure of colonial administration. For the advent of forest management—with the hill conifers being arguably the most valuable forest "property" in India—signalled the state's growing intervention in the day-to-day life of the peasantry. By curtailing customary rights of access and use, scientific forestry drastically affected peasant economic and social organization. In analyzing the development of peasant resistance to these changes, I shall distinguish between two stages. The early period of resistance to forest management and the forced labor system lay in a direct path of continuity with traditional methods of peasant resistance. Resting on appeals to the "customary" obligations of the state, such forms of "avoidance" protest[5] were not successful in bringing commercial forestry to a halt; in consequence, protest rapidly assumed a more militant and confrontational form. And as peasant resistance crystallized into a more widespread movement, it began to use new mechanisms of protest in addition to those used traditionally. These changes in the method of protest were matched by concomitant changes in peasant consciousness, both reflecting the rapidly fading legitimacy of the colonial state. The transition in peasant ideology and forms of protest, and its interrelationship with changing structures of power and authority, will be illustrated by the historical evidence presented in this chapter.

The history of social protest in the Indian Himalaya seriously calls into question the received wisdom on the role of the peasantry in anti-colonial movements in the Third World. The literature on Indian nationalism—in common with that on the Vietnamese and Chinese revolutions—has focused on the role of the vanguard party (in this case, the

Indian National Congress) in initiating and directing movements of agrarian protest.[6] While this bias is in part a function of the historical record—viz., the accessibility of source materials on organized nationalist campaigns—it is also informed by a skepticism of the power of the peasantry to act independently in defense of its interests. Thus, according to a prominent Indian historian, nationalism as represented by the Congress party "helped to arouse the peasant and awaken him to his own needs, demands and above all the possibility of any active role in social and political development."[7]

There are at least two ways in which historical research can challenge a view of peasant nationalism that is centered on the role of a "hegemonic" party. One way, suggested by the pioneering work of the Subaltern Studies school, stresses on the one hand the numerous peasant revolts in the nineteenth and early twentieth centuries, well before "modern" nationalism had penetrated into the countryside, and on the other hand the relative autonomy of peasant participation in later movements formally led and directed by a nationalist party.[8] A somewhat different line of inquiry is suggested by James Scott. According to Scott's hypothesis not only is open rebellion infrequent, it is by no means the characteristic form of peasant resistance. The everyday form of peasant resistance is "the prosaic but constant struggle between the peasantry and those who seek to extract labor, food, taxes, rents and interest from them." It utilizes "the ordinary weapons of relatively powerless groups: foot dragging, dissimulation, false compliance, pilfering, feigned ignorance, slander, arson, sabotage, and so forth. . . . To understand these commonplace forms of resistance is to understand what much of the peasantry does 'between revolts' to defend its interests as best it can."[9]

Although Scott's own work is set in contemporary Malaysia, his formulations can be applied fruitfully in historical analyses of lower-class protest. For the archival record may obscure, but it can never completely eliminate, evidence of "everyday forms" of peasant resistance. As elaborated in this chapter, many of the weapons of the weak described by Scott in reference to Malaysia—including foot dragging, false compliance, feigned ignorance, and arson—were used effectively by Himalayan villagers protesting colonial forest management. At the same time, our evidence suggests that over a period of time, these peasants tended to discard these weapons in favor of more open and confrontational forms of protest, even as they remained relatively independent of the influence of urban nationalists in the Congress party.

The Kumaun case may thus provide a bridge between the two approaches described above: the emphasis on the autonomy of lower class revolt and Scott's own work on everyday forms of resistance. Further, I can ask (and tentatively answer) a question that Scott, somewhat surprisingly, never asks: What are the conditions under which "avoidance" protest turns "confrontational"?[10]

Kumaun: Economy and Society[11]

The Central Himalaya is composed of two distinct ecological zones: the monsoon-affected areas at middle and low altitudes, and the high valleys of the north, inhabited by the Bhotiya herdsmen who had been engaged in trade with Tibet for centuries. Along the river valleys cultivation was carried out, limited only by the steepness of the land and more frequently by the difficulty of irrigation. Two and sometimes three harvests were possible throughout the nineteenth century; wheat, rice, and millets were the chief cereals grown. With production oriented toward subsistence needs, which were comfortably met, there remained a surplus of grain for export to Tibet and southward to the plains. Usually having six months' stock of grain at hand, and with their diet supplemented by fish, fruit, vegetables, and animal flesh, the hill cultivators were described by Henry Ramsay, commissioner from 1856 to 1884, as "probably better off than any peasantry in India."[12]

With animal husbandry being as important to their economy as cultivation, the hillmen relied heavily on the extensive forests for subsistence. Around the villages, the oak forests provided both fodder and fertilizer. Green and dry leaves, which served the cattle as litter, were mixed with grass and the excreta of the animals and once fermented provided manure for the fields. In winter, manure was moulded from dry leaves and subjected to rot. Thus the forest augmented the nutritive value of the fields, directly through its foliage and indirectly through the excreta of the cattle fed with fodder leaves and forest grass. Broad-leaved trees also provided the villagers with fuel and agricultural implements.[13]

In the lower hills, the extensive chir pine forests served for pasture. Every year, the dry grass and pine needle litter in the chir forest was burned to make room for a fresh crop of luxuriant grass. Very resistant to fire, chir was used for building houses and as torchwood. In certain parts, where pasture was scarce, trees were grown and preserved for fodder.[14]

Social anthropologists studying ritual hierarchy in the Indian Himalaya have stressed the similarities between hill society and the rest of
India—seeing the former as a variant of the pan Indian trend.[15] While
this may be true in so far as caste is concerned, there are significant
differences in terms of control over land and the configuration of the
political structure. Kumauni society exhibits an absence of sharp class
divisions; viewed along with the presence of strong communal traditions, this makes it a fascinating exception that does not to fit into
existing conceptualizations of ritual hierarchy in India. The distinctive
agrarian structure of Kumaun is germane to the specific forms taken by
social protest.

The hill land tenure system inherited by the British strikingly differed from the adjoining Indo-Gangetic plain, where large landowners
(and a multitude of small owners, tenants, and landless laborers) predominated. The first commissioner of Kumaun, G. W. Traill, observed
that at least three-fourths of the village land was wholly owned by the
actual cultivators of the land. With the gradual elimination of the few
remaining intermediaries from the pre-British period, by the end of the
nineteenth century fully nine-tenths of all hillmen were estimated to be
cultivating proprietors with full ownership rights. These estimates are
validated by census returns, according to which approximately 80
percent of the total population farmed their own land, largely with the
help of family labor. The extraordinarily low proportion of agricultural
labor (in most districts, less than one percent) confirms the picture of
an egalitarian peasant community: a picture used more often as an
analytical construct than believed to exist in reality.[16]

Its strategic location on the Nepal and Tibet borders and its status as
a recruiting ground for army personnel were reflected in the administrative policies followed in Kumaun. Recruitment had started by the
mid nineteenth century, mostly for the crack Garhwali Regiment
formed in 1890. Essentially, peasant farmers who returned to cultivate
their holdings on retirement enjoyed an enviable record of bravery.[17]
As a reward, British land taxes were extraordinarily light. A rapid
expansion of the cultivated area was watched over by a highly personal-
ized administration under Henry Ramsay, whom fellow Englishmen
hailed as the uncrowned King of Kumaun. In sharp contrast to the rest
of India, the colonial state made no attempt to induce peasants to shift
to commercial crops. Indeed, in the odd year when the monsoon failed,
the administrations were swift in importing and distributing grain (at
remunerative prices) in the interior villages. Such measures may help

explain the absence of agitations related to land policy in either the nineteenth or twentieth centuries.[18]

The inception of commercial forestry, however, signaled a dramatic change in the level of state interference with the everyday life of the peasantry.[19] The landmark in the history of Indian forestry is undoubtedly the building of the railway network. The large-scale destruction of accessible forests in the early years of railway expansion led to the hasty creation of a forest department, set up with the help of German experts in 1864. The first task before the new department was to identify the sources of supply of strong and durable timbers—such as sal, teak, and cedar—which could be used as railway sleepers. As sal and teak were heavily worked out, search parties were sent to explore the cedar forests of the Himalayan foothills.[20] Intensive felling in these forests—1.3 million cedar sleepers were exported from the Jamuna valley between 1865 and 1878—forced the government subsequently to rely on the import of wood from Europe. But with emphasis placed on substituting indigenous sleepers for imported ones, particularly in the inland districts of North India, the department began to consider the utilization of the Himalayan pines if they responded adequately to antiseptic treatment.[21] British interest in the Himalayan forests—dominated by the long-leaved or chir pine—quickened when two important scientific developments were reported by forest officials. The tapping of chir pine for oleo-resin had been started on an experimental basis in the 1890s, and by 1912 methods of distillation had been evolved that would enable the products to compete with the American and French varieties that had hitherto ruled the market. At the same time, fifty years of experimenting with a process to prolong the life of certain Indian woods for use as railway sleepers through chemical treatment finally bore fruit. Of the timbers successfully treated, the chir and blue pines were both found suitable and available in substantial quantities and could be marketed at a sufficiently low price.[22]

These two sets of findings influenced the decision to finally carve extensive reserves in the Kumaun forests. Forest settlements carried out in the three districts between 1911 and 1917 resulted in the constitution of almost 3,000 square miles of reserved forest in the Kumaun Division. Elaborate rules were framed for the exercise of rights, specifying the number of cattle grazed and amount of timber and fuelwood allotted to each rightholder. Villagers had to indent in advance for timber for construction of houses and for agricultural implements, which would be supplied by the Divisional Forest Officer (DFO) from a notified list of species. The annual practice of burning the forest floor for a fresh crop of grass was banned within one mile of reserved forests—since this excluded few habitations in these heavily forested hills, the prohibition made the practice virtually illegal.[23]

Within a few years of commercial working, the Kumaun forests had become a paying proposition. When one full fifteen-year cycle (1896–1911) had revealed that resin tapping did not permanently harm trees, attempts were made "to develop the resin industry as completely and rapidly as possible."[24] Between 1910 and 1920, the number of resin channels tapped rose from 260,000 to 2,135,000, a rate of increase matched by the production of rosin and turpentine. When the construction of a new factory at Bareilly was completed in 1920, production was soon outstripping Indian demand. This put under active consideration proposals for the export of resin and turpentine to the United Kingdom and the Far East.[25]

The First World War provided a fillip, as well, to the production of chir sleepers. The cessation of antiseptic imports proved a "blessing in disguise" when the Munitions Board requisitioned untreated sleepers.[26] In 1914, three large antiseptic treatment centers were established at Tanakpur, Hardwar, and Kathgodam respectively—where the Sarda, Ganga, and Gaula rivers debauched onto the plains.[27] Almost four hundred thousand sleepers were supplied during 1916–18, and the Kumaun circle began to show a financial surplus for the first time, with all stocks being cleared. The government saw mill was unable to deal with all the indents it received—nevertheless, over 5,000 chir trees were felled and sawed annually. The forest department's activities during the war were adequate justification for the recent and controversial forest settlement in the hills.[28]

Early Resistance to Forced Labor

Perhaps the most visible form of state intervention before the inception of commercial forestry was the system of forced labor operated by the British in Kumaun. A legacy of the petty hill chiefs who preceded them, the colonial state took over the system on grounds of administrative convenience in tracts whose physical situation made both commercial transport and boarding houses economically unattractive. Under the system, peasants were required to provide, for government officials on tour and for white travelers, several distinct sets of services. The most common of these involved carrying loads, building temporary rest huts, and supplying provisions such as milk, food, and fuel. Other forms of statutory labor included the collection of material and leveling of sites for buildings, roads, and other public works and transporting the luggage of army regiments on the move. According to the land settlement, villagers were supposed to be reimbursed for these services, but in actual practice they were often rendered for free.[29]

The incidence of forced labor was comparatively slight in the first century of British rule. Nevertheless, its impressment was resisted in various ways. The village headman (himself exempt) occasionally concealed some of the men in his village[30]—alternately, travelers who indentured for coolies found the headman being "openly defied" by his villagers, who refused to supply labor or provisions.[31] When census returns from Garhwal reported a large excess of males over females in the ten to fourteen age group, this discrepancy was traced to the age (sixteen years) at which men were called upon to carry loads or furnish supplies. Thus all those whose age could possibly be understated were reported to be under sixteen.[32] Officials commented too that the hillman's aversion to being made to work under compulsion had led to his earning an undeserved reputation for indolence—while he worked hard enough in his fields, coolie labor, especially during the agricultural season, was performed in a manner that made his resentment apparent.[33] Travelers and soldiers thus often found themselves stranded when villagers failed to oblige in carrying their luggage. Ramsay had to levy a considerable fine on a village near Someshwar in Almora district, which struck against forced labor. Another strike in 1903 led to the imprisonment of fourteen villagers of Khatyadi. Concurrently, opposition to the forced labor system was expressed in newspapers published in the towns of Almora, Naini Tal, and Dehradun.[34] The Kumaun Parishad, based in Almora, took up both the forced labor and forest issues, asking the forest department to hire its own coolies and build more roads.[35]

With the advent of the forest department, the burden of these services on the Kumauni villager increased dramatically. The reservation of the forests and its future supervision involved extensive touring by forest officials who took labor and provisions as a matter of course. Coming close on the heels of the demarcation of the forests, the additional burdens the new department had created evoked a predictable response. Forest officers touring in the interior of Garhwal were unable to obtain grain because villagers, even where they had surplus stock, refused to supply to a department they regarded "as disagreeable

interlopers to be thwarted if possible.''[36] Statutory labor, in the words
of the Kumaun Forest Grievances Committee, was ''one of the greatest
grievances which the residents of Kumaun had against the forest settlement.''[37] When coupled with the abbreviation of community control
over forests, it represented an imposition unprecedented in its scope
and swiftness. Villagers looked back, not altogether without justification, to a ''golden age'' when they had full freedom to roam over their
forest habitat and state interference was at its minimum. These emo-
tions were expressed beautifully by a government clerk who applied for
exemption from forced labor services:

> In days gone by necessities of life were in abundance to villagers . . .
> [and] there were no such Government laws and regulations prohibit-
> ing the free use of unsurveyed land and forest by them as they have
> now. The time itself has now become very hard and it has been made
> still harder by the imposition of different laws, regulations, and
> taxes on them and by increasing the land revenue. Now the village
> life has been shadowed by all the miseries and inconveniences of the
> present day laws and regulations. They are not allowed to fell down a
> tree to get fuels from it for their daily use and they cannot cut leaves
> of trees beyond certain portion of them for fodder to their animals.
> But the touring officials, still view the present situation with an eye
> of the past and press them to supply good grass for their horses, fuels
> for their kitchens, and milk for themselves and their [retinue] with-
> out even thinking of making any payment for these things to them
> who after spending their time, money and labor can hardly procure
> them for their own use. In short, all the privileges of village life, as
> they were twenty years ago, are nowhere to be found now, still the
> officials hanker after the system of yore when there were everything
> in abundance and within the reach of villagers.[38]

As one can discern from this petition, the new laws and regulations
were already beginning to threaten the considerable autonomy enjoyed
by the village community. Here, as in other colonial societies of South
Asia and Southeast Asia, unusual exactions and other forms of state
encroachment upon the privileges of individuals or communities were
regarded as transgressing the traditional relationship between ruler and
ruled. By clashing with his notions of economic and social justice,
increased state intervention breached the ''moral economy'' of the
peasant.[39] Anticipating that the hillman would react by ''throwing his

Forest loads down the khud [ditch] and some day an unfortunate Forest Officer may go after them,'' Wyndham, commissioner of Kumaun, believed that the only way to prolong the life of the forced labor system would be for forest officials to use pack ponies. Government could hardly defend the use of forced labor by a money making department— which, if it continued to avail itself of such labor, would hasten the end of the system.[40] Echoing the commissioner's sentiments, the Garhwal lawyer and legislative council member Taradutt Gairola pleaded for a "vigorous policy of reform" failing which "trouble (would) arise" at the revision of the revenue settlement.[41]

These warnings were to prove prophetic, but, in the meantime, the state hoped to rely on a series of ameliorative measures. The lieutenant governor had in 1916 rejected the possibility of the forced labor system itself being scrapped; while it had caused "hardship" in certain areas, the government, he emphasized, was concerned merely "with checking any abuses of the system."[42] In a move initiated by Gairola, coolie agencies were started in parts of Garhwal; by paying money into a common fund from which transport and supplies were arranged, villagers were not required to perform these tasks themselves.[43] In other parts, registers were introduced to ensure that the forced labor burden did not fall disproportionately on any individual or village. Officers were advised to camp only at fixed places and procure grain from merchants subsidized by the government. Rules were framed prescribing what kinds of supplies could be indented for, and loads restricted to twelve pounds per coolie.[44] In a bid to "raise the status of the soldier," retired and serving members of the Garhwal regiments were granted personal exemption from forced labor in 1900, although they were required to provide a substitute.[45] This was extended during World War I into an unconditional exemption for all combatant members of the 39th Garhwalis and for the direct heirs of soldiers killed in battle.[46] The introduction of these "palliatives which afford a considerable measure of relief," it was hoped, would ensure the continuance of the system itself.[47]

Early Resistance to Forest Management

It is important to understand the dislocations in agrarian practices subsequent to the imposition of forest management. Working a forest for commercial purposes necessitates its division into blocks or coupes, which are completely closed after the trees are felled to allow regeneration to take place. Closure to people and cattle is regarded as integral to successful reproduction, and grazing and lopping, if allowed, are regulated in the interests of the reproduction of favored species of trees. Further, protection from fire is necessary to ensure the regeneration and growth to maturity of young saplings. Thus, the practice of firing the forests had to be regulated or stopped in the interests of sustained production of chir pine. While the exercise of rights, where allowed, was specified in elaborate detail, rightholders had the onerous responsibility, under Section 78 of the Forest Act, of furnishing knowledge of forest offenses to the nearest authority and of extinguishing fires, however caused, in the state forests. In general, as endorsed by the stringent provisions of the forest act, considerations of control were paramount.

There is evidence of protest at the contravention of traditionally held and exercised rights well before the introduction of forest management. Charcoal required for smelting iron in the mines of Kumaun was brought from neighboring forests—where these lay within the boundaries of villages, villagers prevented wood from being cut without the payment of levies.[48] And in the years following the first attempt by the state to regulate village use of the forest, the deputy commissioner (DC) of Garhwal reported that "forest administration consists for the most part in a running fight with the villagers."[49]

Even where discontent did not manifest itself in overt protest, the loss of control over forests was felt acutely. The forest settlement officer of British Garhwal, at the time of the constitution of the reserved forests, commented:

> (The) notion obstinately persists in the minds of all, from the highest to the lowest, that Government is taking away their forests from them and is robbing them of their own property. The notion seems to have grown up from the complete lack of restriction or control over the use by the people of waste land and forest during the first 80 years after the British occupation. The oldest inhabitant therefore, and he naturally is regarded as the greatest authority, is the most assured of the antiquity of the people's right to uncontrolled use of the forest; and to a rural community there appears no difference between uncontrolled use and proprietary right. Subsequent regulations—and these regulations are all very recent—only appear to them as a gradual encroachment on their rights, culminating now in a final act of confiscation. . . . (My) best efforts however have, I hear, failed to

get the people generally to grasp the change in conditions or to believe in the historical fact of government ownership.[50]

As this lengthy extract expresses quite clearly, at the root of the conflict between the state and hill villagers over forest rights lay opposing conceptions of property and ownership. A developed notion of private property did not exist among these peasant communities, a notion particularly inapplicable to communally owned and managed woods and pasture land. In contrast, the state's assertion of monopoly over forests was undertaken at the expense of what British officials insisted were *individually* claimed rights of user. With the "waste and forest lands never having attracted the attention of former governments"[51] strong historical justification existed for the popular belief that all forests within village boundaries were "the property of *the villagers.*"[52]

Discontent with the new forest regulations manifested itself in various other ways. The option of flight was considered by a group of villagers belonging to Tindarpur in Garhwal, who approached an English planter for land, "as the new forest regulations and restrictions were pressing on them so severely that they wished to migrate into another district and climate rather than put up with them any longer."[53] Another time-honored form of protest—noncompliance with imposed regulations—was evident when villagers gave misleading information at the time of the fixation of rights.[54] As villagers were "not in a frame of mind to give much voluntary assistance," one divisional forest officer (DFO) predicted, accurately, "active resentment" at the fire protection of large areas and their closure to grazing and other rights.[55]

In 1916 a number of "malicious" fires were set in the newly constituted reserved forests. In May the forests in the Gaula range of Naini Tal division were set ablaze. The damage reported was exclusively in chir forests, and 28,000 burned trees had to be prematurely felled. For the Kumaun circle as a whole it was estimated that at least 64 percent of the 441 fires that burned 388 square miles (as against 188 fires that had burned 35 square miles in the preceding year) were "intentional."[56]

The "deliberate and organized incendiarism" of the summer of 1916 brought home to the state the unpopularity of the forest settlement and the virtual impossibility of tracing those who were responsible for the fires. Numerous fires broke out simultaneously over large areas and often an occurrence of fire was the signal for general firing in the whole neighborhood. Forty-four fires occurred in the North Garhwal division, almost all in order to obtain a fresh crop of grass. In Naini Tal and in the old reserves of Airadeo and Binsar of Almora district—areas that had been fire protected for many years—an established crop of seedlings was wiped out. The areas chosen for attack had been under both felling and resin tapping operations.[57] In Airadeo, the fire continued for three days and two nights with "new fires being started time after time [as soon as] a counterfiring line was successfully completed."[58] As a result of such "incendiarism," several thousand acres of forest were closed to all rights for a period of ten years.[59]

The protests against the forest settlement were viewed with apprehension in Lucknow, where the lieutenant governor, anticipating the conclusion of World War I, observed that "it would be a pity for the 39th Garhwali [soldiers] to come home and find their villages seething with discontent." Reporting on the situation, the DC of Garhwal concluded, somewhat self-evidently, that government could not but affect village life in every county by taking over the forests. The people's "dislike of the Forest department and the horde of new underlings let loose on the district" was shared by the soldiers, one of whom stated that if the war had ended before they left Europe, they could have petitioned the king to rescind the settlement. The soldiers's discontent was evidently disturbing—for, as the district officer put it, "if we can get them on our side it will be a great thing. . . . They are already a power in the land and will be still more a power after the war."[60] The forest department continued to be complacent that such discontent would blow over when the villagers had "greater familiarity with the true aims of the department."[61] Alternately, they pointed to the strategic and financial results obtained in a few years of commercial working.[62] Percy Wyndham, as the commissioner of Kumaun, the senior official entrusted with law and order, was considerably less sanguine. He preferred that the hills continue to provide "excellent men for sepoys, police and all such jobs"—a situation jeopardized by the forest department, which had demarcated the villages as if "the world were made for growing trees and men were vermin to be shut in." In a situation where the "Revenue Department holds the whole country by bluff," without the help of regular police, Wyndham was clearly not prepared to enforce new rules on a "dissatisfied people," preferring to do away with forest rules and staff altogether.[63]

Contravention of the new regulations concerning lopping, grazing, and the duties of rightholders was, as Table 2 indicates, perhaps the most tangible evidence of the continuing friction. Figures from other

Table 2

Breaches of Forest Law in United Provinces (U.P.), 1911–1922

Circle Year	Western Circle		Eastern Circle		Kumaun Circle[a]	
	A[b]	B[b]	A	B	A	B
1911–12	786	1,798	1,167	2,306	958	2,159
1912–13	881	2,182	1,230	2,424	1,203	3,374
1913–14	1,006	2,091	1,365	2,905	1,309	3,864
1914–15	1,248	2,681	1,646	3,293	1,671	5,857
1915–16	1,401	2,662	1,514	3,029	1,610	5,796
1916–17	1,368	2,517	1,636	2,944	2,023	10,264
1917–18	1,242	2,364	1,530	2,777	2,197	11,046
1918–19	1,153	2,058	1,723	3,167	2,167	11,024
1919–20	1,162	2,120	1,378	2,773	2,136	13,457
1920–21	926	1,618	901	2,154	1,723	10,328
1921–22	1,248	2,437	1,622	839	2,070	3,799[c]

Source: APFD, relevant years.

Notes: [a]The total area of reserved forest in U.P. equalled 4.32 million acres, of which 1.91 million acres lay in the Kumaun Circle.

[b]A is the number of cases; B is the number of convictions (in persons).

[c]Cases dropped due to the recommendation of the Kumaun Forest Grievances Committee.

forest circles are given by way of comparison. While the number of yearly convictions in the Kumaun circle far exceeded those obtained elsewhere, a comparison with "Criminal Justice" in Kumaun itself is no less revealing. Over a ten-year period (1898–1908), an average of only 416 persons were convicted annually in the Almora district, on account of cognizable crime of all kinds, ranging from nonpayment of excise to murder.[64] Indeed, with the absence of an adequate patrolling staff, many breaches of the forest law went undetected.[65] Underlying the stiff resistance to the regulations of the forest department was a tradition of hundreds of years of unrestricted use.[66]

The continuing opposition to forest management bore a strong similarity to traditional methods of social protest in the hills. Traditionally, peasant movements had encompassed two major forms of protest. First of all, peasants refused to comply with imposed rules and resisted the officials who enforced them. Occasionally, when the demands grew excessive and were backed by force, villagers fled to the jungles or across political frontiers into an adjoining chiefdom. Alternatively, they would catch hold of an offending official, shave his head and moustache, put him on a donkey with his face toward the tail and drive him out of the state. Such noncooperation at a local level often culminated in a gathering of men drawn from neighboring villages. Having decided not to cultivate their fields or pay revenue, peasants marched to the capital, accompanied by the beating of drums. Here, they demanded an audience with the king to demand a repeal of the offending laws. [67]

In this tradition, physical violence (barring isolated attacks on officials) was conspicuous by its absence. Its sociocultural idiom was predicated firstly on the traditional relationship between the king and his subjects and secondly on the democratic character of these peasant communities. By protesting in such a manner, peasants actually believed that they were helping the king—to whom they accorded a quasi-divine status—restore justice. Once punishment was inflicted on erring officials, the protest invariably subsided—only to flare up again when fresh cases of tyranny occurred.

Such protests essentially represent a right to revolt sanctioned by custom. Hindu scriptures urged obedience to the sovereign as well as the right to revolt when the king failed to protect his people. A form of rebellion sanctioned by customary law has existed in many precapitalist societies, from medieval Europe to twentieth-century African kingdoms. In the words of Max Weber, ''opposition is never directed at the system as such—it is a case of 'traditionalist' revolution, the accusation against the ruler being that he failed to observe the traditional limits to his power.'' In the area covered by my study, however, the movements embodied a distinctive form of social protest that continued to be used, albeit with variations, in the colonial period. Vestiges of this form of collective resistance can be found in contemporary peasant movements (i.e., Chipko) as well. [68]

Forced Labor and Forest Movements, 1921

Meanwhile, village opposition to the forced labor system was matched organizationally by the establishment of the Kumaun Parishad in 1916. This association of local journalists, lawyers, and intellectuals, chaired in its initial years by local notables professing loyalty to the king emperor, underwent a rapid transformation with the onset of the forest department and the enhancement of the customary labor services. The impact of village-level protest and, indirectly, the upsurges elsewhere in India, contributed to a growing radicalization of the Parishad, best exemplified in the person of Badridutt Pande of Almora. As Shekhar Patnak has compellingly shown, Pande, far more than other Kumaun nationalists was acutely aware of the growing discontent among the peasantry. (However, most Parishad leaders were small landholders, like the majority of their kinsmen, and perhaps less alienated from the villages than urban nationalists in many other parts of India).[69] Convinced of the futility of memoranda presented to the government by a few individuals based in Almora, Pande and his associates sought to establish branches of the Parishad in the villages of Kumaun. Simultaneously, his weekly *Shakti*, published from Almora, became an important forum where the labor system and forest rules were made the butt of strident criticism.[70]

In 1920, *Shakti* reported a strike in the county of Kairarao, with villagers refusing to pay the fine levied on them. At the annual session of the Kumaun Parishad, held at Kashipur in December 1920, a major conflict arose between those who still hoped to negotiate with the state and village representatives who pressed for direct action. After the reformists had walked out, the latter urged Badridutt Pande and other Parishad leaders to come to the Uttaraini fair.[71] Held in mid-January at Bageshwar, (a temple town at the confluence of the Saryu and Gomati rivers) this fair annually attracted 15,000–20,000 pilgrims from all over the hills.

Here matters came to a head. In early January, the conservator of forests was refused coolies at Dwarahat and Ganai and, anticipating a strike, the DC of Almora, W. C. Dible, urgently asked the government for a declaration of its future policy (a request summarily dismissed).[72] At Bageshwar a crowd of over 10,000 heard Badridutt pass on a message from Mahatma Gandhi that, "he would come and save them from oppression as he did in Champaran." When almost all responded to a call to raise their hands to show that they would refuse forced labor, Pande continued: "After abolishing coolie [labor] they would agitate for the forests. He would ask them not to extract resin, or saw sleepers, or take forest contracts. They should give up service as forest guard which involves insulting their sisters and snatching their sickles." Slogans in praise of Mahatma Gandhi and "Swatantra Bharat" [Free India] and cries that the government was "anniyayi" (unjust) rent the air.[73] In a dramatic gesture, village headmen flung their coolie registers into the Saryu.[74]

In the weeks following the fair, several officials were stranded when the villages neighboring Bageshwar declined to supply coolies. Elsewhere, coolies were available only on payment, at extraordinarily high rates. With schoolmasters and other government functionaries extending their support to the movement, Dible hastily summoned regular police.[75] Pathak has uncovered evidence of at least 146 anti-labor meetings in different villages of Garhwal and Kumaun, held between January 1 and April 30, 1921.[76] When the DRO of Almora complained of the continuing difficulties faced by touring officials, he was tersely told that the district administration was not in a position to "give you or your department one coolie."[77] Requests for forced labor were not made in tracts where they were likely to be refused.[78] In a matter of weeks, the state's determination not to dispense with the system itself had broken down, and its abolition followed. In the following year, over 1.6 lakh rupees, a substantial sum, were spent by the exchequer on the transport and stores of touring officials in the hills.[79]

As the press communique issued by the UP government emphasized, the growth of the forest department, with all that this growth implied for the social and economic life of the hill peasant, was at the root of the opposition to statutory labor.[80] Peasant opposition to forced labor was conducted at a different level, and for quite different reasons, from the periodic memoranda, appealing to the instincts of a benign and civilized government, that liberal nationalists continued to submit to the state.[81] An English planter based in Kausani reported that while Hargovind Pant, an Almora lawyer, was asking that coolies not be supplied for forced labor, village leaders were prepared to go even further. Thus local activists insisted that no coolies should be applied at all, i.e., they were against paid coolies as well.[82] After Bageshwar, the DC of Almora was tersely informed by a group of headmen that they had refused to supply coolies in order to compel attention to their grievances, chief among them that their forests were being taken away. Dible reported that proposals for closure to grazing had much to do with this intense feeling. A fund had been created by the villagers—anticipating punitive action—for defending anyone against whom the state had initiated proceedings and for paying fines when they were inflicted.[83] While this unity and sense of purpose necessarily made their actions political, the politics of the peasantry were clearly not derivative of the politics of urban nationalism. Apart from a hazy perception of Gandhi as a saint whose qualities of heroic sacrifice were invoked against the inimical powers of government, the forced labor movements had little identification with the Congress.[84]

The Forest Movement of 1921

Following Uttaraini, Pande and his colleagues toured the different villages of Almora, establishing local branches of the Parishad. Inspired by the success of the antilabor campaign, Pande in his speeches urged the need for direct action in order to recover lost rights over forests. For the "Government that sells the forest produce is not liable to be called a real Government"—indeed, it was precisely these mercenary motives that had made God send Gandhi "as an incarnation in the form of Bania [merchant] to conquer Bania Government."[85] As the reference to Gandhi's caste indicates, the term "bania" evoked images of power as well as deception—by selling forest produce, the state was hastening the erosion of the legitimacy it had enjoyed earlier in the eyes of the peasantry. At Bageshwar, Badridutt had depicted this transition in tellingly effective symbols. When forest resources and grass were plentiful and easily available, villagers had an abundance of food and drink—but now he said, "in place of tins of ghee [butter] the Forest Department gives them tins of resin."[86] Sensing the peasantry's mood after the labor strikes, Dible had, with uncanny prescience, predicted the shape of the impending agitation. "[The] next move will be against the Forest Department. Agitators will make a dead set for resin coolies and contractors' coolies engaged in sleeper work, and try to drive them from this work. The people will be incited to commit Forest offenses and we shall have serious trouble with fires." In the coming months, breaches of the forest law increased daily—these included not merely the firing of forests for grass but also "wholesale cutting of trees."[87] In British Garhwal, too, the popular feeling against the forest policy continued to be "very bitter."[88]

The summer of 1921 was one of the driest on record. The failure of the winter rains had contributed to a poor crop and money was scare for subsistence loans in the hill districts.[89] In Totashiling, where the campaign was to be at its most intense, the local branch of the Kumaun Parishad passed a resolution that the people were themselves to decide whether or not to set fire to forest land falling within old village boundaries.[90] From the last week of April a systematic campaign, especially in the Almora district, had been launched for firing the forest. When called upon (under Section 78 of the Forest Act) to assist in extinguishing these blazes, villagers instead directed their energies toward helping the fire to spread. As a consequence, the attempted fire protection by the Forest Department of commercially worked areas was a major failure. Of 4 lakh acres of forest in which fire protection was attempted, 2.46 lakh acres were burned over.[91] The machinery for control of forest offenses "more or less broke down," and an estimated total of 819 offenses occurred of which 395 were definitely known to be "incendiary."[92]

Several features of a form of social protest summarily labelled "incendiarism" by the state merit comment. On the one hand, the incendiarism represented an assertion of traditionally exercised rights—the annual firing of the forest floor—circumscribed by the state in the interests of commercial forestry. On the other, the areas burned over were almost exclusively chir pine forests being worked for both timber and resin—this wholesale burning of the chir reserves representing, as Wyndham acknowledged, a "direct challenge to Government to relax their control over forests."[93] The intensification of the campaign in Almora and Naini Tal was confined to those areas well served by a network of roads, areas that had been under commercial working for some time. When fires swept through nearly all the areas being logged, young regeneration was wiped out. Covering nearly 320 square miles of forest, these fires destroyed 1.5 million resin channels and 260,000 pounds of resin.[94] At the same time, there is no evidence that the vast extent of broad-leaved forests, also under the control of the state, were at all affected. As in other societies in different historical epochs, this destruction by arson was not simply a nihilistic release but carefully selective in the targets attacked. As Eric Hobsbawm has argued, such destruction is never indiscriminate, for "what is useful for poor men"—in this instance broad-leaved species far more than chir—is spared.[95]

However, as the analysis of court cases by the collector of Almora indicates, burning the chir forests represented a direct confrontation with the colonial authorities. The decision to burn the commercially worked areas was predicated not merely on their containing the locally almost useless (in comparison with oak) chir pine. For, as Badridutt Pande well understood, the export of forest produce by the state clashed strongly with the subsistence orientation of the hill peasant. In the collector's classification, typical in its detail of the colonial state's concern to understand—with a view to suppressing—any sign of protest, the fire cases were broken down into the headings in Table 3.[96]

Further details, which may reveal more about the nature of protest, can be gleaned from summary accounts of the court cases. Gangua,

Table 3

Fires Cases in Almora, 1921

Head			Number of cases	Number of persons involved
I.	INTENTIONAL			
	A)	To paralyze FD by destroying valuable areas	8	21
	B)	To cause loss to FD by way of revenge due to hatred	26	45
	C)	To have good grass for cattle	11	17
	D)	To cause loss to resin mates out of enmity	2	3
	E)	Out of enmity to spite another	3	5
	F)	Which agitation was direct cause of fire	NA	13
		Total	50	104
II.	ACCIDENTAL			
		(This includes smoking or carrying fire within the reserves, the spread of fires from cultivated fields, etc.)	23	45

Source: Forest Department (FD) file 157/1921, UPSA.

aged sixteen, was one of several youths "put up by noncooperators" to destroy "valuable regeneration areas" by fire. Nor was participation restricted to men—thus Durga was sentenced to one month in jail when she "deliberately set fire to Thaklori forest." In at least four different instances, witnesses set up by the prosecution were "won over" by noncooperators, and the cases had to be dropped. Chanar Singh and four others of the Tagnia clan of Doba Talla Katyur were "affected by lectures" by "Non-cooperators and a Jogi" and set fire to regeneration areas. This tantalizingly brief reference to the yogi (who was later prosecuted) leads to speculation that the peasantry sought (as in the Uttaraini fair) a moral-religious sanction for their acts. No such sanction was required by Padam Singh and Dharam Singh of Katyur, awarded the maximum sentence of seven years imprisonment, who expressed their opposition to state monopoly in no uncertain terms. In the words of the Magistrate: "The compartment fired was near the village and used by them. They resented the work of the Department in this compartment since it interfered with their use of the compartment. Therefore they set fire to it deliberately."[97]

The firing of pine needles for grass occurred in Garhwal as well. With commercial forestry and the protection of regeneration areas from grazing and fire as yet restricted in its operations, the damage to state-controlled forests was not as widespread as in Almora. Yet the DC had convicted 549 persons, 45 for "direct or indirect incendiarism," and 504 for refusing to extinguish fires, before the recommendations of the Grievances Committee led to all pending cases being dropped. Fires were reported to be most acute in the areas bordering Almora and in the southern counties of Landsdowne Subdivision in the outer hills. With resin-tapping in its infancy, fires were most often started with the goal of obtaining fresh grass.[98]

While all social groups participated, the involvement of soldiers in the forest movement of 1921—in the same way as the participation of village headmen in the forced labor campaign—bore witness to the failure of the attempt by the colonial state to create an indigenous collaborating elite. In Garhwal, the fires were most often started by soldiers on leave, but as "99 per cent of the population sympathized with them" their apprehension by the authorities became an impossible task. Four soldiers of the 39th Garhwalis were arrested for threatening or assaulting forest officials.[99] After the Uttaraini fair, ex-soldiers were active among those who helped the Kumaun Parishad form branches in the villages of the Kosi valley. One soldier said in his speeches that "government was not a Raja, but a Bania and Rakshasi [demonic] Raj and the King Emperor was Ravan [demon god]." Recounting his experiences in Europe where he was wounded the pensioner described the visit of the king emperor to his hospital bedside. Asked to state his grievances, "he complained against *Patwaris* [revenue officials] and forest guards but all that has been given is the Rowlatt Act and Martial Law."[100] No longer was the king perceived as having the quasi-divine powers of intervening to restore justice and a harmonious relationship between the state and the peasant. As expressed through the symbolism of the epics, the government now embodied not merely the rapacious *bania* (merchant) but the evil-intentioned demons of Hindu mythology. Ravan, the very personification of evil, was equated with the king emperor, whose failure (or inability) to stem the expansive growth of the Forest Department and its minions had led to a rapid fall from grace.

Kumaun and the Sociology
of Peasant Protest

I have tried here to explain the form social protest took in Kumaun in the early decades of the twentieth century and show that prior to the reservation of forests, hill society could be described as a conglomeration of village communities with control over the means of production and over the resources needed to reproduce itself. Commercial forestry and the changes it brought in its wake initiated a process whereby the Kumaun peasantry began to lose control over these resources. The response of the peasantry to these profound dislocations ranged from incipient, "unorganized" forms of protest—such as flight, breach of forest rules, and so on—to an open confrontation with the state as witnessed by the labor and forest campaigns of 1921.

One striking fact about these movements is the absence, comparatively speaking, of violence (certainly physical violence). The methods of protest characteristically used by the hill peasants were strikes and burning the forest floor. In this context, one may refer again to the unusual political and economic structure of Kumaun, where the state dealt directly with the relatively egalitarian village communities without the help of an intermediary class enjoying a vested interest in land. The dreaded triad of "Sarkar, Sahukar, and Zamindar [state, moneylender, and landlord] (which) was a political fact rooted in the very nature of British power in the subcontinent," was here conspicuous by its absence, as indeed was the "total and integrated violence" of rebellion observed elsewhere.[101] Although "impatient of control,"[102] the hill man enjoyed an *autonomy* rarely found elsewhere in India, as this description of the "Garhwal village paharee" [hillman] by a British health officer testifies: "I suppose it would be difficult to find any peasantry in the world more free from the *res angustae domi* (i.e. straitened circumstances at home): he is the owner of a well built stone house, has as much land as he wants at an easy rental, keeps his flocks and herds, and is in every sense of the word, an independent man."[103]

The absence of a culturally distinct buffer class (as the Hindu zamindars were to the tribals in peninsular India) between the body of cultivating proprietors and the state, and the comparative autonomy the former continued to enjoy, are germane to the particular forms taken by conflict between the peasantry and the constituted authority of the state, and the manner in which these conflicts were represented in popular consciousness. Undoubtedly, the first century of British rule and the paternalist style of Ramsay and Co. may have seen a partial transference of an allegiance earlier owed to the king. Traditionally, peasant protest in the pre-British period had taken the form of collective resistance to tyranny by officials, and concomitantly, a call to the monarch to restore justice. Such forms of "avoidance" protest continued to be used; simultaneously newer and more militant forms of resistance emerged with the onset of forest management. Forest administration introduced a notion of property—one integral to colonial rule but previously foreign to Kumaun—that ran contrary to the experience of the village communities in which different castes shared a "remarkable amity," symbolized by their sharing of the common pipe.[104] The affirmation of a state monopoly and its corollary, the sharp diminution of community rights over forests, breached the notions of economic and social justice that scholars have called the "moral economy" of the peasant.

To be comprehensive in scope, the sociological analysis of peasant protest must incorporate the vitally important dimension of change. As I have shown in this study, the weapons of the weak are neither uniform nor unchanging. While the early period of resistance to colonialism lay in a direct path of continuity with traditional mechanisms of protest, there was a marked change in the later period, with the peasantry coming into sharp conflict with state authority. Nowhere was this change more explicitly manifested than in the radicalization of an organization originally set up to mediate between the state and the peasantry. Established in the afterglow of the Coronation Durbar of 1911, the Kumaun Parishad initially swore undying loyalty to "George Pancham" [George V]. But the pressure from below, as it were, egged them to adopt a more directly confrontationist position. And in July 1921, their philosophy was being described as "the anarchist doctrine of direct action, which has been attempted in England by Bolshevist Labour Revolutionaries."[105] Clearly such a situation had been brought about by the "inherent" elements of folk or popular ideology impinging upon, and transforming in the process, the "derived" elements originating in organized politics.[106]

For the Kumaun peasant, the cohesion and collective spirit of the village community provided the mainspring of political action. The wide ranging campaign of 1921, though differing from a modern social movement in its aims and methods, was far from being a spontaneous outburst of an illiterate peasantry, representing a blind reaction to the expropriation of a resource crucial to their subsistence. It expressed, albeit in a far more heightened way, the motivations that underlay the sporadic and localized protests in the early years of forest administration. Expressed through the medium of popular protest were conflicting theories of social relationships that virtually amounted to two world views. One can contrast state monopoly rights with the free use of forest by members of the village community as sanctioned by custom—a pattern of use, moreover, regulated by the community as a whole. The exploitation of the pine forests on the grounds of commercial profitability and strategic imperial needs was at variance, too, with the use of natural resources in an economy oriented toward subsistence. The invocation of the symbols of Bania (merchant) and Rakshas (demon), with all that they stood for, were a natural consequence of this discrepancy. As the paternalist state transformed itself into an agency intruding more and more into the daily life of the peasantry, so its claim to legitimacy floundered. While early resistance did not seriously question the legitimacy of a government separated from its subjects by a gulf of race, class, and language, the cumulative incursions of forced labor and commercial forestry culminated in the organized and widespread campaigns of 1921. And, as the success of these movements testifies, in this instance at least, "primitive rebellion" proved to be several steps ahead of "modern nationalism."

Notes

1. See A. Mishra and S. Tripathi, *Chipko Andolan* (New Delhi, 1978, mimeographed); B. Dogra, *Forests and People* (Rishikesh: Himalaya Darshan Prakashan Samiti, 1980).

2. P. Mason, *A Matter of Honour* (London: Cape, 1975), p. 451.

3. E. P. Stebbing, *The Forests of India* Vol. III (London: John Lane, 1922–27), p. 39.

4. E. A. Smythies, *India's Forest Wealth* (London: Humphrey Milford, 1925), p. 84.

5. Cf. Michael Adas, "From Avoidance to Confrontation: Peasant Protest in Precolonial and Colonial Southeast Asia," *Comparative Studies in Society and History* 23 (1981); J. C. Scott, *Weapons of the Weak: Everyday Forms of Peasant Resistance* (New Haven: Yale University Press, 1986).

6. See Sumit Sarkar, *Modern India, 1885–1947* (New Delhi: Macmillian, 1983) for a historiographical review.

7. Bipan Chandra, *Nationalism and Colonialism in Modern India* (New Delhi: Orient Longman, 1979), p. 345.

8. Ranajit Guha, ed., *Subaltern Studies: Writings on South Asian History and Society*, Volumes I to IV (New Delhi: Oxford University Press, 1982–85).

9. Scott, *Weapons of the Weak*, p. 29.

10. Although, as the argument and evidence of this essay will make clear, Scott's

earlier work does provide some valuable leads in this regard.

11. In this essay, Kumaun refers to the British civil division comprising the districts of British Garhwal, Almora, and Naini Tal. In the precolonial period, the latter two districts constituted the chiefdom of Kumaun, while British Garhwal formed part of the chiefdom of Garhwal. The Kumaun Division (hereafter KD) was separated from Nepal in the east by the river Kali, from Tibet in the north by the Himalaya, from the state of Tehri Garhwal in the west by the Alakananda and Mandakini rivers, and from the adjoining district of Rohilkhand in the south by the outer hills.

12. H. G. Walton, *Almora: A Gazetteer* (Allahabad: Government Press, 1911), pp. 57–9; S. D. Pant, *The Social Economy of the Himalayans* (London: George Allen and Unwin, 1935), p. 137; "Correspondence Relating to the Scarcity in Kumaun and Garhwal in 1890," in *British Parliamentary Papers* 59 (1890–92).

13. This paragraph is based on Franz Heske, "Problem der Walderhaltung in Himalaya" (Problems of forest conservation in the Himalaya), *Tharandter Forstlichen Jahrbuch* 82 (1931); 545–94. I am grateful to Professor S. R. D. Guha for help with translation from the German.

14. *Ibid.*, pp. 555, 564–65; E. K. Pauw, *Report on the Tenth Settlement of the Garhwal District* (Allahabad: Government Press, 1894), pp. 23, 47.

15. The classic studies are Gerald Berreman, *Hindus of the Himalayas* (Berkeley: University of California Press, 1963); R. D. Sanwal, *Social Stratification in the Rural Kumaun* (New Delhi: Oxford University Press, 1976).

16. G. W. Traill, "Statistical Sketch of Kumaun," *Asiatic Researches* 16 (1828; rprt. New Delhi: Cosmo Pub., 1980); J. H. Batten, editor, *Official Reports on the Province of Kumaun* (1851; rprt. Calcutta: Government Press, 1878); *Census of India*, 1911 and 1921.

17. See Mason, *A Matter of Honour*, pp. 384, 418–22.

18. A. S. Rawat, "Administration of Land Revenue in British Garhwal (1856–1900)," *Quarterly Review of Historical Studies* (Calcutta) 21 (1981–82).

19. For a detailed analysis of colonial forest policy, science, and legislation, see my articles "Forestry in British and Post British India: A Historical Analysis," *Economic and Political Weekly* (hereafter EPW), in two parts, 29.10.1983 & 5–12.11.1983, and "Scientific Forestry and Social Change in Uttarakhand," EPW, Special Number, 1985.

20. G. P. Paul, *Felling Timber in the Himalayas* (Lahore: Government Press, 1871).

21. D. Brandis, "Memorandum on the Supply of Railway Sleepers of the Himalayan Pines Impregnated in India," *Indian Forester* (IF), 4:4, 1869.

22. Puran Singh, "Note on the Distillation and Composition of Turpentine Oil From the Chir Resin and the Clarification of Indian Rosin," *Indian Forest Records* (IFR), Vol. 4, Part 1 (Calcutta, 1912); R.S. Pearson, "Note on the Antiseptic Treatment of Timber in India, With Special Reference to Railway Sleepers," IFR, Vol. 3, pt. 1 (Calcutta, 1912).

23. Details of these rules can be found in A. E. Osmaston, *Working Plan for the North Garhwal For. Div., 1921–22 to 1930–31* (Allahabad: Government Press, 1921), Appendix.

24. E. A. Smythies, "The Resin Industry in Kumaun," *Forest Bulletin No. 26* (Calcutta, 1914), p. 3.

25. Imperial Institute, Indian Trade Enquiry, *Report on Lac, Turpentine and Resin* (London: Imperial Institute, 1922), pp. 29–51. India was the only source of oleo-resin within the British dominions.

26. Stebbing, III, pp. 658–59.

27. J. E. C. Turner, "Antiseptic Treatment of Chir Pine Sleepers in the Kumaun

Circle, UP,'' IF, Vol. 40 (1914), pp. 427–29.

28. *Annual Progress Report of Forest Administration in the United Provinces* (hereafter APFD), for 1916–17, pp. 20, 28, 35; APFD 1917–18, pp. 22–23.

29. Shekhar Pathak, ''Uttarakhand mein coolie begar pratha, 1815–1949'' (The system of forced labor in Uttarakhand, 1815–1949), unpublished Ph.D. thesis, Dept. of History, Kumaun University, Naini Tal, 1980. Also his ''Kumaun mein begar anmulan andolan'' (Movements against forced labor in Uttarakhand), paper presented at Seminar on Peasant Movements in Uttar Pradesh (UP), Jawaharlal Nehru University, New Delhi, 19–20.11.1982. These are hereafter referred to as Pathak(1) and Pathak(2) respectively.

30. J. H. Batten, ''Final Report on the Settlement of Kumaun'' in *idem*, ed., *Official Reports of the Province of Kumaun*, p. 270.

31. ''Mountaineer,'' ed., *A Summer Ramble in the Himalaya* (London: Hurst and Blackett, 1860), p. 167.

32. Census of India, 1891, Vol. 16, pt. 1, NWP & O, General Report, pp. 29–30.

33. V. A. Stowell, *A Manual of the Land Tenures of the Kumaun Division* (1907; rprt. Allahabad 1937), pp. 150–56.

34. See Pathak(2), pp. 4–14.

35. See Letter from Comm. KD, to Chief Secretary, UP, dt. 18.9.1916, in FD File 164/1916, UPSA.

36. Doc. No. 10X, dt. 6.2.1917, from DFO, North Garhwal to Conservator of Forests (CF) Kumaun Circle, GAD File 398/1913, UPSA.

37. *Report of the Kumaun Forest Grievances Committee* (hereafter KFGC), in Progs. A, June 1922, Nos. 19–24, File No. 522/1922, Dept. of Rev. & Agl. (Forests), NAI, p. 2.

38. Petition to Sir James Meston, Lt.-Gov., UP, by Pandit Madan Narayan Bist (Village Ulaingad, Patti Wallawigad, Almora), clerk on duty at the office of the Director-General of Archaeology at Ootacamund, dt. 17.5.1913, GAD file 398/1913. Grammar and punctuation as in original.

39. J. C. Scott, *The Moral Economy of the Peasant* (New Haven: Yale University Press, 1976).

40. ''Note on transport of forest officials by Uttar and pack ponies,'' by Comm. KD, dtd. 17.8.1919, in File No. 21 of 1918–19, Dept. XV, Regional Archives, Naini Tal (RAN).

41. ''Report of the Kumaun Sub-Committee of the Board of Communications of coolie utar and bardaish in Kumaun''; Sd/-P. Wyndham, Chairman, dtd. 9.10.1919; note on above report by T.D. Gairola, dtd. 17.10.1919, GAD file 739/1920, UPSA.

42. Speech by Sir James Meston at Darbar held in Naini Tal on 30.9.1916, in GAD file 108/1918, UPSA.

43. See, for example, ''Annual Report of the Coolie Agencies in Garhwal District for 1911–12,'' in GAD file 398/1913.

44. No. 6544/XV/50, dtd. 10.9.1916, from Comm. KD to Chief Secretary UP; ''Rules for touring officials in the hill pattis of the Kumaun Division,'' Sd/-Comm. KD, 18.10.1916. Both in *ibid*.

45. No. *6056* dtd. 19.6.1900, from Comm. KD to Chief Secretary, XVI–19 NWP & O; No. *2503* dtd. 4.8.1900, from Chief Secretary NWP & O, to 1–303B' Deputy Adujtant-General, Bengal, both in File No. 19 of 1899–1900, Dept. XVI, RAN.

46. No. 1165/III/398, dtd. 5.6.1916, from Chief Secretary, UP to Officers commanding 1st and 2nd Cos, 39th Garhwal Rifles, GAD File 398/1913.

47. See note by Under Secretary to Chief Secretary, UP, dated 17.8.1913, in *ibid*.

48. J. O. B. Beckett, ''Iron and Copper mines in the Kumaun Division,'' report dated 31.1.1850, in *Selections*, Vol. III (Allahabad 1867), 31–8. ''There is *not a single*

malgoozar of any of the villages in the neighborhood of the iron mines, who has not at one time or other endeavored to levy a tax on *all* the charcoal burners" (*ibid.*, 36, emphasis added).

49. "Note on forest administration for my successor" by McNair, DC Garhwal, dated Feb. 1907, in FD file 11/1908, UPSA.

50. J. C. Nelson, *Forest Settlement Report of the Garhwal District* (Lucknow, 1916, mimeographed), pp. 10–11.

51. Pauw, "Settlement Report," p. 52.

52. Gairola, "Selected Revenue Decisions," p. 211.

53. District and Sessions Judge, Moradabad, to Pvt. Secretary to Lt.-Gov., UP, dtd. 2.3.1916, in FD file 163/1916 (Forest Settlement Grievances in the KD), UPSA.

54. According to the settlement officer, "much was omitted and much exaggerated, much extenuated and much set down in malice," while quarrels over rights "were unfortunately always very bitter," Nelson, Forest Settlement Report, pp. 2–4, 13, 25.

55. Osmaston, "North Garhwal WP," p. 67.

56. *Report on the Administration of the United Provinces of Agra and Oudh, 1915–16* (Allahabad: Government, 1916), p. viii.

57. APFD 1915–16, p. 7.

58. H. G. Champion, "Observations on some effects of fires in the *chir* (Pinus longifolia) forests of the West Almora Sivision," *Indian Forester* Vol. 45 [1919], pp. 353–63.

59. H. G. Champion, *WP for the Central Almora for Div.* (1922), pp. 13–14.

60. J. C. Meston (Lieutenant Governor) to Comm. KD, dated 5.3.1916; DC Garhwal to L-G, dtd. 27.3.1916; "Note on the Forest Settlement and the Garhwali Officers of the Regiment," by DC Garhwal, dated 20.3.1916, all in FD file 163/1916.

61. G.O. No. 197/XIV/163, dated 14.2.1918, appended to APFD, 1916–17.

62. See G.O. No. 114/XIV/172 of 1918 dtd. 4.2.1919, appended to APFD 1917–18.

63. Wyndham to Meston, dtd. 26.6.1916; same to same, dtd. 3.7.1916; "Subjects for discussion at the conference of selected officers to be held at Government House Naini Tal at 10.30 a.m. on the 28th August 1916"; Sd/-P. Wyndham, dtd. 14.8.1916, all in FD file 163/1916.

64. Figures calculated from Walton, "Almora," Appendix.

65. See, for example, G.O. No. 1237-XIV-209, dated 2.11.1922, appended to APFD, 1921–22.

66. See APFD, 1919–20, p. 8; Osmaston, "North Garhwal WP," p. 89.

67. I am grateful to the veteran historian of Garhwal, Shoorbeer Singh Panwar, for being the first to point out to me the cultural significance of the protests known as *dhandak*. This account of the *dhandak* is based on my archival and field research on peasant movements in the princely state of Tehri Garhwal. For reports on *dhandaks*, see, inter alia, Foreign Dept. Internal B. Progs, October 1907, Nos. 37–9, National Archives of India (NAI), New Delhi; T. D. Gairola, "The Disturbance in Rawain (Tehri)," *The Leader*, 3.8.1930. Cf. also Anon., "Mass Demonstrations in the Hills," *Indian States Reformer* (Dehradun), 22.5.1932.

68. See Ramachandra Guha, *The Unquiet Woods: Commercial Forestry and Social Protest Movements in the Indian Himalaya*, forthcoming from Oxford University Press, ch. VIII.

69. See G. B. Pant's evidence to the *Royal Commission on Agriculture in India* (London: Government Press, 1927), Vol.VII, p. 360.

70. Shekhar Pathak, *Badridutt Pande aur unka yug* (Lucknow: Government Press, 1982), pp. 12–24, hereafter Pathak(3).

71. Pathak(2), pp. 22–24. Prominent among the village activists was Mohan Singh Mehta of Katyur.

72. DC No. C.3, dated Bageshwar, 17.1.1921, from DC, Almora to Comm. KD. Extract from confidential fortnightly report of Comm. KD; dated 10.1.1921, both in Police Department (PD) File 1151/1921, UPSA.

73. Summary of Badridutt Pande's speech at Bageshwar, by S. Ijaz Ali, Deputy Collector, Almora, in *ibid*.

74. Pathak(2), p. 28.

75. DC, Almora, to Comm. KD, No. C.3, dated 17.1.1921; same to same, No. C.4, dated 20.1.1921; No. 43, CI, 21, dated 29.1.1921, from Comm. KD, to Chief Secretary UP, all in PD file 1151/1921.

76. Pathak(1), Appendix III.

77. No. 42, C.I.21, dated 28.1.1921, from Comm. KD, to DFO, Almora, in PD file 1151/1921.

78. Comm. KD, to Secretary to Government UP, dated 4.3.1921, in GAD file 739/1920.

79. Resolution passed by UP Legislative Council on 5.3.1921. Table on transport of Officers in camp, 1921–22, enclosed with D.O. No. 215, dated 17.6.1922, from Comm. KD, to Deputy Secretary, GAD, UP, both in *ibid*.

80. "In recent years, mainly owing to the rapid expansion of the Forest Department, the demands for utar have greatly increased and the obligations of furnishing utar have caused growing resentment." Press Communique, dated 1.2.1921, Sd/-HS Crosthwaite, Secretary to Government, UP in *ibid*.

81. See Memorandum on Coolie utar submitted by Kumaun Association (Ranikhet branch) to Lt.-Gov., UP, dated 16.10.1920, in *ibid*.

82. Letter from R. G. Bellaire, Colonization Officer of Soldier Settlement Estates, Kausani, to DC Almora, dated 1.2.1921, in PD file 1151/1921.

83. DC Almora to Comm. KD, dtd. 17.1.1921; same to same, No. C.15, dtd. 24.1.1921, both in *ibid*., Wyndham was clear that "the root of the whole evil and discontent is "our d----d forest policy" (No. 2. C.II, 21, dtd. 1.2.1921, from Comm. KD to Chief Secy. UP in *ibid*.).

84. Cf. Govind Chatak, *Garhwali lok geet* (Dehradun: Yugvani Press, 1956), pp. 261–62.

85. "Report of Pandit Badridutt Editor's speeches to Villagers in Almora District," in PD file 1151/1921.

86. See Criminal Case No. 7 of 1921, King Emperor vs. Motiram, Budhanand and Badridutt of Totashiling, at Police Station Palla Boraran, in the court of W.C. Dible, District Magistrate, Almora, dated 7.7.1921, in FD file 157/1921 ("Forest fires in Kumaun"), UPSA.

The implication, if it needs to be spelled out, was that while the forests had earlier supplied products like ghee and thus contributed to the local economy, now they were used to produce resin which was of no use to villagers. The use of such a metaphor, it may be added, reiterates the strong emphasis placed on village autonomy.

87. DC, Almora to Comm. KD, No. C.15, dated 24.1.1921; same to same, No. C.63, dated 2.3.1921, both in PD file 1151/1921.

88. Extract from fortnightly D.O. from Comm. KD for second half of March 1921, FD file 157/1921.

89. See File No. 56 of 1921, A Progs., Nos. 1–2, May 1921, Dept. of Revenue and Agriculture (Famine), NAI.

90. See resolution printed in the *Shakti* of 12.4.1921 (extract found in FD file 157/1921: all archival sources in the rest of this essay, unless mentioned otherwise, are from this source).

91. Fortnightly DO No. 13.CY.21, dated 23.5.1921, from Comm. KD to Chief Secretary, UP; DO. No. 348, dated 28.5.1921, from Chief Conservator of Forests (CCF), UP to Governor, UP; No. 53-CC/XIV-1, dated 2.6.1921, from Offg CF. Kumaun Circle, to CCF, UP.

92. APFD, 1921–22, pp. 7–8.

93. D.O. No.31.C.VI.21, dated 9.6.1921, from Comm. KD, to Home Member, UP.

94. SB Bhatia, *WP from the East Almora For Div. 1924–25 to 1933–34* (Allahabad: Government Press, 1926), p. 41.

95. See his *Primitive Rebels* (3rd ed., Manchester: Manchester University Press, 1974), pp. 25–26.

96. This extremely revealing classification and the following paragraph are taken from the two "Statements on fire cases in Almore," Sd/-W. C. Dible, dtd. 23.7.1921 and 3.11.1921 respectively. Unfortunately, similar details could not be traced for Naini Tal and Garhwal.

97. Cf. Eric Hobsbawm on the Luddites: "In some cases, indeed, resistance to the machine was quite consciously resistance to the machine in the hands of the capitalist." See his *Labouring Men* (London: Weidenfeld, 1964), p. 10.

98. "Fire cases in Garhwal district," Sd/-P. Mason, DC Garhwal, dated 9.9.1921; DC Garhwal to Secretary, Government of UP, dated 29.12.1921; D.O. No. 31.C.V.21, dated 9.6.1921, from Comm. KD to Home Member, UP.

99. DC Garhwal, to Secretary to Government, UP, dated 7.9.1921.

100. Source cited in fn. 96.

101. Ranajit Guha, *Elementary Aspects of Peasant Insurgency in Colonial India* (New Delhi: Oxford University Press, 1983), pp. 27, 157. These two aspects are repeatedly stressed by Guha. See *ibid.*, pp. 6–8, 84–85, 92, 112–13, 158, 160, 226, etc.

102. KFGC, p. 2.

103. Dr. F. Pearson, "Report on Mahamurree and smallpox in Garhwal," in *Selections*, Vol. II (Allahabad: Government Press, 1866), p. 300.

104. G. R. Kala, *Memoirs of the Raj Kumaun* (New Delhi: the author, 1974), p. 20.

105. Dible to Wyndham, D.O. No. C.355, dtd. 24.7.1921, in FD file 157/1921.

106. Cf. George Rudé, *Ideology and Popular Protest* (London: Lawrence and Wishart, 1980). Rudé, like some other historians, is rather more conscious of instances where so-called "modern" ideologies have helped the process of political self-awareness on the part of the peasantry.

4

The Conspiracy of Silence and the Atomistic Political Activity of the Egyptian Peasantry, 1882–1952

Nathan Brown

In 1909, a British official writing from Egypt complained of growing lawlessness in Egypt. Among the most shocking incidents, he mentioned the following: "One of the overseers on Prince Hussein's estates was returning home in the evening at the head of over 100 cotton pickers when a man stepped into the middle of the road and shot him dead. No one made any attempt to seize the assassin."[1] Several decades later, Henry Ayrout, an often astute observer of the Egyptian peasantry, noted an attitude that makes this incident seem almost routine: "When a usurer, a landowner, or a *nazir* [overseer] has carried his exactions too far, and is murdered with public approval, the finest sleuth cannot discover the murderer, so close is the conspiracy of silence."[2] While such incidents may have been common in the countryside, they have rarely drawn more than passing attention from social scientists studying Egypt or other countries.

Because of their concentration on the more dramatic and revolutionary moments in peasant history, social scientists have unwittingly joined their own conspiracy of silence over peasant political behavior.[3] Most social and political resistance by peasants has been ignored or recast—by both contemporary authorities and later writers—as crimi-

I would like to thank Nancy Bermeo, Forrest Colburn, Judith Kohn, James Scott, and John Waterbury for their comments and assistance on earlier drafts of this essay.

nality.[4] Thus all but a few Egyptian social historians have missed an entire tradition of activity by the Egyptian peasantry.[5] This tradition consisted of what might be called atomistic, or primitive, activity. Atomistic action refers to acts by individuals or small groups involving little coordination (though minimal planning may be in evidence sometimes); it generally involves attempts to defeat or attack immediate enemies.

While social scientists have largely overlooked this sort of activity, they have not completely ignored it. In particular, James Scott has discovered a vital history of ''everyday forms of peasant resistance'' in a Malaysian village. Scott uses this term to refer to those forms of resistance that are ''the nearly permanent, continuous, daily strategies of subordinate rural classes under difficult conditions.''[6] Scott considers the war of words, ideologies, and symbols as well as acts of pilfering and vandalism.

Atomistic activity refers to a broader range of actions than Scott's everyday forms of peasant resistance. The actions of the Egyptian peasantry include vandalism, cattle poisoning, and murder. The targets of these actions were local representatives of the social and political order. In short, atomistic activity consisted of attempts by individuals or small groups to strike out at local manifestations (and perceived injustices) of the prevailing order. Such atomistic actions were widespread in Egypt, and they must be seen as stemming from more than individual self-interest. The actions must also be seen in the context of a general atmosphere, a consensus that encouraged and supported those peasants defending themselves against perceived threats. Atomistic acts, therefore, are of interest not only because of the specific (and far from random) targets chosen, but, more importantly, because a careful reading of the community reaction to such acts reveals much about Egyptian peasant society and politics. The passive support of peasant communities made atomistic action widespread; it thus became of interest to those concerned with peasant politics.

The focus of this essay is therefore similar to Scott's ''everyday forms of peasant resistance.'' Yet it is important to stress that there are differences between atomistic action and everyday resistance. Scott primarily discusses intravillage conflicts and rarely considers peasant-state relations directly. The present focus, however, includes peasant relations with the local authorities—and thus the local manifestations of peasant relations with the state.

Additionally, the events that draw Scott's attention are more routine than most events of interest in Egypt. He considers, for example, battles over symbols and ideology (as well as vandalism and theft). While the forms of activity considered here do fall far short of open rebellion, they are not quite so commonplace or continuous as Scott's everyday forms—although they might have a common etiology. The murder of a village mayor, while a surprisingly common event in rural Egypt, was never an "everyday" occurrence.

Revolutions involve overturning the existing order. Atomistic action is more limited in its aims and effects than revolution or rebellion; it is limited because the power of peasants is limited. The course of rebellion is rarely open to peasants. Atomistic action comprises the political repertoire of peasants who have to cope with perceived injustice on a daily basis. If peasant rebellions often seem millennial, atomistic acts do not transcend the mundane.

Even if atomistic action often seems less significant because of its local focus, it can still be important at the national level. Scott claims that even though "everyday forms of resistance make no headlines" the cumulative effect of numerous such acts can interfere with the ambitions of states and rulers.[7] What is remarkable about the Egyptian case is that atomistic activity did make headlines (though as crime, not as resistance).

Atomistic Activity, Criminality, and the Egyptian State

Indeed, the newsworthiness of atomistic activity provides the ultimate proof of its significance at the national level. (It was always important to individual peasants and peasant communities.) Those ruling Egypt, along with the entire Egyptian landowning elite, displayed an awareness that something was seriously wrong in the countryside. They were fully aware of the tradition of atomistic political activity among the peasants they ruled. Or rather they were aware of the seriousness of crimes that had a social and a political dimension. For in the eyes of those who controlled the country, almost any challenge that was made to the social and political order—no matter how local—was criminal. And criminality was very much on the minds of Egypt's rulers; the poor state of public security in the countryside constituted one of their major worries. In his Annual Report for 1907, Lord Cromer, the British Consul-General (and effective ruler of the country), declared of crime in general: "I have no hesitation in stating that this increase of crime, to which I have frequently alluded in former reports, is the most unsatisfactory feature in the whole Egyptian situation.''[8] And it was primarily rural crime that concerned Cromer (and others); the rural crime rate consistently surpassed the urban crime rate. The year following Cromer's statement the question of rural security in Egypt was even raised in the British Parliament.[9]

It was not only the British who saw rural crime as a leading issue. In 1908 Prince (later Sultan) Husayn Kamil expressed the view that the lack of security in the countryside was disrupting agricultural production.[10] Indeed, if contemporary newspapers are an indication, rural crime was always an important—sometimes the most important—national issue.

Rural crime frightened those who ruled Egypt for two reasons. First, crime posed a direct threat to the safety of the Egyptian elite. Large landowners, their agents, and local officials could not help but notice that a disproportionate share of crime was directed against them. While authors differed on the reasons, many shared the opinion that peasants were shockingly bold in resorting to violence against landowners and their agents. Muhammad al-Babli, director-general of the Police Academy, wrote about the "repetition of incidents of aggression on owners and overseers of farms and others." Such people were targets of "murders, beatings, and other offenses for nothing except merely taking legal measures" such as confiscating or forcing the sale of crops, filing criminal charges, or "even refusing to lower rents which have been agreed upon or to postpone repayment of debts."[11]

A prominent lawyer recorded his (probably exaggerated) complaint in the Cairo daily *Al-Ahram* in 1944 that

> if a man of means wants to invest his money in the purchase of land then the first question confronting him would be "What is the security situation in the area? How many murders have occurred? How many thefts? How many incidents of crop damage? How many cases of cattle poisoning?" And so forth and so on until the value of land in some areas has decreased by half because of the instability of the security situation there.[12]

Sir Thomas Russell Pasha, a high official in the Egyptian police until 1946, discovered the extent to which landowners were afraid of attacks when he suggested to an Egyptian landowner that without books to read, life in the evenings on their country estates must hang heavily, and that an easy chair and a good book on a cool veranda would make life much more agreeable. My friend said at once: "You don't think that a landlord in the districts could sit out on a veranda after dinner with a bright light over his head, do you, and not get shot?" I might have thought of that myself.[13]

Yet there was a second, more profound reason why rural crime troubled Egypt's rulers so much. Criminality was not only a threat to the persons and property of the Egyptian elite; it represented a rejection of the political structure the rulers wished to impose. The late nineteenth and early twentieth centuries witnessed an ambitious attempt to expand the Egyptian state and extend its direct control throughout Egyptian society. Egypt's rulers began this effort to expand the state before the British occupied the country in 1882, but the British gave the endeavor new impetus and direction. After direct control over the state apparatus returned to Egyptian hands in 1922 there was no relaxation of the effort to project state authority farther out into Egyptian society and to penetrate more deeply the daily lives of the Egyptian population.

While both British occupiers and members of the Egyptian elite participated in this state-building enterprise, the Egyptians were more ambitious than their occupiers. The British focused on constructing a state characterized by sound finances and fair administration. Many members of the Egyptian elite desired not only an efficient but a strong state, able to develop the Egyptian economy and to remold the population into a responsible citizenry.

Thus, during the period of British occupation, the tax burden in rural areas was lightened but collections were put on a regular schedule. A civil law code (based on the French law code) was promulgated before the British occupation (and then rewritten under the British). Civil courts were established as the state began to assert its control over adjudication of disputes and criminal matters. The Egyptian state created a national police force as well and began to assert direct control over local security officials such as village guards.

Before the turn of the century telephones were installed in many villages to keep local police and other officials in direct and immediate contact with their superiors. Automobiles were introduced and seemed to make the police and other officials ubiquitous. Decisions about agricultural production and irrigation that had previously been made locally now became matters of state policy enforced by agricultural and irrigation inspectors who reported to their ministries in Cairo. And, especially important to the Egyptian elite, primary education came within the purview of the state for the first time; the purpose was to transform the Egyptian population into a literate and responsible citizenry.

Indeed, many of these efforts were based not only on the desire to foster responsibility among the citizenry; they actually required a responsible citizenry—responsible, that is, to the Egyptian state. This need for responsibility was felt especially in the new structures of criminal investigation and law enforcement. Egyptian peasants had often been asked for their labor and the fruits of their labor; now they were asked for loyalty as well. Burdens previously imposed on the peasantry required only passive resignation; the new institutions required active cooperation. Crimes had to be reported to the police. Witnesses had to testify truthfully to both the police and the courts. Crime, rural or urban, hardly represented a new phenomenon in Egypt. Yet the definition, investigation, and punishment of rural crime had always been concerns for local notables, officials, and families to deal with. Now the state assumed responsibility for these tasks. In this sense, the period saw the nationalization of crime. Criminal acts were no longer violations of local standards of conduct; they became offenses against the state.

Local officials (particularly village mayors) were reluctant to accept the diminution in their authority and autonomy implied by the nationalization of crime. Indeed, well into the twentieth century, village mayors were frequently suspended or fined for their failure (or refusal) to report and refer crimes to higher authorities.

Yet the attitudes and actions of the peasantry posed the greatest obstacle to the successful nationalization of crime. Most peasants responded with silence to the call for responsible cooperation with the state and its officials. Contemporary observers often attributed this silence to the ignorance of the Egyptian peasantry—that is, to their ignorance of their public duties. In retrospect it seems just as accurate to describe the peasant response as deliberate and resentful silence.

These, then, are the two reasons crime troubled and frightened Egypt's foreign and native rulers. First, crime threatened their persons and property. Second, crime threatened their ambitions. Peasants showed no inclination to behave in a way their rulers considered responsible. Peasant noncooperation represented a rejection of the new order. Whether those acts that the state defined as criminal were regarded locally as legitimate or illegitimate, rural residents refused to cooperate with the nationalization of crime. They often reacted instead by forming a conspiracy of silence that protected political and social protesters (as well as simple thieves).

The distinction between these two reasons for the Egyptian rulers' concerns about crime seems clear, yet it was rarely made at the time. Atomistic activity and the conspiracy of silence that encouraged such activity seemed to represent the active and passive aspects of an identical phenomenon: the refusal of the peasantry to support the new order. Peasants acted as if they wanted to limit the penetration of the Egyptian state. A few did so by criminal acts; most did so with silence about such acts. This refusal of the Egyptian peasantry never threatened the existence of the state. Yet it frightened those who controlled the state and seemed to frustrate their ambitions.

This peasant refusal is why atomistic resistance was newsworthy in Egypt. As the authorities began to take more notice of crime they also began to count and tabulate murders and other offenses for the first time. These official statistics seemingly constitute attractive data for the scholar. This essay will not rely on such data, however, as it is impossible to discern the motives and nature of crimes from aggregate crime statistics. In the eyes of the state, killing an official was murder (for peasants this was not always the case). Official statistics take no special notice of social and political crimes. Consequently, uncritical use of contemporary statistics constitutes a partisan act. It implies acceptance of the state definition of crime.

An alternative use of official crime statistics might be to accept them as measuring not crime but resistance. This alternative means considering as resistance all actions counted as criminal by the state. Such a perspective captures the contemporary worries about crime but must also be eschewed. It risks attributing to crimes social and political motives of which neither perpetrator nor victim were aware. Therefore using official statistics to demonstrate the level of peasant resistance (as some have done) is misleading.[14] As Stanley Cohen has observed of the issue of studying crime, "The methodological problem here is to do justice to social meaning without romantically elevating it into something we would prefer it to be."[15] Indeed, the official statistics are probably more a measure of state penetration—that is, of the degree to which the state was able to ensure that crimes were reported and recorded—than of peasant discontent.

Because of the great attention paid to rural crime it is possible to avoid reliance on aggregate official statistics by using more revealing and detailed data. Since atomistic action made news even as it was viewed as crime, newspapers throughout the period contained extensive information on relevant incidents. The details contained in newspapers generally make it possible to distinguish social and political crimes from those with other motives; they also make it possible to gauge the reaction of peasant communities to acts deemed criminal by the authorities. The level of detail thus makes possible a systematic study of atomistic action by peasants. Newspapers accounts typically mentioned the victim, the circumstances of the crime, and generally followed the course of the police investigation (including speculation on the perpetrator and motive, and testimony—or lack thereof—of witnesses).

The remainder of this essay analyzes these social and political crimes, relying primarily on a systematic recording of all such acts mentioned in the daily newspapers for twenty of the years between 1882 and 1952. (Table 4 presents a breakdown of these incidents by year and type.) All incidents were recorded in which notables, authorities, or state property were attacked. Incidents in which it seemed possible that robbery was the motive were discarded, however (in spite of the fact that some robberies should be seen as political). Newspapers did not report most of the atomistic activity that occurred, but they did report a significant portion.[16]

A Tradition of Atomistic Action

Throughout the period between the nationalist uprising of 1882 and the 1952 revolution, Egyptian peasants showed remarkable ingenuity in dealing with adversaries. As direct confrontation with powerful adversaries was generally inadvisable, peasants pursued a wide variety of individual strategies in attempting to enforce their wishes on those who seemed more powerful. In some years, Egyptian newspapers recorded more than 100 incidents of attacks on landlords and their agents, government property and personnel, and local authorities. Just as remarkable as the endemic nature of atomistic action is the resourcefulness peasants demonstrated in pursuing it.

As weak as they might have been, Egyptian peasants were not completely devoid of the power to strike out at those with whom they were in conflict. The effect of their weak condition was to force peasants to use weapons of social and political expression that social scientists are accustomed to consider as criminal.

A primary weapon used by peasants was direct physical—often murderous—attack. Assassinations of local officials and notables unsettled many landowners and other members of the elite. Their distress was well founded. In 1933, for example (a particularly violent year), the daily *Al-Ahram* mentioned 23 attacks on the persons or property of village mayors or members of their families (there were between 3,500 and 4,000 village mayors in the country), 10 attacks on local notables, merchants, or foreigners, 5 on landlords, 8 on officials from outside the village, 13 on village officials (other than village mayors), and 28 on agents of large landowners and estates. Many of these attacks were anonymous, but almost all were believed to have a political or economic grievance behind them. In short, some peasants seemed inclined to kill those who offended them.

It should not be so surprising that peasants resorted to murder as they had few other weapons to use in conflicts with adversaries. Both economically and legally, peasants had little power or voice as individuals. The endemic nature of murder can be seen as a result of this weakness: individual peasants, with distressing regularity, moved conflicts into an area where they could win. Those who evicted tenants, raised rents, confiscated crops, or acted in a high-handed manner generally had the law on their side. That did not protect them, however, from shootings, stabbings, beatings, or vandalism. Many landowners and village officials traveled with armed guards to protect themselves from those who had grievances against them, but attempts on their lives did not cease.[17]

If the high incidence of murder is itself not surprising, perhaps more remarkable is the resourcefulness peasants showed in attacking those who offended them. Direct attacks were effective but still somewhat risky. Peasants in Egypt therefore obtained revenge or pressured adversaries with a wide variety of less direct methods. What these methods offered was safety through anonymity. Direct confrontation with an adversary (and the law) could be avoided in several ways.

Primary among these was the hiring of professional criminals. Writing in 1941, Muhammad al-Babli noted that the use of professional criminals was a recent phenomenon but had become widespread and accepted. Hiring these criminals or scoundrels (as they were termed by both press and police) gave the instigator of the crime an alibi and made his apprehension more difficult. Although their fees were low enough for peasants to afford, such criminals were true professionals who had

Table 4

Incidents of Atomistic Action for Selected Years

Incident	1891	1897	1901	1908	1911	1914	1915	1918	1920	1922
Attack on mayor, his family, reputation, or property	2	1	2	13	4	12	13	7	9	6
Attack on notables, foreigners, their families, or property	2	0	3	4	5	8	5	1	12	4
Attack on landlord or his property	0	1	2	3	1	5	3	0	12	2
Attack on employee of an estate, his family, or property	0	0	1	2	2	6	6	3	5	7
Attack on village official, his family, or property	0	1	2	2	2	6	5	1	16	5
Attack on external official or government property	0	0	0	0	1	2	1	3	4	3
Attack on means of transportation or communication	0	0	2	1	0	0	5	0	17	4
TOTAL	4	3	12	25	15	39	38	15	75	31

Note: This table tabulates the atomistic acts I recorded in a survey of newspapers for selected years during the period. I relied chiefly on the Cairo dailies *Al-Mugattam* and *Al-Ahram* for the following years: 1891, 1897, 1901, 1911, 1914, 1915, 1918, 1920, 1922, 1926, 1931, 1933, 1936, 1941, 1944, 1948, 1949, 1950, and 1951. In addition, I recorded all events for January and February 1919 and the first six months of 1952—that is, before the outbreak of the 1919 Rebellion and the July 1952 Coup. I only recorded those atomistic acts where robbery was not the chief motive.

1926	1931	1933	1936	1941	1944	1948	1949	1950	1951	1952 (Jan-June)	Total
5	19	23	15	3	1	8	6	8	7	4	168
7	15	10	20	2	3	3	4	5	10	6	129
1	10	5	8	0	1	2	7	4	2	7	76
5	11	28	11	3	3	9	3	8	10	4	127
2	10	13	17	0	2	4	3	10	7	0	108
2	8	8	14	0	0	2	1	1	3	2	55
8	9	2	20	0	0	1	5	0	6	0	80
30	82	89	105	8	10	29	29	36	45	24	743

The newspapers obviously did not report all such acts. It is difficult, however, to tell how many acts went unrecorded in the newspapers. Perhaps indicative is that the number of *officially reported* offenses involving the railroad (probably the best reported of all crimes because it relied on railroad officials rather than peasants to report) generally numbered between 30 and 60; the number of such offenses mentioned in the newspapers ranged from 0 to 20.

learned how to exploit police weaknesses and evade the surveillance often placed on them. In some villages Al-Babli claimed that the number of professional criminals stood at one percent of the village population.[18]

A less direct weapon was vandalism directed against the crops, livestock, and equipment of officials and landowners. Indeed, crimes of vandalism were far more common than direct physical attack in Egyptian villages. (There were, for example, generally two to four times as many instances of reported crop destruction as there were murders.[19]) Indeed, vandalism could also be used in any dispute among villagers—which is perhaps the best evidence of the preference of villagers for direct solutions over those requiring involvement with official institutions and processes. Thus a conflict between two individuals or groups in a village often resulted in a series of acts of vandalism and theft rather than an appeal to the authorities. Accustomed to resorting to vandalism in disputes among themselves, peasants found few difficulties in using the same weapons against officials, landowners, and creditors. And, as with murder, they would also pay others to vandalize and steal for them. For instance, *Al-Ahram* reported on June 16, 1920 that a group of criminals uprooted crops on a landowner's farm near Tukh. Often other forms of vandalism were used. In numerous cases vandals stole the belt to an irrigation pump used by a landowner, thus rendering the pump temporarily useless.

A more ingenious weapon was sometimes employed against local officials, which involved an attack not on their persons or property but on their reputations. The target of these actions would be those officials (particularly village mayors) responsible for maintaining local security. Murders or acts of vandalism occurring within their area of responsibility would reflect badly on such officials and often result in their dismissal. Seizing on this, villagers would occasionally intentionally commit crimes—generally senseless in themselves—solely to endanger the reputation and standing of a local official.

Most common in this regard were attacks on the railroad. Except during the uprising of 1919 and some national elections, most attacks on railroads can be considered indirect attacks on the standing of local officials. For instance, in 1915 a group of villagers from Safay (in Abu Qurqas district, Minya province) uprooted the train tracks running near the village. An express train derailed causing some deaths and many injuries. The investigation following the event determined that the villagers' intent was to have the Mayor of Safay accused of inability to maintain law and order.[20] In most years between 1882 and 1952 between thirty and sixty such acts of vandalism against the railroad were reported, although few resulted in as many casualties as the 1915 Safay incident.

The peasant arsenal consisted not only of attacks on officials, landlords, their agents, and their property. Peasants could also react in less active and direct ways. That is, they could ignore or evade unfavorable policies; they could slack off if they received too little for their crops or labor. Such passive resistance has been held responsible for completely disrupting economic policies over much of the continent of Africa in recent years. Peasants in Egypt were never that effective (although that may be changing now).[21] Although their passive resistance never brought the social or political order to the brink of collapse, neither did it escape notice. Three examples are relevant here.

The first example involves daily labor on estates. Yusif Nahhas, writing in 1902, attributed endless patience to Egyptian peasants. Egyptian peasants—unlike the European worker—could not be pushed into strikes or revolution. They could only defend themselves with indirectness and subterfuge.[22] According to Nahhas, it was daily laborers who bore special watching for such strategies. Having no stake in the results of their labor, they had to be supervised very closely.[23]

What concerned Nahhas was that dissatisfied laborers, rather than refusing to work, would choose instead to slack off (or worse). No union was necessary; no formal demands for higher wages had to be made. Peasants could individually and silently express their wishes, knowing that they would be supported by their fellows.

Such strategies were best suited to wage labor as workers were generally paid by the day rather than piece-rate. Thus laziness or vandalism, so long as it remained undetected, brought no costs. Wage labor, though widely used, was nevertheless rarely the primary means landowners used to exploit their property. So there was little chance of bringing down the existing order by slacking off. Yet it still could be a cause for concern—not only in 1902 when Nahhas wrote, but all throughout the period.

Indeed, landowners not only worried about wage laborers slacking off. They also faced the danger that angry peasants would switch from deliberate laziness to a more active form of resistance—sabotage. In the fall of 1951 (a time of great political agitation in urban Egypt over negotiations concerning British troops in the Suez Canal Zone), one British resident of Egypt suggested that it was still such slackness and petty vandalism that worried large landowners far more than any nationalist issues:

> All accounts available to me agree that no one in the provinces cares a damn whether troops stay on in the [Suez] Canal [Zone] or not. But they are rife in many areas for agrarian agitation, for which political riots in Cairo and/or other cities would be the occasion. I quote Chalaby Sarofeen out of many landowners, not because I like old Victorian complexes, but because I am sure he is truthful and think it likely he is good to his tenants. He has not dared to leave with his family for Switzerland for the reason that he could not trust his peasants to pick instead of destroying the cotton crop if he were not present, and even so he is going to arrange with the Mudir [provincial governor] for a display of troops in readiness on the outskirts of his land.[24]

While Sarofeen's reaction seems extreme, his fears were probably quite widespread among those who employed peasant labor.

The second example of passive defiance involves state requisition of crops and animals. During World War I, the British enacted a policy of requisitioning grain and pack animals for the war effort. This was the only time during this period that such a policy was adopted on a national scale. While the long-term effect was to contribute to the 1919 uprising, the immediate reaction of the peasantry was to evade the policy. Rather than directly oppose the requisitions—something they were too weak to do—peasants sold or concealed what they were afraid would be taken. Immediately after the outbreak of the war a rumor spread in Sharqiyya province that the government was confiscating all chickens and sheep. Villagers rushed to sell or slaughter as many of these animals as they could in order to escape the rumored confiscations.[25] In March 1915, rumors spread throughout Minufiyya province that British troops were confiscating and slaughtering cattle, sheep, and chickens. Residents reacted by hiding cattle in their houses or by selling their animals at whatever price they could get.[26]

The final example of passive defiance involves state restrictions on the sale of crops. During the Great Depression, it became increasingly more difficult for the state to collect the land tax. In 1933 the state therefore adopted the policy of prohibiting peasants from bringing their crops to local markets unless they had paid their taxes. Guards were posted on the roads with orders not to let peasants pass with their crops unless they had a permit from the village tax collector (indicating that taxes had been paid). Those responsible for the policy never made clear how peasants were to pay taxes before selling their crops. Yet peasants found a way to evade the policy, again without a direct assault. The British consular agent in Damanhur explained the obvious strategy:

> The Ghaffirs [guards] have quite distinct orders, that the Fellah may come so far and no further, but there is no restriction on merchants going within the precincts and bringing grain out or sitting by the road under a shady tree, sending a partner into a village to say he is there and starting a daily business. This is becoming general.
>
> Other corn merchants have opened shops in villages to receive grain.
>
> It must be borne in mind that Fellahin selling under these conditions are at a disadvantage.[27]

Peasants may not have obtained the full market price for their crops but they did evade successfully a curious policy that threatened their livelihood.

Indeed, all these forms of resistance were similar in that they aimed at evasion, not confrontation: they were passive rather than active defiance. In that they differed from other atomistic acts. Like those acts they were carried out by individuals and thus required no formal organization. Yet in the same sense as the active forms of resistance, many of these forms of resistance must be seen against the background of a general atmosphere of resistance. They then seem to form a common strategy if not an organized one.

Atomistic Action and Peasant Communities

It is therefore clear that individual peasants frequently acted to defend their interests through means that frustrated and even frightened Egypt's rulers. This reveals something about the individual peasants and something about state ambitions, but what does it reveal about peasant society in Egypt? Why are these actions political rather than self-interested acts of anger or aggrandizement? This question is a general one that can be applied to all forms of individual acts of peasant resistance: how can political motives be separated from self-interested ones? In an essay that deals with some of the conceptual and methodological difficulties of the study of peasant resistance, Michael Adas writes of strategies of collusion, concealment, and under-reporting that "the extent to which under-reporting or cheating on tribute payments represented corruption for individual gain, as opposed to resistance to demands that were perceived to be excessive is difficult to determine."[28] The problem is how to distinguish those actions that are criminal and self-interested from those that are genuinely political.

In the Egyptian case this is a false problem. Peasant political actions and criminal actions never constituted entirely separate categories. Those who wrote the law ensured that all forms of peasant political action (petitioning and voting excepted) were criminal. Had the conceptions of right and wrong that were prevalent in peasant society been taken by the state as a basis for law, this would not have been the case. And almost all political acts were self-interested in the sense that they were designed to redress individual grievances.

Atomistic acts should not be considered political because they were not fundamentally criminal or self-interested. They were almost always both. Atomistic actions should be considered political because they were made thinkable by the consensus and support of the community. This is true not only of atomistic action but also of most forms of peasant political action. Scott writes that most everyday forms of peasant resistance "cannot be sustained without a fairly high level of tacit cooperation among the class of resisters."[29]

Atomistic actions were those that, while perhaps consistent with the self-interest of the actors, still cannot be understood as isolated acts of self-help. Such acts were made thinkable by the support of the consensus of the community. A shoplifter helps himself in a way that is not political. A group of shoppers who, acting in an atmosphere of distress over high prices, simultaneously refuse to pay for their groceries or stand back while a few attack the grocer are helping themselves in a communitarian—and political—fashion. And villagers who engaged in these strategies of passive defiance generally relied on the silence and even the sympathy of their fellow villagers. Often they could count on such sympathy because their fellow villagers were engaged in similar actions. (It is the existence of such sympathy and support in other peasant societies that have led some, like Hobsbawm, to conclude that some rural banditry should be seen in a similar light.[30] Without delving into the controversies provoked by Hobsbawm's argument, it is enough to observe here that such "social banditry" did not exist in Egypt; there is little evidence of community support or glorification of the numerous bandits that existed.[31])

The peasant arsenal thus contained weapons that often allowed the users to avoid open confrontation. These weapons were employed out of weakness, but their use demonstrates the resourcefulness of peasants and their ability to make the best of their inferior position. And the tacit support of the community made use of these weapons feasible. It also made their use of interest to those studying peasant politics and society. Accordingly it is to the supportive atmosphere that I now turn.

The Conspiracy of Silence

The arsenal of the peasantry consisted mainly of acts defined as criminal by the state. In effect, the authorities and the peasantry clashed over the definition of crime. Peasants resisted the state both in matters of law making and law breaking. And it was the silence of the peasantry in matters of crime that created the circumstances in which individual peasants could often get away with murder.

The peasantry's conspiracy of silence consisted of three elements: the refusal to report crime, the refusal to identify criminals, and the refusal to tell the truth about crime. In a sense, when Egypt's rulers complained about the failure of the peasantry to cooperate with the authorities, they did so with good reason. Even at the end of the period, with the Egyptian state's greater ability to project its authority, peasants displayed a surprising stubbornness on this matter. For instance, in January 1950 a group of fifteen armed men stopped a car which belonged to a sugar estate near Al-'Araki in Naj' Hamadi district, Qina province. They robbed the passengers and kidnapped one of them who worked as treasurer of the estate. The authorities reacted by sending a large force to the area and launching a thorough investigation. They discovered that a whole series of kidnappings of local residents had occurred but not until the treasurer was kidnapped did anyone notify the police.[32]

The second element of the conspiracy of silence consisted of the frequent refusal of the peasantry to identify those who had committed crimes. Complaints about this were as common as those concerning the refusal of peasants to report crimes.[33] Once crimes did come to the attention of the authorities there was little hope of obtaining the cooperation of the local population in apprehending the culprits. In 1909, when the British momentarily felt they had finally begun to realize some progress in the reporting of crime, one official noted that this hardly sufficed:

> The judicial adviser to the Egyptian Government has recently expressed the opinion that at no time has the proportion of unreported crime been so small, and that the public shows an increasing readiness to bring offenses to the knowledge of the authorities. Unfortunately all such readiness evaporates as soon as specific evidence in a court of law is required.[34]

Much more often, the readiness evaporated long before cases reached court. This was true even of misdemeanors. Three years before this statement, a British irrigation inspector was insulted in Minufiyya by a group of men he had ordered to stop drawing water from a canal. The British official summoned the headman of a nearby estate to identify them. The shaykh came but refused to identify the men even after one began pelting the inspector with bricks.[35] Such refusal to identify criminals and give testimony served to undermine the efforts of the authorities to control the countryside.

The peasantry's refusal to cooperate with the authorities could go beyond silence to false testimony. Judging from the newspaper accounts of the investigation of crimes, this was fairly common. Charges were filed and then had to be dropped; suspects were arrested and then had to be released; contradictory and incredible testimony was commonplace. Those who did not trust the state seemed to place no value on being truthful to it.

Less frequently, matters went beyond false testimony by individuals to organized perjury. So, at least, the authorities believed. The conspiracy of silence was transformed on occasion into a conspiracy of lies. Russell claimed this occurred in cases in which a professional murderer had been hired: "I have known cases where every detail of the intended murder has been rehearsed beforehand with accomplices taking the parts of police and Parquet officials, so that everyone under interrogation after the crime would be word-perfect in their replies."[36] A British official working in the European Department of the Egyptian Interior Ministry voiced a similar complaint in 1933: "I am told that after a murder of a European occurs in the provinces, the enemies of the murdered man generally gather to concoct alibis, get up false evidence, etc., with the result that the investigators are completely baffled."[37]

The prevalence of these three strategies to evade and confuse authorities should not be taken to mean that peasants never cooperated with the authorities. On rare occasions, peasants even complained about local officials who tolerated—or seemed implicated in—criminal activity.[38]

Yet these cases remained exceptional. The climate that prevailed in the countryside made it possible for most of those who broke the law to escape punishment.

Two statistical measures support this impression. First, the rate of unsolved crimes was consistently high. A report issued by the Interior Ministry on public security during the 1930s revealed that investigations had to be suspended in approximately 60 percent of the reported murders each year. The record on thefts was little better.[39] Second, peasants were always underrepresented in the prison population. In the first decade of the twentieth century, for example, generally 85 to 90 percent of the felonies reported each year occurred in the rural provinces. Yet of those convicted and sent to prison each year only around one-half had agricultural occupations.[40] The most plausible (if not the only) conclusion is that peasant offenders were more likely than others to escape arrest and imprisonment. The statistical evidence by itself is far from conclusive but in combination with official complaints and peasant actions (as detailed in newspapers) a clear picture emerges.

The picture that emerges is that of a tradition of atomistic action consisting of more than a series of crimes. The crimes would not have been possible without a peasantry willing to support lawbreakers with silence (and sometimes protection).

Indeed, it is the attitude of the peasantry that suggests using the term "tradition" in reference to atomistic action. The activity was atomistic only in the sense that it required positive action only from individuals or small groups. However, such activity cannot be understood without reference to passive community support, that is, to an atmosphere of quiet support and acquiescence. The peasantry as a whole formed a protective covering for those willing to break the law in order to enforce their individual and concrete ideas of justice. The desire of the peasantry to escape the state was even strong enough at times to extend the protective covering to those pursuing personal gain at the expense of peasants. The authorities naturally felt frustration with a peasantry that seemed at best passively resistant and at worst positively hostile. This frustration, so often expressed in public, is the best indicator of the success—limited and local as it was—of the tradition of atomistic action.

What is meant, then, by the tradition of atomistic action is not that all peasants in Egypt desired to kill their landlords or village mayors or to vandalize their property. Instead the tradition was a climate that made such murders and acts of vandalism thinkable to many. These acts were thinkable because of the attitude of the community. The actions were often not criminal in the eyes of the peasantry; they were individual attempts to right wrongs. There were probably some who took advantage of this climate to engage in activities that the peasantry probably did consider criminal, but still avoided reporting to the resented police. Thus the real meaning of atomistic activity was to give the peasantry the only advantage it had in confronting its enemies.

Those who pursued atomistic action in effect changed the terms of conflict—and here lay the advantage. They were economically weaker than their landlords and, of course, politically weaker than them (and local officials) as well. Thus they moved the conflict from the political and economic realm into the realm of physical force. Here the conflict became more equal. A village mayor or landlord had the police and often a private guard to defend him, but a would-be assassin or vandal could rely on the anonymity granted him by the conspiracy of silence.

The climate that made peasants fearful and suspicious of the state sometimes caused them to attempt to defeat or outwit it—not through direct confrontation or open defiance but through individuals acts of avoidance. Scott has noted that these sorts of acts draw on the few strengths the peasantry has—loose organization and isolation.[41]

Fear and Loathing in the Egyptian Countryside

The existence of a conspiracy of silence can thus be demonstrated by reference to the complaints of Egypt's rulers, the actions of peasants, and the failure of the authorities to suppress atomistic action. Yet what lay behind this conspiracy? What is it that led peasants to form the protective covering, allowing individuals to act to redress personal grievances?

Certainly fear played a role in reinforcing the conspiracy of silence—fear both of some of those involved in domestic action and of the state agents attempting to suppress them. It is clear from many contemporary writings that the authorities felt peasants were simply too cowardly to cooperate with them. Those who did cooperate by reporting crimes and testifying in court might themselves become targets of vandalism or worse. This fear underscored the observation that peasants saw the state as neither trustworthy nor a source of protection and security. Peasants did not look to the state or its agents for protection.

Yet more than fear was involved in silencing peasants. Feelings of antipathy and alienation toward the state were every bit as important in keeping peasant mouths shut. Three observations underscore this.

First, the increasingly extensive and intensive presence of agents of the state did not lead peasants to cooperate with them. Village mayors slowly accepted their duty of reporting crimes; the police became more powerful and capable; state authorities began to monitor closely and directly events within villages. As the state became a more active presence it did not become a more attractive one. With the greater ability of the state to project its authority, those who previously may have wished to cooperate could do so with more confidence. The opportunity for cooperation was there. Few took it.

The inability of the state to protect peasants was not as resented as its penetration. A more imposing presence therefore provoked not cooperation but continued silence. Frustration with this silence was still frequently expressed in the press and the writings of officials. Peasants seem to have been motivated by antipathy toward the agents of the state as much as they were motivated by fear of being hunted by the agents of the state.

A second indication that the conspiracy of silence was motivated by alienation as well as fear is that on a number of occasions the conspiracy moved beyond silence. In these instances, peasants protected accused criminals with more than feigned ignorance. In February 1948, in the village of Mit Tamama, the administrative chief of the district accompanied a police force to arrest some villagers accused of theft. The force was met not with gratitude and cooperation or even fear; it was met by a hostile crowd. One villager was killed and several injured in the ensuing battle.[42] The following October a similar battle erupted in the village of Kamshush when police attempted to confiscate rifles from residents who did not have permits for them. One police officer was killed and several injured.[43]

What is striking is that such incidents became much more common as the police presence increased. Peasants in Egypt had frequently resisted land and crop confiscations by mass action but in the 1940s instances of mass actions simply against state agents became common as well. Between 1948 and 1950 newspapers recorded twelve pitched battles between crowds of villagers and police resulting from the following provocations: arrests of individual villagers (for theft or possession of narcotics), arrival of fire fighters during a fire, and a police order to extinguish lights. (These occurred in addition to the standard clashes over rents, wages, access to land, and irrigation.) It did not matter that Egyptian rather than British officials now ran the courts and police; it was state interference, not nationalism, that was at issue.

A third and final indication that peasants were motivated by more than fear in their refusal to cooperate with the police is the frequency and nature of official complaints. Peasant villages and families had their own standards of justice and means to enforce them. They did not refer disputes or perceived offenses of any sort to the authorities and preferred their own methods. Those who felt wronged preferred direct action to involving the police. Such a preference is hardly the mark of a fearful peasantry. Murder of a family member provoked an attempt to kill those responsible, not a call to the police. Ahmad Muhammad Khalifa, a prominent lawyer and prosecutor, wrote as late as 1954 that "frequently those obliged to avenge a murder (*ashab al-dam*) attempt to take their revenge on their antagonist immediately, even while he is being held by police or investigators."[44] For the authorities, the refusal of peasants to turn to the police was a backward and ignorant practice. Yet this refusal—and the audacity often displayed in the process—is convincing evidence that for peasant families matters of crime and punishment were far too important to leave in the hands of the police and the courts.

The atomistic activity of the Egyptian peasantry—and the conspiracy of silence that made it possible—thus can almost be seen as a social movement. Since it did attract attention from the authorities and other observers (though not as a social movement), there is sufficient information available to discern some of the patterns that this movement followed.

Patterns of Atomistic Action

It is possible to discover in the atomistic action of Egyptian peasants patterns that reflect the nature of the peasant political outlook. Through their behavior Egyptian peasants displayed an alienation from the state, aversion to open confrontation, and a tendency to view political and economic issues in concrete, personal, and parochial terms.

Peasant alienation from the state had both a positive and negative aspect. The positive aspect consisted of attacks on officials—most frequently on the most immediate representatives of the state. Attacks of this nature were regular occurrences in the Egyptian countryside. In some years these attacks were especially widespread—in each of the depression years newspapers reported dozens of physical attacks on officials, their families, and their property. These attacks were not simply random acts occurring out of general rage or antisocial impulses. Where the attacker was apprehended he was almost always discovered to have a concrete and personal complaint against his victim.

Yet the negative aspect of peasant hostility to the state is much more indicative of the general peasant reaction to the state. Resistance to the state through attacks on officials involved a small number of individuals; the majority of peasants resisted—or at least displayed their contempt for, alienation from, and fear of—the state through the conspiracy of silence. This conspiracy—in addition to the frequency of complaints about the failure of the peasantry to cooperate with the authorities—offers convincing evidence of a sullen peasant hostility to the state.

The silence of peasants is also strong evidence of the second aspect of their political outlook—an inclination to avoid confrontation with powerful enemies. Silence inhibited the authorities and frustrated them, but still fell short of an open challenge demanding a direct—and repressive—response. In order to overcome the barriers posed by uncooperative peasants the authorities could speak only of reeducating them.

Beyond this, the silence of the peasantry made it possible for individuals who chose the path of active resistance to do so, while minimizing the dangers of confrontation. Those who attacked authorities and landowners ran a much smaller risk because of the refusal of the peasantry to cooperate with the state.

These two elements of the peasant outlook—antagonism toward the state and an avoidance of confrontation—combined to form the atmosphere of quiet resistance. And it was this atmosphere that made individual acts of active resistance possible. It also led some to take advantage of the safety thus granted to rob indiscriminately. The refusal of the peasantry to cooperate with the state allowed criminals—whether motivated by social concerns, individual grievances, or greed—to operate relatively freely. In the conflict between lawmakers and lawbreakers, peasants preferred neutrality.

The third aspect of the peasant political outlook—a local and concrete focus—obtained no matter how much the plight of peasants may have been a result of national (or even global) forces. The actions of the peasantry demonstrated that local officials and landowners were held personally responsible for their behavior toward peasants. Attacks on officials—or even landowners—who did not have direct contact with peasants were extremely rare. In the few instances in which peasants did attack high officials, such concrete and personal motives were generally involved. For instance, in March 1932, two peasants murdered the administrative head of the Badari district of Asyut province. The two were convicted, as were six others accused of giving false testimony in the case. On appeal it was revealed that the official had previously been directly involved in torturing his two assassins (presumably in order to obtain confessions for a previous crime).[45]

The vast majority of incidents remained within the village. Peasants viewed economic matters as personal ones as well. This was true even to the extent that estate residents were far more likely to attack overseers—with whom they had daily contact—than the estate owners whom the overseers served. Russell observed:

> At one time most agricultural estates in Egypt were run by a Greek *nazir* (superintendent): today I doubt if there are any left, they have all been either shot or frightened away. Even an Egyptian nazir takes severe risks when he tries to enforce discipline on an estate by punishing or dismissing a laborer for laziness or disobedience, often paying for it with his life.[46]

Russell was correct that Egyptian nazirs were prone to attack just as were foreign ones. He was incorrect in suggesting that there were no more foreign nazirs to attack. In May 1952 (only a few months before the land reform that forced the dismantling of most large estates), two foreign overseers were killed in separate incidents in Buhayra province.[47]

Similarly, migrant workers were more likely to strike out at the labor contractors who brought them to the estates than anyone on the estate itself—for it was through the contractors that the workers were employed and paid. The few incidents involving agricultural workers were all attacks on contractors.[48]

This is not to say that landlords were immune from the wrath of peasants. Like the head of Badari district, if they were directly linked to a perceived injustice they could be victims of peasant attacks. For instance, in December 1922, the owner of a 500-acre estate in Fayyum province was shot dead along with her accountant. Although the murder occurred in front of the residents in broad daylight they all claimed ignorance of the identity of the criminal. It was finally ascertained that the owner of the gun used in the double murder belonged to a former resident of the estate who had been evicted by the owner.[49] Similarly, in 1912 a French estate owner was riding with his daughter and another woman near Disuq when the two women were shot. The culprits were two estate residents—one who claimed the landowner owed him money, while the other had just been evicted from the estate by the owner himself.[50]

This tendency of peasants to view disputes in highly personal terms is further underscored by incidents in which peasants reacted contrary to any spirit of peasant solidarity. When losing land, for example, or upon dismissal from a position as a paid guard, peasants could attack those who had evicted or fired them—but they also could attack those who replaced them. For example, in January 1936, in Abu Tij district a renter was evicted from his land after being late in paying the rent. He and his brother reacted by attacking the new renters and their families.[51]

Whether they felt treated unfairly by officials, landlords, their agents, or their fellow peasants, peasants held responsible the person with whom they had direct contact. These atomistic actions are therefore best seen as responses to perceived threats and injustices. Most of the accounts of atomistic actions stress their angry and vengeful nature. Those who shot their landlords did so not only to decrease their rents but also to strike back at those who had offended them.

Conclusion

General statements on peasants in other areas based only on evidence gathered on Egypt must, of course, be made with great caution. Nevertheless, the Egyptian case suggests much about the significance of small-scale forms of peasant political activity.

First, attention should be paid not solely to the acts of resistance but also to the general community reaction. This is necessary not only in order to shed light on peasant society and politics, but it may also be necessary to understand the acts themselves. For in Egypt, and perhaps elsewhere, atomistic action was intimately tied to the atmosphere created by the peasants' rejection of the state. The tools of resistance examined here generally served the purposes of those who employed them. Yet the support of communities proved to be as crucial as the interests of individuals in provoking peasants into defending their interests. The conspiracy of silence brought the costs of resorting to atomistic action far lower than they would have been without community support. The values and culture of the peasantry should not be ignored even when studying the actions of individuals.

Second, the Egyptian case suggests that atomistic activity can be significant on a national level. By stealing, vandalizing, and murdering, Egyptian peasants frightened their rulers. By lying and concealing these acts, Egyptian peasants added frustration to their rulers' fear. The cumulative effects of numerous atomistic acts greatly troubled those who commanded the Egyptian state.

Indeed, the cumulative significance of small-scale actions has been alluded to frequently in the growing literature on everyday resistance. Kerkvliet, for instance, states that "the cumulative effects of everyday resistance can thwart the plans of those with more power and status."[52] The link between the actions of individual peasants and the failure of the state's ambitions is appealing and should be made. Those interested in development policy, approaching the issue from the perspective of the state rather than that of the peasantry, have already begun to note this same link between individual action and policy failures. It is noteworthy that scholarship on the peasantry has reached conclusions that dovetail with scholarship on state policy.

The development is noteworthy, but two notes of caution must be added. First, and more obvious, the national significance of small-scale resistance must be investigated rather than assumed. In Egypt thousands of thefts and murders did have national effects. Yet those effects were limited to provoking fear and unease among the rulers; the fears of the rulers had solid foundations but were not fully realized. At most, the Egyptian state's penetration of rural society may have been slightly slowed. Egyptian peasants tried to solve local and concrete problems not to establish an anarchist utopia.

This leads to the second note of caution: focusing on the significance of atomistic action to national politics and economics, while attractive, should not induce us to leapfrog the separate question of the significance of atomistic action to peasants. Since the actions under consideration were motivated by local and concrete concerns they must be understood in that context before larger (and probably unintended) cumulative effects are considered. It is proper to ask what effect atomistic action had on the state; it is also essential to ask what atomistic action reveals about peasant politics and culture.

Indeed, demonstrating the usefulness of posing just these questions is the final way in which the Egyptian case can shed light on the general study of peasant politics. The atomistic activity of the Egyptian peasantry—and the conspiracy of silence that fostered and protected it—

provide the most reliable evidence that exists on how peasants viewed and experienced politics. And since peasants are generally silent in the historical sources on which we must rely, the study of those small-scale actions that have been recorded will likely provide the most promising evidence on how peasants experienced politics elsewhere.

The study of peasant rebellion leaves mute the vast majority of peasants who never rebelled. The best way to break this silence is to study the more mundane forms of political activity. Larger, national political implications might arise from such a study. Yet no such implications are necessary to justify the effort to overcome peasant silence and discover how peasants experience politics. Criticisms of equating state politics with peasant politics is precisely what motivated many scholars to study everyday forms of peasant resistance in the first place. The importance of peasant politics on development should not, therefore, obscure the broader study of peasant politics.

Notes

1. Graham to Grey, 5 September 1909, Foreign Office Records, Public Record Office, London, FO 371/34675, file 663.

2. Henry Ayrout, *The Egyptian Peasant* (Boston: Beacon Press, 1963), p. 211.

3. For a similar observation see James Scott, *Weapons of the Weak* (New Haven: Yale University Press, 1985), pp. 36–37.

4. Even Gabriel Baer in his seminal article refuting the myth of the submissiveness of Egyptian peasants only considered rebellions and jacqueries. See "Submissiveness and Revolt of the Fellah," in *Studies in the Social History of Modern Egypt* (Chicago: University of Chicago Press, 1969).

5. 'Ali Barakat has written most extensively on these forms of activity. See "AlQarya al-Misriya fi A'qab Ma'rakat al-Tall al-Kabir [The Egyptian Village in the Wage of the Battle of Al-Tall al-Kabir]," *Al-Siyasa al-Duwaliya* 19 (1983), 38; and "Al-Fallahun bayna al-Thawra al-'Urabiya wa-Thawrat 1919 [The Peasantry Between the 'Urabi Revolt and the 1919 Revolution," *Al-Majalla al-Ta'rikhiya al-Misriya* 22 (1975), 201.

6. Scott, *Weapons*, p. 273.

7. *Ibid.*, p. 36.

8. Lord Cromer, *Report by His Majesty's Agent and Consul-General on the Finances, Administration and Conditions of Egypt and the Soudan*, 1907, p. 85.

9. FO 371/45416, file 451.

10. *Al-Muqattam*, 5 October 1908.

11. Muhammad al-Babli, *Al-Ajram fi Misr Asbabuha wa Turuq 'Ilajuha* [Crime in Egypt, Its Causes, and Methods of Treating It] (Cairo: Matba'at Dar al-Kutub, 1941), p. 235.

12. 'Aziz Khanki, "Hawadith al-Ightiyal fi al-Aryaf [Incidents of Assassination in the Countryside]," *Al-Ahram*, 23 October 1944.

13. Sir Thomas Russell Pasha, *Egyptian Service, 1902–1946* (London: John Murray, 1949), p. 33.

14. See, for example 'Abd al-Wahhab Bakr, *Adwa' 'ala al-Nashat al-Shuyu'i fi*

Misr [(Throwing) Light on Communist Activity in Egypt] (Cairo: Dar al-Ma'arif, 1983), pp. 12–16.

15. Stanley Cohen, "Bandits, Rebels or Criminals: African History and Western Criminology," *Africa* 56 (1986), p. 477.

16. See note for Table 4.

17. That many village mayors and large landowners traveled with guards is clear from the accounts of attempted murders in the newspapers.

18. Muhammad al-Babli, *Al-Ajram fi Misr*, pp. 192–209. On several occasions throughout the period, the state attempted to eradicate this phenomenon either by internal exile of all known or suspected professional criminals or close supervision of them. None of these attempts succeeded.

19. Yearly crime statistics are recorded in the *Annuaires Statistiques* issued by the Finance Ministry.

20. *Al-Ahram*, 26 August, 6 October, and 27 November 1915. The motive may have involved resentment of confiscations of livestock and impressment into the Labour Corps during World War I. The campaign of confiscation and conscription was carried out through village authorities.

21. See Richard Adams, *Development and Social Change in Rural Egypt* (Syracuse: Syracuse University Press, 1986).

22. Yusif Nahhas, *Al-Fallah* [The Peasant] (Cairo: Khalil Matran, 1926; originally published 1902), pp. 52–53.

23. *Ibid.*, pp. 111–12.

24. Campbell to Stevenson, 14 September 1951, FO 141/1433, file 1011. I am grateful to Joel Gordon for bringing this letter to my attention.

25. *Al-Ahram*, 13 September 1914.

26. *Ibid.*, 12 March 1915.

27. Butler to Campbell, 16 June 1933, FO 141/704, file 719, no. 6. A similar strategy was adopted for cotton. See "Memorandum on the Economic Situation in the Provinces and Its Possible Reactions on Public Security," 20 November 1933, FO 371/J2712/39, file 17015.

28. Michael Adas, "From Footdragging to Flight: The Evasive History of Peasant Avoidance Protest in South or South-east Asia," *Journal of Peasant Studies* 13 (1986), 71.

29. See Scott's essay in this volume. For a more general argument along these lines, see Scott, *Weapons of the Weak*, pp. 291–97.

30. Eric Hobsbawm, *Bandits* (Harmondsworth: Penguin Books, 1985).

31. I have discussed Egyptian banditry in greater detail in my doctoral dissertation *Peasants against the State: The Political Activity of the Egyptian Peasantry, 1882–1952*, Department of Politics, Princeton University, 1987.

32. *Al-Ahram*, 30 January and 31 January 1950.

33. See, for example, 'Ali Mitwalli, "'Awdat al-Ashqiya' li-l-Jara'im al-Mukhilla bi-l-Amn al-'Amm [The Return of Criminals to Crimes Distrubing Public Security]," *Al-Ahram*, 24 January 1920.

34. Graham to Grey, 5 September 1909, FO 371/34765, file 663.

35. Findley to Grey, 7 July 1906, FO 141/397, no. 113.

36. Russell, *Egyptian Service*, p. 32.

37. Letter from Boyd, December 13, 1933, contained in "A Precis of the Reports of Finance Inspectors on the Condition of the Fellaheen," 8 October 1933, FO 141/7231, file 1006.

38. Muhammad Ibrahim al-Shawarbi, *Dawr al-Fallahin fi al-Mujtama' al-Misri fima bayna 1919–1952* [The Role of the Peasantry in Egyptian Society between 1919 and 1952], Ph.D. dissertation, Department of History, University of Alexandria,

n.d., ch. 5, mentions petitions from peasants complaining that their *'umdas* concealed crimes.

39. Wizarat al-Dakhiliya, Idarat 'Umum al-Amn al-'Amn, *Taqrir 'an Halat al-Amn al-'Amn fi al-Qutr al-Misri 'an al-Mudda min Sanat 1930 ila Sanat 1937* [Report on the State of Public Security in Egypt in the Period from 1930 to 1937] (Bulaq: Al-Matba'a al-Amiriya, 1939), pp. 14 and 18.

40. *Statistical Yearbook of Egypt*, 1909.

41. See Scott, *Weapons of the Weak*, pp. 35–36.

42. *Al-Ahram*, 1 March 1948.

43. *Ibid.*, 20 October 1948.

44. Ahmad Muhammad Khalifa, *Usul 'Ilm al-Ajram al-Ijtima'i* [The Principles of the Social Science of Crime] (Cairo: Dar al-Nashr li-l-Jami'at al-Misriyya, 1954), p. 94.

45. The case attracted national attention and eventually led to the resignation of 'Ali Mahir, then Minister of Justice. For details, see Lorraine to Simpson, 31 December 1932, and memo by G. W. Booth, 13 January 1933, FO 371/J57, file 17007.

46. Russell, *Egyptian Service*, p. 33.

47. *Al-Ahram*, 4 May and 31 May 1952.

48. See, for example, *ibid.*, 20 June 1933.

49. For example see *ibid.*, 12 December and 16 December 1922.

50. The driver of the landowner's carriage was also charged with complicity. The three were acquitted in an Egyptian court, however, probably due to political and nationalist overtones of the case. See FO 371/28824/27338, file 1363, 1 July 1912.

51. *Al-Ahram*, 6 January 1936.

52. Benedict J. Tria Kerkvliet, "Everyday Resistance to Injustice in a Philippine Village," *Journal of Peasant Studies* 13 (1986): 120.

53. See, for example, Goren Hyden, *Beyond Ujamaa in Tanzania* (London: Heinemann, 1980); and Robert Bates, *Markets and States in Tropical Africa* (Berkeley: University of California Press, 1981).

5

Class, Gender, and Peasant Resistance in Central Colombia, 1900–1930

Michael F. Jiménez

"The awakening of agriculture is notable," Jesús del Corral told a gathering of large landowners in Bogotá on May 1, 1914. "Land values are rising. We Colombians are soon to be on that royal road of the world, the Panama Canal, and we must fully prepare ourselves . . . to attend the magnificent banquet of civilization."[1] A decade after economic crisis and civil war at the turn of the century, Colombia's planter elites were in a celebratory mood. Growing demand for their coffees in international markets seemed to provide the foundation for unparalleled political stability and social progress in that northern Andean nation.[2] Yet the lecturer plainly intended to sound a warning that conditions in the coffee plantation districts just to the southwest of the capital might well provoke a "leveling rebellion" by the peasantry. He complained that the fines, labor demands, and persecutions inflicted on the rural poor by owners and local officials violated "the imperatives of morality and justice which ought to reign in any Christian republic"

Earlier versions of this essay were delivered at the Princeton University Women's Graduate Colloquium in April of 1986, the Fourth Annual Latin American Labor History Conference at Yale University in April of 1987, and a research seminar at CINEP (Centro de Investigación y Educación Popular) in Bogotá in August of 1987 where the author received helpful criticism. The author extends his appreciation to Forrest Colburn, Mauricio Archila, Emilia Viotti da Costa, Laura Englestein, Elizabeth B. Clark, James Scott, and Julie Taylor for their comments and encouragement in this project. He also wishes to recognize the generosity of the people of Viotá and other municipalities of southwestern Cundinamarca who shared their public and private histories with him during 1980.

and were likely to spawn dangerous protests in that vital region.

Having reproached his fellow planters for their "veritable feudal regime," Jesús del Corral insisted that the greatest threat to social order was the physical and moral state of the poor. He described the rural populace as "lacking in clothes, sustenance, and proper hygiene . . . struck down by the scourges of drink and tropical anemia . . . given to degrading vices, and filled with silly superstitions." For him, the crisis originated in the weakness of the family as an institution, for the "vast majority of peons and tenants live together unmarried, therefore not occupying themselves with the formation of a home nor the care and education of their children."[3] In the three decades before the Great Depression, observers found peasants in central Colombia's coffee zones indifferent, even hostile, toward efforts to civilize them. Illegitimate births, as high as 75 percent in some large plantation municipalities at the turn of the century, had fallen only slightly on the eve of the depression,[4] and it was reported that the rural poor fled from church missionaries teaching Catholic doctrine and seeking to sanctify common law marriages.[5] The "incautious women," as Jesús del Corral referred to them, were judged to have contravened upper-class conceptions of the ideal, male-dominated household, thereby indirectly challenging upper-class rule.

Elite apprehension about the apparent incoherence of family life in the great estate coffee districts suggests a complex intertwining of class and gender in the jostling between the rural poor and the planters during the first three decades of the twentieth century. This chapter explores the ways in which gender shaped what James Scott has referred to as the "transcript" of class during the height of export capitalism in central Colombia, simultaneously fueling peasant resistance to landlords and the state and precluding the creation of an oppositional culture that would encompass the needs and aspirations of both men and women.[6] The focus is on materials from the department of Cundinamarca and the large coffee plantations of Viotá. The argument here is that while patriarchy was proclaimed by elites and male peasants alike as the basis of sexuality, family structure, and the division of labor within the household, several factors prevented the consolidation of a unequivocally male-dominated peasant society in the shadow of the great estates.[7] The organization of export production, notably fragile institutions of social control, and the sexual predations of estate owners and managers influenced conditions of peasant life, causing men and women to oppose planter domination and assert autonomy in different, sometimes congruent, and occasionally antagonistic, ways. In effect, what Joan Scott has described as the impact of gender on the "the very construction of class" significantly affected the terms of peasant resistance to central Colombia's coffee planters in the first third of the twentieth century.[8]

Planters, Peasants, and Coffee Estates in Central Colombia

In the last quarter of the nineteenth century, Colombian entrepreneurs embarking on export agriculture on the western slope of the country's eastern highlands were hardly optimistic about the human material at hand. The semitropical region known as the "hot country" was a rugged series of valleys and gorges stretching eastward from the Magdalena River to the edge of the highland plateaus. While large populations were dominant features of the northern Andes plateaus since the sixteenth-century conquest, the semitropical region was sparsely inhabited by peons and tenants on cattle ranches and sugar plantations and by small holders not easily pried loose from their farms to work on the newly established coffee estates. Foreign observers called attention to the tropical diseases that ravaged the slope's inhabitants and to their alleged predilection for strong local brews made from fermented sugar on which they purportedly spent "all of their wages in drunken orgies."[9] The people of these districts were seen as indolent, given to vagrancy, banditry, and gambling; Federico Aguilar lamented in 1886 that "if it were not for the extreme apathy of its inhabitants, it would be possible to export three times what is now gathered."[10]

To solve the labor problem, coffee entrepreneurs turned to the eastern highlands. In 1878, a Viotá landowner suggested recruiting workers "from Boyaca where the population is large, where there is great poverty and the salaries are very low."[11] The traditional core of Colombian society was undergoing a severe social crisis caused by demographic expansion, the erosion of cottage industries by imported manufacturers, and liberal land reforms leading to the consolidation of large estates.[12] Consequently, beginning in the 1860s and reaching a peak in the first two decades of the twentieth century, a substantial segment of the mixed-blood highland peasantry journeyed to the plantation districts in the west.

These migrants were portrayed as superior to the "hot country" inhabitants; the German geologist, Alfred Hettner, reported that the

highlanders were, like his own countrymen, "most industrious workers," possessed of "serious and tranquil" personalities, unlike the
lowlanders who, as the French, were given to "rowdy diversions."[13]
The migrants, apparently well-schooled in the tightly organized and
hierarchical communities in the eastern highland core, were seen as fit
for the rigors of commercial agriculture; geographer and naturalist
José Vergara y Velasco reassured the elites that the highlander was
"hard-working and tireless, submissive and worthy . . . a machine, for
he serves all with equal passivity and duty."[14]

"Hot country" estate owners were nonetheless at a constant disadvantage in their efforts to acquire and maintain a cheap, disciplined
labor force. In the half-century before 1930, planters complained long
and bitterly about the scarcity of hands. Often the flow of migrants from
the eastern highlands was insufficient and, in later decades, planters
were undercut by better paying jobs in cities and on public works
projects as well as opportunities in new agricultural frontiers to the
west. Moreover, the new coffee elites after the 1870s regularly suffered
from inadequate monetary resources; fluctuating world markets, high
interest rates, and rising production costs rendered it impossible for
most planters to attract and keep workers by offering high wages.[15]
Finally, Colombia, unlike other major Latin American coffee producing countries, was able neither to attract nor coerce a disciplined labor
force for its great estate agriculture; European immigrants were not
drawn to the Andean republic on the scale to which they were when
they entered Brazil before World War I, and the Colombian state did not
develop an apparatus for impressment of the peasantry into servitude
such as evolved in early twentieth-century Guatemala.[16]

In response to these obstacles, there emerged a payment structure
and management system that provided the basis for—and ultimately the
undoing of—successful large-scale coffee cultivation in central Colombia for several generations. A growers' manual published in 1892
recommended the use of wage labor and cautioned against sharecrop-
ping, rentals, or other forms of tenancy.[17] But such advice was best for
small or medium-sized holdings, and prior to 1930 only a handful of
larger estate owners had sufficient liquid capital to employ wage labor.

By the early decades of the twentieth century most larger planters
had settled on service tenancy to attract and retain the bulk of their
permanent labor force. In this system, tenants worked in the coffee
groves under direct supervision for approximately fifteen days a
month; in exchange, they were allotted a small parcel, usually between

five and seven acres, on which they were permitted to grow only foodstuffs.[18] As the estate expanded, more land served as a wage bill of sorts; in Viotá, by the early 1930s, one-fifth of the municipality was given over to tenancies, and on some of the larger estates as much as 20 to 40 percent of their territories had been allocated in this manner.[19] With a substantial portion of land and labor power outside the direct control of the planters, it is hardly surprising that they cultivated a style of estate management that was hierarchical and arbitrary. Under such circumstances, efficacious use of peasant labor depended on administrators, foremen, and straw bosses disciplining their workers through a systematically capricious, arbitrary code of job regulations, tenancy contracts, and forms of payment.[20] This management style was informed by a paternalism where benevolence and injury were in uneasy balance. In this brutal intimacy, the provision of gifts and special deals to assure the loyalty and affection of subordinates combined with a crueler pedagogy that included brutal beatings, whippings, evictions, and sexual abuse.[21]

"Living at the whim of the lords," as Jesús del Corral put it, the service tenants seemed in an unenviable position.[22] This was especially true, as a Viotá planter reported early on, if compared to day laborers who, following harvests and avoiding estates with reputations for mistreatment, "earned more and suffered less . . . (and) looked down on the tenants with disdain and sadness."[23] Yet the arbitrariness and brutality of tenancy arrangements bespoke the weakness of the large plantation as an effective vehicle for social control. Paradoxically, what was economically rational ultimately proved to be socially untenable. Service tenancy was an expedient way of acquiring and retaining labor, but land as payment caused relatively autonomous small holder units to become embedded in the great estates, placing those enterprises at risk. This became patently clear in the late 1920s and 1930s when central Colombia's rural poor formed leagues and unions that fought for reduced labor obligations, higher recompense, and, in the end, for proprietorship over their tenancies and other estate lands. These depression-era protests in central Colombia possessed similar organizations and ideology of revolutionary agrarianism such as emerged in China and other parts of the world in those years. Yet they were preceded and indeed distinguished by intensive bargaining between peasant and planter, which is the focus of this chapter. On the peasants' side these negotiations were usually carried out on an individual basis, occasionally collectively, yet seldom in an overtly ideological or political manner. Thus, the "machines" from the highlands proved to be far less malleable than the coffee planters had expected, balking early on at the disciplines of export agriculture and constantly attempting to establish independent small-holderships.

The most direct, repeated confrontations between estate managers and the rural poor occurred in plantation workplaces where levels of supervision and evaluation were commonly high. In coffee groves and processing centers, peasants confronted a meticulously organized and increasingly demanding production process intended to satisfy the requirements of North Atlantic markets;[24] by the 1920s, Colombian coffees had achieved repute abroad partly because of the labor intensive, systematic pruning of the coffee bushes and the individual picking of beans as they ripened over a several-week harvest period.[25] Confronted by these circumstances, the peasants resisted the pace and design of closely watched gang labor in customary ways. Constantly renegotiated piecework was met by foot dragging and slipshod performance; foremen attempting speedups or encouraging competition among workers were checkmated by threats and community pressure. There was also friction over output and remuneration, with the counterpoint of peasants mixing gravel with the coffee beans and administrators reducing the size of the measuring boxes while retaining the same payment schedule.[26] Most significantly, however, tenant efforts to reduce their labor obligations led to constant wrangling over their completion, the negotiation of specific jobs in lieu of gang labor, and, for those with sufficient resources, hiring substitutes to fulfill their work dues.

For tenants, escape from such obligations meant greater opportunities to consolidate the household economy based on the land allotments that served as payment for their labor. If the planters expected these plots merely to provide the basic necessities of their permanent work force, they failed to appreciate the ambitions, energy, and cleverness of the rural poor. While only the most daring challenged estate sanctions against coffee production, many tenants produced foodstuffs, charcoal, cigarettes, brown sugar loaves, and cane-based liquors to sell in nearby towns and in market hamlets where, early in the twentieth century, there were reports of gatherings of "two to three thousand persons making transactions for considerable sums."[27]

The peasant economy that evolved within the great estates became the focus of tense, sometimes volatile, encounters between planters and the rural poor. There was, of course, constant bargaining over labor requirements, which included the estate denial of marketing privileges for tenants who had yet to complete their obligations. Also, bitter disputes broke out over compensation for improvements made by tenants to their plots; though planters initially resisted, by the 1920s such payments were fairly commonplace. Tenants and planters were always sparring over the use of estate resources. Much of the tension concerned access to uncultivated meadows and forests surrounding the plantation core that were transformed into commons where tenants hunted and collected wood for charcoal production and building materials. Moreover, pilfered great estate cane, the molasses allowance given fieldhands, and sugar cultivated on the tenancies became the foundation for the extensive small-scale manufacture of brown sugar loaves and fermented and distilled beverages in great demand throughout the coffee districts.[28] Finally, as these households prospered, the planters' attempts to siphon off tenant wealth into estate coffers through fines, license fees, and tolls on goods passing through the estates on the way to market were met by all kinds of evasions and trickery.

Beyond the coffee plantations, however, the tenant's encounters with the state turned out to be equally uneasy and explosive, perhaps more so. Civil society was scarcely an arena within which to press claims against planters who were often in collusion with local bureaucrats; the boundary between estate rules and the legal system was thin indeed as authorities meted out punishments for infractions of estate regulations. Moreover, early twentieth-century municipal government in central Colombia still relied heavily on the corvée; unmet obligations resulted in fines, embargoes on peasant goods, and even physical punishment. As the tenant economies crystallized, they seemed to be an even more attractive target for the state. In order to avoid the revenue collection agents, the peasantry developed extensive networks to protect a contraband economy based primarily on the production and sale of untaxed liquors. In 1911, a departmental official characterized those evading excise taxes as "a sort of brotherhood . . . audacious, aggressive, full of subtleties and surprising capabilities."[29] By the end of the decade, after various episodes of mobs sacking excise offices and releasing offenders from jail, a departmental spokesman deplored the fact that "excisemen, reduced in number and lacking authority, simply cannot visit certain areas where the contrabandists live constantly on the alert and are prepared for combat, well armed and resolved to defend their industry."[30]

The estate owners were not unsympathetic to the plight of the peasants on this score. One observer noted that additional burdens such as the corvée raised "the specter of rebellion among these dark laborers, simple spirits . . . (so that) they just break the chains, and abandon their plot."[31] Taking flight was an extreme, though not unusual, response to the pressures from departmental officials, but certainly disturbing to the planters desiring stable work forces. Equally problematic was the consternation caused in the coffee districts by the campaigns to enforce the excise taxes, particularly with sweeps of police and special task forces put together for revenue collection. This led estate owners to denounce the representatives of the state as "parasites who live off the farmer, neither working nor allowing others to do so" and even charge them on occasion with fomenting unrest.[32] Paradoxically, the planters had come to rely on the stability and viability of the tenant households and made common cause with the rural poor against the state even as the peasantry was threatening the integrity of their institutions from within.

While concerned about threats to the public order caused by government pressures on the rural poor, the planters themselves relied on a somewhat flawed, but still resilient, paternalist code deeply rooted in Colombia's eastern highland culture and redesigned in the export-oriented plantation districts on the western slope during the nineteenth century. On the one hand, the separate and unequal positions of landowner and peasant on the social hierarchy were acknowledged on both sides, as symbolized by workers' greeting planters on bent knee. Landlords humiliated their dependents through verbal and physical abuse and sexual harassment. Yet theirs was also a close identification because the two classes had lived and worked together in the coffee groves during the last quarter of the nineteenth century. Peasant men considered themselves worthy of their lords, bound to them less by servility than by common endeavors and mutual affection; the planters displayed proper decorum and even conviviality toward the men on whose labor they so relied for their wealth. Such paternalism was obviously marked by deep contradictions.[33] Yet these tensions were effectively managed because, as one local bureaucrat later recollected, the most effective landlords were those who knew how to "treat" their dependents with a subtle blend of liberality and firm acknowledgment of their superiority.[34] In effect, in the early stages of estate formation, planters cultivated what Richard Sennett has called paternalism's inherent "false love" between master and servant as assiduously as they did their precious coffee groves.[35]

However, after the turn of the twentieth century, this solvent of class antagonism was losing its effectiveness. The rapid expansion of the work force on the larger estates after 1900 and the growing pressures in the plantation workplace, together with the widened horizons of the tenants and the absence of planters who were in Bogotá offices and on grand tours of Europe, set in relief the deep tensions inherent within paternalism. While some administrators were quite adept in the "treating" of their peons and tenants, the spirit of mutual deference between owners and their workers was being seriously strained. As suggested, the rural poor responded by husbanding their resources for their households. But they also asserted their identity and self-esteem in seemingly irrational, more symbolic ways. Thus, the carcass of a prize steer with a message carved on the hide—"don't mess with us"—or the felling of a stand of expensive, imported eucalyptus by a gang of youths were more than acts of mischief. They signaled that the social code that had long governed the relations between the classes in the large coffee plantation districts was becoming badly fractured.

The foundations of elite rule were thus profoundly shaken even before the tenants formed the first peasant leagues in the late 1920s upon joining forces with urban radicals. As one former tenant explained years later, "the landowners wouldn't even greet us, considering themselves a different breed." A group of tenants therefore decided not to extend their greetings, causing their employer to complain of his workers' rudeness. One of the tenants responded: "Look, sir, why should we waste our time greeting you? Better to greet a tree which at least waves back!" In telling this story, the old man clearly recognized that the terms of social interaction between the classes were being rewritten. "Thus began a certain forcefulness," he recalled, "a certain form of rebellion. Yes, that's how it was."[36]

The Problem of the "Skirts"

After the turn of the century, conflicts over gender roles and sexual norms—between the peasants and their superiors and among the peasants themselves—were central to the reworking of the transcript of class relations on the great coffee plantations. In 1928, the first contract signed between a tenant organization and a Viotá estate owner included a provision that "the bosses will take the required measures, in so far as possible, to assure that their employees will not be disrespectful nor attack the tenants nor their families."[37] The article was apparently intended to shelter workers from the brutal, often capricious physical abuse that generally characterized estate management. However, male peasant negotiators clearly wanted resolution of the "problem of the skirts," mostly understood as the rape and seduction of their women-folk by the owners and managers of Viotá's largest coffee enterprise. For these men, their self-respect was linked to wresting from the planters undisputed control over their families in general and their women in particular. The deep anxiety aroused by planters' sexual predations was certainly as responsible for fueling the organized opposition of the rural poor in the following decade as demands for the alteration of work obligations or efforts to guarantee the autonomy of the peasant household.

This was an ancient point of contention between lord and peasant in central Colombia. Following the Spanish conquest in the sixteenth century, the reconstruction of gender relations in the populous eastern highlands accompanied the creation of a senorial society in which the white upper classes exercised control over the conquered populations through networks of landlords, local bosses, and priests.[38] Traditional native societies had been characterized by premarital sexual relations, a plurality of intimacies in adult life for both sexes, and independent access by women to economic resources. The renovated gender system set in place by the European colonizers and sanctioned by the Catholic Church was intended to assure the unequivocal subordination of women and their families to men. During four and a half centuries after the conquest, landlords and clerics, in collusion with male-dominated clans created under their aegis, sought to enforce conformity to a patriarchal system within the peasant family.[39] Yet, even as the elites encouraged patriarchy among the rural poor, the intimacy forced by white men on Indian women was commonplace, resulting in rapid miscegenation throughout most of the eastern highlands and institutionalized interclass sexual relations, which undercut male authority among the peasantry. Young peasant women often paid sexual tribute to their lords prior to marriage and customarily served as concubines for men of substance in the thickly populated region north and east of Bogotá.[40] Finally, the legal norms regarding women, which remained in place into the twentieth century, disallowed them either from testifying in courts against their husbands or making legal contracts while married, and left the administration of their property in the hands of male family members.[41]

Thus, from the outset, the elite's stance regarding sexuality and family organization among their dependents was deeply contradictory. By the early twentieth century, there was growing concern among the elites that the lower classes, as the governor of Cundinamarca wrote in 1906, had forgotten "their responsibilities to God and their families, letting thus the impulses of primitive custom—erasing all moral laws— hold sway."[42] Soon after, the Catholic Church initiated its first massive campaigns to salvage the souls and families of the poor.[43] This sensibility was certainly echoed in the pleas of Jesús del Corral for the reaffirmation of patriarchy among the rural poor as he urged fellow planters not to employ unmarried couples on their estates.

But his condemnation of the "demons of seduction" stalking the countryside in pursuit of young women probably fell on deaf ears. The presumption of unchallenged access by the elite to lower-class women so commonplace in highland society was easily transplanted to the frontier plantation districts from the 1870s onward. There was neither a lack of targets for coercive sexual relations, especially considering the large numbers of unattached adolescent girls arriving to work in the coffee groves and the processing houses, nor a short supply of explanations or excuses. Prevailing racist ideologies noted the unharnessed sexuality of the poor in general, and women in particular.[44] Local folklore gave ample evidence of the peasant women's natural promiscuity; for example, tales of abductions and rape of women by bears implied the consent of the victims.[45] Finally, sexual coercion may have represented perhaps the most powerful, if dangerous, weapon at the disposal of the planters in imposing their will on the workers; the resulting divisiveness and demoralization of the peasant household was consistent with the goals of maintaining control over subordinates through arbitrary decisions, in this case directed at the very core of their personal and family existence. In effect, forced intimacy was neither a mere ahistorical embodiment of male lust nor a simple vestige of *señorialism.* Rather it represented a deeply rooted cultural norm given new vitality as an integral part of the process of labor control, which emerged on the western slope's largest coffee plantations.

Not surprisingly, the resistance of the rural poor, and of men in particular, occurred within the framework of the gender ideology elaborated by the upper classes and incorporated into peasant culture from the mid-sixteenth century onward. While not discounting the affection and mutual respect between the sexes, which was surely maintained among the rural poor, peasant men acknowledged the propositions of the patriarchal model, namely that women were ruled by a near-demonic sexuality, which made them different from men and that they were to be regarded ultimately as possessions of the latter. This view appears to have given peasant men wide latitude to use their womenfolk in the complex psychological combat in which they were engaged with the coffee planters of the western slope in the early twentieth century. On occasion, they collaborated in the sexual predations of their masters. The revelries that sometimes accompanied planter visits to their estates included intimate, often forced, encounters with peasant women arranged for by peasant men.[46] In pawning women to the planters and the administrators, these men may have hoped to curry favor or gain privilege. But there was perhaps more to such exchanges than obeisance, rather a sense of empowerment in which the bosses' passions had made them vulnerable to manipulation by those who provided the instruments for their pleasure. The masters in their lust were thus momentarily at a disadvantage to lower-class men.

However, more commonly, peasant men sought to "protect" their womenfolk, which meant at least corralling them for their own desires and interests. Ironically, the central presumption of the patriarchal model, that a man's worth depended upon his ability to possess women, whether mates or daughters, set male peasants on a collision course with their social superiors. In the treacherous social landscape of the great estates, the predatory sexuality of the owners and managers put male self-esteem at risk. Peasant men were thus in a continual state of alarm regarding sexual advances to their womenfolk by those in command. By the 1920s, the situation was probably more volatile than ever before because the absentee landlords had virtually ceased cultivating the intimacies of paternalism, so that the intrinsic savagery of class relations became ever more salient. Peasant men tried to prevent such intrusions into their families, concealing young girls from estate owners and managers, attempting to exclude women from workplaces without familial supervision, and reporting scandalous incidents to the authorities. When these tactics were of no avail, they called on the supernatural for protection. For example, at the approach of a planter or administrator, men would begin to sing, warning women and seeking to engage the spirits on their side in battle with the masters.

> Rattler, little rattler
> Wandering in the cane
> Bite the boss' foot
> Which stepped on my rosebush.[47]

While shoring up the entitlements of patriarchy against the estate owners and their representatives, peasant men were also on the alert against the threats to their womenfolk from another quarter. The male heads of service tenants' households, fast becoming the most enduring and stable peasant institutions on the western slope, especially feared the wandering casual laborers; harvest time was a particularly tense period, during which sexual encounters and pregnancies appear to have increased.

Though elite and peasant men alike shared the vision of a male-dominated family, this patriarchal ideal was hardly achieved in its totality. Illegitimacy rates on the western slope remained persistently high throughout the period; in 1906, three-quarters of the births in Viotá were illegitimate, falling to only 63 percent by the late 1920s.[48] So high a proportion of births out of wedlock might be seen as resulting from the subordinate position of lower-class women in the region and the fragility of social institutions to protect their interests as wives and parents, a view articulated by Jesús del Corral and others in the first decades of the twentieth century. On the other hand, illegitimate motherhood may very well have reflected choices made by women to have relationships with men where the women possessed greater personal autonomy in the private and public spheres. Some peasant women appear to have calculated the possibilities for protection or self-improvement sometimes accruing from intimacy with landowners and managers. Visits by planters and their friends not only broke the monotony of plantation life, but also provided opportunities for the exchange of sexual favors by young peasant women for material goods such as a pair of shoes or a dress or escape to a potentially better life in the city as a servant girl, seamstress, or prostitute.[49] The possibilities of such changes in fortune for young women who faced a life of utter misery and wretchedness were not always easy to forego. In this way, despite the obvious dangers to peasant women seeking autonomy through intimacy with those above them, their consent to such relations represented another divergence from the social norms of patriarchy, the women defying domination by peasant men who considered themselves as shamed and dishonored by such encounters.[50]

The apparent anomaly of such choices by peasant women where patriarchy had such a firm grip on the imagination of rich and poor alike is explicable on various levels. In the first place, peasant women drew upon an alternative gender ideology with deep historical roots. Prior to the conquest, women in the populated eastern highlands had possessed considerable sexual autonomy and economic independence. The patriarchal project of colonial society was intended to redesign gender relations, as landlords, priests, and peasant men drew boundaries around the private and public lives of women. Yet the solidity of the male-dominated family imposed by the European elites and the Catholic Church was undercut early in the colonial period by population decline, the transfer of males to work in locales away from their villages, and the dependence on female labor in the household economy. Patriarchal institutions likely crystallized with the demographic surges and economic prosperity in the highlands during the eighteenth century, although by the third quarter of the nineteenth century economic stagnation and demographic expansion caused an uprooting of the peasantry and a probable weakening of the male-dominated family among the rural poor.[51] Despite several centuries during which a relatively stable highland peasantry within a *señorial* order emerged in central Colombia, preconquest patterns of intimacy and family organization, based on relative gender equality and considerable female autonomy, survived. Despite severe sanctions, there was a range of alternatives for women in their relations with men, including premarital sexual encounters, single motherhood, common-law marriages, and concubinage.[52] These relations remained underground for several centuries, operating at the margins of a peasant clan structure and a wider social order where patriarchy was in command.

This alternative gender ideology, which sanctioned greater autonomy for women in private and to a lesser extent the public realms, flourished during the establishment of export agriculture on the western slope from the last quarter of the nineteenth century onward.[53] The patriarchalism of the highland peasant family did not survive intact its transplantation to the coffee districts where the reassertion of clan-centered conformity was quite difficult. Arriving from many different highland regions, these migrants were not easily melded together into a coherent peasant society over several generations of continual movement onto the frontier southwest of the capital.[54] Moreover, entire families did not usually journey together to the coffee districts. Most commonly, young men following harvests would make deals with landowners for longer-term employment and then send for a sister or cousin to assist in the cultivation of a garden plot and preparation of meals. Many young women also came on their own to the coffee plantations.[55] Migrants were thus entering a frontier society where the pressures of patriarchal family organization were considerably diminished. A measure of the weakness of male-dominated clans in the region was the relative paucity of fictive kinship relations, which might have complemented or shored up patriarchy.[56] Finally, young women coming into the coffee districts were most certainly at some advantage, in terms of choosing partners, given the greater numbers of men than women in the coffee districts than in the highland communities from whence they came. In the latter, for example, women were some 52 to 55 percent of the population, while these percentages were reversed in the lowlands.[57]

While migration itself disrupted traditional family structures and relations, the highlanders arrived in a world which was only several hundred miles distant, but a universe away from the villages and manors they had left behind. According to Gutiérrez de Pineda, family systems informed by this ideology took root in an environment "far away from the religious controls and social pressures which they had previously endured."[58] Indeed, the elite paternalism that had propped up patriarchal relations among the lower classes in the highlands showed itself to be quite weak on the western slope. The trinity of paternalist institutions—landlord, state, and church—was neither strong enough nor its separate parts sufficiently cooperative with each other to guarantee a disciplined and conformist population in the coffee districts, especially with regard to gender orthodoxies. The increasing absence of planters traveling on business or pleasure in the nation's capital and abroad made it difficult, as we have seen, for the currency of paternalism to maintain its value on the plantations themselves. Further, the relative shallowness of state power in central Colombia's tropical lowlands before the Great Depression partly accounts for the social laxity there, as opposed to the eastern highlands. Bitter antagonisms in the coffee plantation districts between the conservative regime and the mostly liberal landowners made it difficult to establish an enduring partnership of the export-oriented upper classes and the government to control the lower classes or other tasks of governance. There was constant friction between large coffee growers and the authorities over taxes, public labor obligations for tenants, responsibilities for road maintenance, and real estate assessments.[59]

This divide between planters and the state had major consequences for the enforcement of the cultural orthodoxy that had prevailed in the eastern highlands where the Conservative party held sway. In the first place, the Catholic Church was unable to attach itself to the customary armature of class rule in these districts. The alliance of lord and local cleric was manifestly weak in many communities on the western slope; the handful of priests in the region rarely attended the spiritual needs of the poor, who, as Jesús del Corral reported, ran away from Catholic missionaries.[60] Moreover, the efforts of the church to establish even a modicum of orthodoxy in the coffee towns and hamlets of the western slope ran into serious obstacles among largely liberal residents who proved to be an intractable lot.[61] And, as landlords retreated from civic responsibilities in these often isolated districts, the local petty bourgeoisie filled the resulting political vacuum; these local tradesmen, professionals, and merchants often had radically republican and anti-clerical sensibilities.[62] They were also likely to be sympathetic to the claims of the rural poor on whose purchasing power they depended for their livelihoods.[63] With landlords absent much of the time, government bureaucrats unable to rule effectively, and priests viewed with suspicion, the rural poor were often left to their own devices, less encumbered by institutions and norms which had sustained paternalism—and in turn, patriarchy—in the highlands. Further, they were able to find, at least tentatively, some common ground with townsfolk who were, by interest, if not by temperament and ideology, skeptical about the claims of traditional elite power in central Colombia.

But it was on the great estates themselves that the "gender transcript," so to speak, was most dramatically rewritten in the decades before the Great Depression. Of greatest significance was the acquisition of greater economic autonomy by peasant women, resulting in conflicts with their social superiors as well as their fellow male peasants. Just as the rural poor were divided by differential access to land, work arrangements, skills, and favors from the planters, so too they were divided by gender, in other words, by the sometimes differing interests of peasant men and women and the women's ambivalence toward patriarchal norms.

In the first place, work arrangements on the plantations freed women from the constraints of familial supervision. In the highlands, women worked largely within the context of the peasant household well into the twentieth century. Most women's labor on the great estates there, aside from obligations of service in the manor house, was performed under the supervision of male family members. Grain cultivation and cattle raising allowed the family to remain intact as an economic unit, thereby reinforcing the customary sexual division of labor in the highlands. In contrast, the production process on the large coffee enterprises precluded such close familial vigilance of women at work, with men and women often segregated. The latter, prized for their nimbleness and alacrity, were congregated in bean-sorting work sheds at the main processing centers or in harvesting gangs. Peasant men were uneasy about these arrangements, partly because such work assignments drew women away from household work on the tenancies, but also because they rightly feared the advances of managers and foremen in such environments. Doubtless, young peasant women found themselves torn in such circumstances. On the one hand, they were surely anxious about sexually predatory administrators and the intense workplace demands at probably the most critical point in the production process, where quality control was especially important. Yet, bean sorting provided additional income and young women probably found pleasure and security in the particular solidarities of the processing barns.

Indeed, women in those close and emotionally tense workplaces appear to have possessed a greater autonomy and likely presented the planters with quite costly and problematic resistance before the 1930s. Significantly, women were among the first group of peasants who, as workers, not necessarily as aspiring small holders, opposed the estate administrations in an organized and sustained manner during the following decade. Like their early unionized sisters in the large coffee processing firms of the port cities, the young women of the sorting sheds experienced the intertwining of class and gender and thus helped make those places the tinder of rebellion during the depression era protests.

The service tenancies were the most important vehicle by which women achieved autonomy in the large coffee plantation districts. Males were obliged, as we have seen, to work away from their small plots for days or weeks at a time, thus leaving women with considerable responsibility for household management. The emergence of these small production units as relatively dynamic enterprises during the first three decades of the twentieth century relied heavily on female energy and entrepreneurship. For example, women burned felled trees from the expanding groves or at the high altitudes of the estates in order to make charcoal. In addition to charcoal, they sold fruits, vegetables, and corn in the town centers and in the smaller markets established at the edges of the plantations. They were also often contracted by the estate management to feed day laborers. In hamlets throughout the coffee districts, women succeeded in accumulating some capital and establishing connections with local merchants in order to open small stores and grog shops.

Women participated extensively in the contraband economy that flourished in the coffee zones after the turn of the century. Some women manufactured and distributed cigarettes in nearby towns in violation of revenue laws, but, most importantly, they were key players in the production and marketing of local fermented and distilled liquors, which were in great demand in districts where it was reported in 1926 that residents consumed on an average of four quarts daily.[64] Cosme R. Acuña, the prefect of Tequendama, reported that "mothers of families" were the principals involved in the illegal liquor business. Departmental authorities were alarmed by the large numbers of women indicted for violating excise tax laws. In 1919, women represented 40 percent of arrests for tax fraud. Officials refused to acknowledge that women were major independent actors in the contraband economy, with the departmental treasurer arguing that "in the majority of cases, the male contrabandists make it seem as if the woman is responsible for the fraud" and recommending that male heads of household be made legally responsible for the illicit actions of their womenfolk.[65] Throughout the following decade the problem persisted; between 1925 and 1928, almost half of all indictments for excise tax violations in Viotá were against women.[66]

Finally, women found themselves in another kind of conflict with the authorities in the 1910s and 1920s when, as traditional healers and providers of medicinal herbs, they were proscribed by health reformers moving into the rural areas. This was especially important in the coffee zones where campaigns against anemia and other tropical diseases resulted in difficult encounters with sanitation campaign officials.[67]

Women played a major role in the consolidation of the peasant household economy within the great estate complexes of the western slope. The position of men as essentially part-time proletarians provided peasant women with the kind of space and independence necessary to convert the tenancy plots into efficient units of production, at least partially on the women's terms. The substantial income streams brought into these households by women acting as contracted food provisioners to the estates, as petty merchants, as small store owners, and as major players in the underground economy meant that they were in a position to demand greater control over economic decision making within the family. This situation also enabled them to carve out a place within the commercial networks to which they were connected in the decades before the depression.

But women's autonomy within the peasant household and their external participation were fraught with danger. Women suffered badly at the hands of their menfolk on the discovery of unsanctioned intimacies. Adolescent girls were beaten to near death, poisoned, or driven to suicide by calumny and ostracism, the more so if such encounters resulted in children. Rape and other physical violence against peasant women by peasant men were commonplace; and brawls between the sexes occurred in homes, market hamlets near the great estates, and in the coffee groves.[68]

The frenzied responses by males to real or imagined sexual liaisons must be seen in the context of women's empowerment by the circumstances of export capitalism even as men struggled against the indignities and exploitation of daily life on the large coffee plantations. Men's rage against women among the rural poor, as great as that of the peasant men against the planters, suggests that many peasant women did not share the patriarchal assumptions that they were the property of men or the unresisting object of the latter's passions. While women remained charged with child rearing, the tenancy's dependence on their labor and entrepreneurship before the Great Depression undermined the ideal of patriarchy so deeply rooted among peasant males who resented the independence their womenfolk had achieved by virtue of their position as major contributors to the household.

Women thus lived in great peril. They were hardly shielded by intimacies with their social superiors. While paternalism allowed a close identification between male peasants and their overlords, the sexual exchanges between peasant women and estate owners or administrators were not similarly cushioned. Peasant men could rely in some measure on the male bonding built into paternalism, but women were far more vulnerable to their superiors' caprice. Furthermore, they were usually not formal parties to tenancy arrangements nor heirs of assets or plot occupancy upon the death of a male tenant, a situation which often resulted in vagrancy among women. Ironically, the accumulation of sufficient wealth—to which women were major contributors—allowed tenants to hire substitutes for their labor obligation, thereby bringing men more directly and consistently into household management. This resulted in the turning inward of some peasant women toward domestic life, partly by the decision of the male head of household and partly by their own desire to escape the dangers of life and work on the great estates. Finally, government officials were unlikely to be responsive to their plight, especially given the legal status of women. Moreover, their participation in the underground economy caused many of them to be in constant scrapes with the authorities; certainly, the punishments meted out to these women, up to seven months on a corvée road gang, placed them in dangerous and, according to the bureaucrats, corrupting circumstances.[69]

Gender, Class, and the Dialectics of Everyday Resistance

In early 1928, a coalition of middle-class radicals, artisans, and labor activists was organizing among the workers and tenants on coffee estates throughout central Colombia. Female militants, in particular, urged peasant women in these districts to participate alongside men in the "coming global movement."[70] Several score of women from Viotá's great estates answered the call, saying that "we were aware of none of these things in this isolated place where we know only work day and night, covered in ignorance and wasting our energies for the benefit of the vampires who use us." They invited Leonilde Riaño, the Red Flower of Tequendama, to teach them about the "sublime cause of socialism . . . [to] bring a little ray of light to help us escape the darkness in which we are forced to submit to the will of our oppressors."[71]

In placing themselves at the disposal of the outside organizers, Viotá's rural women joined a rebellion that was to culminate two decades later in the dismantling of the large coffee plantations and the emergence of a Communist-led village of independent small holders. Two powerful streams of protest shaped by the complex social construction of gender in the region deeply influenced the rebellion, particularly in its early phases: the rage of peasant men at the abridgement of their patriarchal prerogatives by the sexually predatory planters combined with women's efforts—through participation in strikes, land invasions, boycotts, and support for armed insurrection—to protect the autonomous small holder economy that they had nurtured for several decades. However, with the triumph of the peasant household after the middle of the twentieth century, there was an erosion of women's autonomy and the reorganization of the peasant family along more patriarchal lines. Although women had been major contributors to the local social revolution that occurred in a handful of central Columbian municipalities in the wake of the depression, they did not, however, entirely reap the benefits of their struggle. In a cruel twist of fate, not long after the victory over the great estates, women began to be locked into family relations and sexual norms that looked not very different from the highland patriarchy from which their grandmothers had fled two generations or earlier.

The affirmation of patriarchy that accompanied a successful local peasant rebellion in the 1930s and 1940s in Viotá was due to several factors. The organization and ideology of the Communist-led movement, the fairly rapid acquisition of land titles by the small holders requiring legally clear terms of inheritance, and the replacement of local liquor production by beer and soft drinks served to undercut the gains made by women during the decades prior to the Depression. Equally important, however, was the legacy of peasant opposition to planter rule that had evolved in the first decades of the century, a rule that included a contradictory set of social constructions of class and gender that underwrote a successful local uprising even while limiting the economic and personal autonomy of women peasants. In terms of the dimensions of everyday resistance laid out by Scott—material resources, identity and self-esteem, and a subculture of resistance—it is evident that the opposition of the rural poor to both landlord and the state depended on a complementary and contradictory relation between class and gender.

In the first place, women made major contributions in the struggles over the "redistribution of control over property," playing significant roles at the nodes of production and exchange in order to guarantee the integrity of the peasant household. Paradoxically, however, women's involvement—in poaching, tax evasion, and the like—strengthened a small holder economy that came to be dominated by men who eventually pushed or cajoled women back into purely domestic, familial tasks.[72] At the same time, the assertion of dignity by peasant men and women in the face of constant humiliation often put them at cross-purposes, especially regarding expressions of sexuality. As women evolved a complicated usage of sex in everyday class combat with their social superiors, male peasants found their own voices to assert their self-esteem. Sometimes the sexually predatory planters and estate managers would be the objects of their rage, but just as frequently their anger was displaced toward easier targets such as wives, sisters, daughters, and lovers seen as having deeply humiliated their menfolk. Out of this tangled emotional web, it is difficult to identify an oppositional culture that could include women on equal terms to men. Thus, while the bruises inflicted on paternalism by the everyday resistance of both sexes might have suggested common ground between men and women, the persistence of the patriarchal ideal among the peasantry undercut its capacity to sustain a full range of opposition to the dominant culture. As with property, the legal order, and other issues, the "little" and "big" traditions shared a common stance with regard to gender identities and relations. While this might have given some legitimacy and vitality to the everyday resistance from below, it also appears over the long term to have been a limiting factor for peasant rebels, before and after their opposition acquired more recognizable political shape in terms of organization and ideology.

Despite the reasserted patriarchy in this district, the longer-term impact of the gendering of the "class transcript" should not be discounted. The escalation and near consolidation of peasant women's economic autonomy and sexual independence in the first three decades of the century and women's liberation ideals propounded by the Communists appear to have provided a kind of subtext in Viotá which is not altogether obvious. In short, the mixing of these elements may have created the liniments in Viotá of what Judith Stacey, in referring to the impact of the Chinese Revolution on gender relations and the family, has called "democratic patriarchy" in which women have significant, if limited, autonomy within a still male-dominated household.[73]

In the late 1970s, the traces of the alternative gender ideology in this village were evident in the interstices of a modified patriarchal order. One of the municipality's principal business figures was Waldimira Vásquez, the daughter of a tenant and peasant league leader; the "millionairess," as she was known, was a fitting descendant of the women who participated in the contraband networks of the 1920s. But there was another, more overt political way in which the alternative gender culture insinuated itself into the life of this coffee municipality of the Columbian Andes, a great plantation district that had become a predominantly small holder community in two generations. The once prosperous small farms located on the former tenancies confronted population pressure, lower coffee prices, land tax increases, and high production costs, especially for new technologies. Women were being forced to work outside the home or migrate to the nearby capital to jobs in industry and household service.[74]

The mobilizations of the rural leagues in the town square at first seemed an odd contrast of old hopes and new claims. Amid the tattered red flags emblazoned with the names of peasant martyrs fluttering above the crowd, women hoisted placards calling for day-care. The peasant leadership, largely male, had attempted unsuccessfully, for several years, to develop a collective response to the erosion of the viability and independence of the small farms. The market, as opposed to the landlords of yesteryear, proved an elusive adversary and the political experience of a generation of protagonists to the great plantations seemed unable to provide a compass for effective cooperative responses to the economic crisis among these independent-minded mountaineers. Yet with the involvement of women and the nature of their demands, ancient claims were being given new life and a modern design. Thus, whether the terms of resistance are everyday and often hidden from view or more explicitly political, the experience of Viotá's men and women suggests that the efforts to rectify the inequalities of wealth and power are intimately connected to the alterations of what Paul Thompson referred to as the "balance of power between the sexes."[75]

Notes

1. Jesús del Corral, "Por los siervos de la gleba," *Revista Nacional de Agricultura* 9:120, Special Edition (June 1914):7.

2. For a description of the economic and political situation in Colombia at the end of the first decade of the twentieth century, see Charles W. Bergquist, *Coffee and Conflict in Colombia, 1886–1910* (Durham, N.C.: Duke University Press, 1978).

3. Jesús del Corral, "Por los siervos de la gleba," p. 11.

4. C. H. Arboleda, *Estadística de la República de Colombia* (Bogotá: Imprenta Nacional, 1906), p. 65; República de Colombia, *Anuario estadístico de Colombia* 13 (Bogotá: Imprenta Nacional, 1929), pp. 87–90.

5. Jesús del Corral, "Por los siervos de la gleba," p. 12.

6. James C. Scott, *Weapons of the Weak: Everyday Forms of Peasant Resistance* (New Haven: Yale University Press, 1985), pp. 184–88.

7. The use of the term "patriarchy" here follows that of Judith Stacey as "a family and social system in which male power over women and children derives from the social role of fatherhood and is supported by a political economy in which the family unit retains a significant productive role." *Patriarchy and Socialist Revolution in China* (Berkeley: University of California Press, 1983), p. 12.

8. Joan Scott, "On Language, Gender, and Working Class History," *International Labor and Working Class History* 31 (1987): 10.

9. Walter Röthlisberger, *El Dorado: estampas de viaje y cultura de la Colombia suramericana*, 2nd. ed., (Bogotá: Banco de la República, 1963), p. 50.

10. Federico Aguilar, *Un paseo de verano en Peñalisa, Girardot, y La Pradera* (Bogotá: Imprenta de I. Borda, 1886), p. 50.

11. Letter of Carlos Abondano. November 12, 1878. In Juan de Dios Carrasquilla, *Segundo informe que presenta el comisario de la agricultura nacional al poder ejecutivo para el conocimiento del congreso, año de 1880* (Bogotá: Imprenta de Medardo Rivas, 1880), p. 42.

12. For a discussion of the crisis in the highlands, see William P. McGreevey, *An*

Economic History of Colombia, 1830–1930 (Cambridge: Cambridge University Press, 1971), Part II.

13. Alfred Hettner, *La cordillera de Bogotá: resultados de viajes y estudios*, translated by Ernesto Guhl. (Bogotá: Banco de la República, 1966), pp. 312–13.

14. F. J. Vergara y Velasco, *Nueva geografía de Colombia*, 2nd edition, Vol. III (Bogotá: Banco de la República, 1974), p. 666.

15. For an extended discussion of the problems confronting large coffee growers in central Colombia from the 1870s through the 1920s, see Marco Palacios, *Coffee in Colombia, 1850–1970: An Economic, Social, and Political History* (Cambridge: Cambridge University Press, 1980).

16. For contrasts with the Colombian case, see for Brazil, Thomas Holloway, *Immigrants on the Land: Coffee and Society in São Paulo, 1886–1934* (Chapel Hill: University of North Carolina Press, 1980); and for Guatemala, J. C. Cambranes, *Coffee and Peasants: The Origins of the Modern Plantation Economy in Guatemala, 1853–1897* (Stockholm: Institute of Latin American Studies, 1986); David McCreerey, "Coffee and Class: The Structure of Development in Liberal Guatemala," *Hispanic American Historical Review* 56 (1976): 438–60; and Carol Smith, "Local History in a Global Context: Social and Economic Transformation in Western Guatemala," *Comparative Studies in Society and History* 26 (1984): 193–228.

17. Nicolás Sáenz, *Memoria sobre el cultivo de café* (Bogotá: Imprenta de la Luz, 1892), p. 21.

18. For descriptions and analyses of the service tenancy arrangements, see Palacios, *Coffee in Colombia*, Chs. IV and V; and Malcolm Deas, "A Colombian Coffee Estate: Santa Barbara, Cundinamarca, 1870–1912," in Kenneth Duncan and Ian Rutledge, eds., *Land and Labor in Latin America: Essays in the Development of Agrarian Capitalism in the Nineteenth and Twentieth Centuries* (Cambridge: Cambridge University Press, 1977), pp. 269–98.

19. Federación Nacional de Cafeteros, *Censo Cafetero, 1932*. A full discussion of this estate structure and its economic and social implications are in Michael F. Jiménez, "Traveling Far in Grandfather's Car: The Life-Cycle of Coffee Estates in Central Colombia. The Case of Viotá, Cundinamarca, 1900–30," *Hispanic American Historical Review* 69 (May 1989): 185–219.

20. The labor management systems on the western slope estates had important similarities with the kinds of relations between employers and workers in small-scale firms described by Richard Edwards in his work, *Contested Terrain: The Transformation of the Workplace in the Twentieth Century* (New York: Basic Books, 1979), Ch. 2.

21. The following discussion of the organization and system of labor management on the large coffee plantations is drawn from interviews with former landowners, tenants, agricultural laborers, merchants, and local officials in Viotá and Bogotá who were knowledgeable about the history of the district before 1930. Additional material was also available in a short municipal history written by José Benigno Galindo, *Monografía de Viotá* (n.d.). A congressional report written in the wake of a violent confrontation between the police and peasants on July 31, 1932, contains much information and observations on estate life and relations between tenants, workers, managers, and estate owners, "Informe que rinde la comisión encargada de estudiar los sucesos ocurridos en Viotá al 31 de julio de 1932," *Anales de la Cámara de Representantes* (19 September 1932). There are two particularly insightful documents on these questions: first, a letter from Francisco José Chaux to the "Sindicato general de propietarios y empresarios agrícolas del Comité de Cafeteros de Colombia," Bogotá, 16 June 1933, 21 pp. *Archivo Olaya Herrera* Section 5, Folder 46. The second is the legislation for the tenancy contract and discussion of its main points which was drawn

up at the Ministry of Industries, "Exposición de motivos sobre 'Proyecto de ley sobre contratos de arrendamientos de tierra y servicios, entre propietarios de fincas rurales y estancieros.'" 1 June 1933, *Archivo Olaya Herrera*, Section 5, Folder 13.

22. Jesús del Corral, "Por los siervos de la gleba," p. 7.

23. Gabriel Ortiz Williamson, "Policia rural," *Revista Nacional de Agricultura* 10 June 1909, p. 185.

24. The pressures on planters to produce a high quality bean for the North American markets are revealed in Sociedad de Agricultores de Colombia, "El café colombiano y las proporciones de su consumo en los Estados Unidos," *Revista Nacional de Agriculturas*, July–August 1922, pp. 5–7; and "Colombian Coffee Trade Conditions Promising," *Spice Mill* (February 1924), which reported that " Colombians . . . have grown considerably in favor with the progressive roasters all over the country," p. 152.

25. Compare this to tree care and harvesting in Brazil described by Stanley J. Stein, *Vassouras: A Brazilian Coffee County, 1850–1890* (Cambridge: Harvard University Press, 1957); and Holloway, *Immigrants on the Land*, pp. 31–32. Between 1905 and 1929, prices for Colombian coffees were on the average some 3.3 cents higher per pound than for Brazilian varieties; in the mid-1920s, the differential was as much as 6 cents a pound. Robert C. Beyer, "The Colombian Coffee Industry: Origins and Major Trends, 1774–1940." Unpublished Ph.D. thesis, University of Minnesota, 1947, pp. 356–85.

26. For an intriguing examination of similar forms of workplace bargaining in a plantation society, albeit somewhat different because of slavery, see James Oakes, *The Ruling Race: A History of American Slaveholders* (New York: Random House, 1983), especially ch. 6.

27. Gabriel Ortiz Williamson, "Región de Subia," *Revista Nacional de Agricultura*, November 1906, p. 270.

28. Ortiz Williamson wrote in his 1906 portrait of the Viotá district that "throughout the region there is a very high number of cane pressers producing molasses and brown loafed sugar. There are some estates which have twenty to thirty each." Gabriel Ortiz Williamson, "Región de Subia," p. 270.

29. Cundinamarca, *Informe del gobernador a la asamblea del departamento, 1911*, pp. x-xi.

30. Cundinamarca, *Informe del secretario de hacienda al gobernador, 1918*, p. 44.

31. *Revista Nacional de Agricultura*, 1 April 1908, p. 353. See also Gabriel Ortiz Williamson's comment on this problem in "Trabajo Personal," *Revista Nacional de Agricultura*, 10 June 1909, pp. 185–87.

32. *Revista Nacional de Agricultura*, 1 April 1908, p. 353. For example, in February 1918, a political demonstration in Viotá's main square turned into a pitched battle between peasants and departmental police during which liquor tax violators were released from prison. For a report on the incident, see Cundinamarca, *Memoria del secretario de gobierno de Cundinamarca, 1918*, p. 22. In the following year, there was apparently quite harsh repression of peasants involved in contraband activities. On 17 March 1919, J. Abondano and M. Lartignan, two Viotá planters, complained to the departmental authorities about the abuses of excisemen against the local population. See Palacios, *Coffee in Colombia*, p. 287.

33. For a theoretical discussion of the design and tensions within paternalism see Howard Newby, "The Deferential Dialectic," *Comparative Studies in Society and History* 17 (1975): 139–64.

34. Interview with Helí Paramo, Bogotá, 15 April 1980. For a suggestive discussion of "treating" in another historical context, see Isaac Rhys, *The Transformation of Virginia, 1740–1790* (Chapel Hill: University of North Carolina Press, 1982).

35. Richard Sennett, *Authority* (New York: Random House 1980), ch. 2.

36. Interview, Emilio Pineros, Viotá, 6 February 1980.

37. *Buenavista* agreement, in Registraduría de Tierras, La Mesa, *Libro de Registro*, Vol. I, Folio 409.

38. For materials on this insufficiently studied region of Colombia, see Orlando Fals Borda, *Historia de la cuestión agraria en Colombia* (Bogotá: Ediciones La Rosca, 1975) and the classic history of the formation of the senorial system in the highlands, Guillermo Hernández Rodríguez, *De los chibchas a la colonia y a la república* (Bogotá: Universidad Nacional de Colombia, 1949).

39. For a discussion of a similar process by which women were subordinated in peasant society in the central Peruvian highlands, see Florencia Mallon, ''Patriarchy in the Transition to Capitalism: Central Peru, 1830–1950,'' *Feminist Studies* 13 (Summer 1987): 379–407.

40. This process is carefully outlined in Virginia Gutiérrez de Pineda, *Familia y cultura en Colombia* (Bogotá: Coediciones Tercer Mundo y Universidad Nacional de Colombia, 1968), pp. 58–71. For a similar experience in highland Peru in the post-conquest period, see Irene Silverblatt, *Moon, Sun, and Witches: Gender Ideologies and Class in Inca and Colonial Peru* (Princeton: Princeton University Press, 1987).

41. For materials on the legal position of women, see María Cecilia Osorno Cárdenas, *La mujer colombiana y latino-americana* (Medellín: Imprenta Marin, 1973), pp. 64–76; and Josefina Amezquita de Almeyda, with the collaboration of Magdalena León de Leal and Lilian Motta de Correa, ''Condiciones de la mujer en el derecho de familia,'' in Magdalena León de Leal, comp., *La mujer y el desarrollo en Colombia* (Bogotá: Asociación colombiana para el estudio de la población, 1977), pp. 273–317.

42. Eliseo Medina made this assessment in his report on the state of affairs in western Cundinamarca following the War of a Thousand Days (1899–1902). Cundinamarca, *Visita del gobernador del departamento de Cundinamarca a las provincias de Sumapaz, Girardot y Tequendama* (Facatativa: Imprenta del departamento, 1906), p. 16.

43. For materials on the emergent church concern about the moral state of the lower classes in the early twentieth century, see *Conferencias episcopales de Colombia, 1908–1953* (Bogotá: Editorial El Catolicismo, 1956).

44. See, for example, the literature on racial degeneration in Colombia and especially the work of the noted psychiatrist Miguel Jiménez López, *Nuestras razas decáen* (Bogotá: J. Casis, 1920) and *La inmigración de la raza amarilla a la América* (Bogotá: Editorial Minerva, 1929).

45. *El Tiempo*, 21 September 1938, reported that a woman in nearby San Bernardo had been abducted and cared for by a bear for eleven days. Interestingly, Natalie Zemon Davis notes that liaisons between women and bears were the theme of festivities in the Pyrenees during the fifteenth and sixteenth centuries. See, ''Women on Top,'' in *Society and Culture in Early Modern France* (Stanford: Stanford University Press, 1975), p. 137.

46. A helpful essay on the issue of the women as objects of sexual exchange, see Gayle Rubin, ''The Traffic in Women: Notes on the 'Political Economy' of Sex,'' in Rayne Rapp Reiter, ed., *Toward an Anthropology of Women* (New York: Monthly Review Press, 1975), pp. 157–210.

47. This ditty was sung during interviews with elderly peasants in Viotá during 1980. It also appears in a study of the folk culture of the eastern highlands by Octavio Quiñones Pardo, *Cantares de Boyaca* (Bogotá: Libreria Atena, 1937), p. 89. In a preface to that volume, Germán Arciniegas wrote that the peasantry ''reduced to silence and passivity . . . sought almost magical ways to escape the eyes and powers of their masters,'' p. xxxi. For an extended discussion of the use of magic as a vehicle for

social struggle, especially in the context of gender, see Silverblatt, *Moon, Sun, and Witches*, ch. XI.

48. See footnote 4.

49. There is impressionistic evidence concerning the crisis in the eastern highlands but as yet no full-scale study of the breakdown of the the traditional order there in the late nineteenth century. See Orlando Fals Borda's community study in which he makes broad generalizations about the highlands, *El hombre y la tierra en Boyaca: desarrollo histórico de una sociedad minifundista* (Bogotá: Editorial Punta de la Lanza, 1973). See also McGreevey's analysis of the data on vagrancy in different regions of Colombia, *An Economic History of Colombia*, p. 175; Palacios' summary of the literature on this subject in *Coffee in Colombia*, pp. 68–71; and a monograph on a region of Boyaca, Fernando López G., "Evolución de la tenencia de tierra en una zona minifundista," *Centro de estudios sobre desarrollo económico* 29 (November 1975).

50. For a discussion of these various forms of sexual intimacy and family organization, see Gutiérrez de Pineda, *Familia y cultura en Colombia*, pp. 71–95; and the following studies of the legal status of concubinage in Colombia in the nineteenth and twentieth centuries, Humberto Ruíz, "El concubinato como fuente de relaciones jurídicas," unpublished thesis, Universidad Nacional, 1955, and Pedro Alejo Cañón Ramírez, *Derecho civil: sociedad conyugal y concubinato*, Tomo 1, Vol. II (Bogotá: Editorial ABC, 1983). For comparisons in the development of family structure of Colombia with other areas in Latin America, notably Ecuador and Argentina, see Eduardo Archetti, "Rural Families and Demographic Behavior: Some Latin American Analogies," *Comparative Studies in Society and History* 26 (1984): 251–79.

51. It should be noted that the illegitimacy rate in the highlands remained remarkably low, both compared to the departmental average and to those in the coffee zones. Caquezá, for example, a traditional small holder village to the east of Bogotá, had an illegitimacy rate of only 21.8 percent in 1905, falling to 17.5 percent by 1927. This is at least an indication of the persistence of patriarchal norms in the highlands in a period during which birth out of wedlock remained remarkably resistant to alteration in the tropical lowlands. Arboleda, *Estadística general de la República de Colombia*, p. 65; and *Anuario estadístico de Colombia* 33, pp. 87–90.

52. Gutiérrez de Pineda suggests that this was a pattern that developed in the traditional senorial order in the highlands and persisted in the lowlands. *Familia y cultura en Colombia*, p. 65. Silverblatt notes a similar process in post-conquest Peru where women "used the contacts that their sexuality offered to gain favors from men in positions of power. . . . Prostitution or concubinage was a path that some native women chose to add a measure of security to their meager lives." Irene Silverblatt, *Moon, Sun, and Witches*, p. 146. Similarly, in her study of rapid social change in late eighteenth- and early nineteenth-century New York, Christine Stansell argues that such apparent violations of social norms have been understood largely as acts "imbued with hopelessness and pathos. Such an understanding, however, neglects the fact that this was a society in which many men still saw coerced sex as a prerogative. In this context, the prostitute's price was not a surrender to male exploitation but a way of turning a unilateral relationship into a reciprocal one." Christine Stansell, *City of Women: Sex and Class in New York, 1789–1860* (New York: Pantheon, 1986), p. 185.

53. Interviews with a number of individuals in Viotá suggested that the "problem of the skirts" was more complicated than the view of unrestrained abuse and exploitation which Jesús del Corral painted in his 1914 lecture. Both men and women indicated that during those years many unattached young women had intimate relations with estate managers, foremen, and the owners themselves and that there was an element of reciprocity in those relations. Evidence on this and other issues involving gender relations comes from, among others, the following interviews conducted in Viotá

during 1980. Cecilia de Castro, Viotá, 12 March 1980; Laura Agudelo, Viotá, 12 April 1980 and subsequent conversations; Emilio Piñeros, Viotá, 6 February 1980 and subsequent conversations; Jaime Muñoz, Viotá, 22 July 1980; and Francisco Bernal, Bogotá, August 1987.

54. The source for materials on migration of women and their role on the great estates is Cecilia de Castro, small holder and caretaker of Hacienda Costa Rica, who arrived in Viotá just after the turn of the century from the highlands. Interviewed in Viotá, 12 March 1980.

55. This was brought to my attention by Viotá's town historian and librarian, José Benigno Galindo. Interviewed in Viotá, 4 February 1980 and subsequent conversations.

56. Colombia, *Anuario estadístico de Colombia, 1936*, pp. 65–66.

57. *Familia y cultura en Colombia*, p. 39.

58. For a discussion of the conflicts between planters and the Conservative state before 1930, see Michael F. Jiménez, "The Limits of Export Capitalism: Economic Structure, Class, and Politics in a Colombian Coffee Municipality, 1900–1930," unpublished Ph.D. thesis, Harvard University, 1985, ch. III.

59. In contrast with the shallowness of church authority in the large coffee plantation districts near Bogotá was the Antioquian corridor in western Colombia where priests and men of substance of small-holder coffee communities successfully enforced cultural conformity. See Christopher Abel, "Conservative Politics in Twentieth Century Antioquia, 1910–1953," *Latin American Center, St. Anthony's College, Oxford, Occasional Paper III* (1973), pp. 743–46; and Gutiérrez de Pineda, *Familia y cultura en Colombia*, pp. 274–95.

60. An example of the friction between the predominantly liberal communities on the western slope and the Catholic Church was the conflict between Fr. Obdulio Chala, the parish priest, and the largely liberal townsfolk. Chala complained to the conservative authorities that one of the schoolteachers had married a liberal and that this would prejudice her teaching. The town was in considerable turmoil over his interventions and vigorously protested his partisanship to the departmental officials. *El Tiempo*, 8 March 1927.

61. The local petty bourgeoisie, who shared the management of local government with the conservative appointees, were, for example, reluctant to force collection of fines for liquor tax violations on the local service tenants and small holders who were their principal customers. In 1922, the conservative mayor of Viotá, General Rafael Galvis pronounced that there was "an absence of public morality, of any judicial or social concept" in the municipality after he discovered 1,600 fines for liquor tax violations which had never been collected. Cundinamarca, *Informe del gobernador a la asamblea, 1922*, p. 97.

62. For a discussion of these women workers see Charles Bergquist, *Labor in Latin America: Comparative Essays on Chile, Argentina, Venezuela, and Colombia* (Stanford: Stanford University Press, 1986), pp. 351–52.

63. Cundinamarca, *Informe del administrador principal de hacienda*, January 1927, p. 15. For a wider discussion of the alcohol consumption patterns in Colombia in this period, see Luis Cuervo Martínez, "Consumo de alcohol en Colombia," *Reportorio de medicina y cirugía* 4 (1913): 229–53.

64. Cundinamarca, "Informe del Prefecto de Tequendama, La Mesa. Febrero 7, 1919," in *Informe del secretario de gobierno al gobernador de Cundinamarca, 1919*, p. 114.

65. Cundinamarca, *Informe del secretario de hacienda al señor gobernador, 1919*, p. 99. This complaint was repeated in 1930 when the report suggested lowering the public works sentences from their normal four to seven months in order to make

"honest" women out of these transgressors of the law. Cundinamarca, *Informe del secretario de hacienda al señor gobernador, 1930*, p. 92.

66. *Gaceta de Cundinamarca*, 1925–1928.

67. On the problem of the local healers, see "Prefectural report dated February 7, 1919," in Cundinamarca, *Informe del secretario de gobierno al gobernador, 1919*, p. 113.

68. Interview. Helí Paramo, Bogotá, 15 April 1980. There are no municipal court records available for these years which would allow for a reconstruction of the full nature and extent of these encounters in the coffee districts, but the indictment announcements in the *Gaceta de Cundinamarca* between 1920 and 1929 reveal that the highest incidence of these, after liquor fraud violations, were for beatings.

69. Cundinamarca, *Informe del secretario de hacienda al señor gobernador, 1919*, p. 99; and a report in *Ruy Blas* 13 January 1928 concerning a dozen women, many with infants, imprisoned for liquor fraud violations in the Facatative jail.

70. *El Diario Nacional*, 23 February 1928.

71. *El Nuevo Diario*, 15 March 1928.

72. Similarly, for the case of the Peruvian highlands, although under very different circumstances, Mallon concludes that "at least initially, the transition to capitalism seems to have provided some 'openings' or opportunities for women of all classes, yet, in the end, none of these transitional alternatives seems to have developed into a basis for longer lasting independence. Quite the contrary, as commodity production became dominant it tended to be defined as an exclusively male sphere, and women's substantial economic activities were relegated to increasingly 'marginal' status within the subsistence sector." Florencia Mallon, "Patriarchy in the Transition to Capitalism," p. 397.

73. Stacey, *Patriarchy and Socialist Revolution in China*, ch. 4.

74. For materials on the contemporary situation in Viotá, see Ingrid Acosta de Mesa, "La Pequeña producción cafetera de Viotá, Cundinamarca: Producto de luchas campesinas," unpublished thesis, Universidad de Los Andes, 1979.

75. Paul Thompson, "Women in the Fishing: Roots of Power between the Sexes," *Comparative Studies in Society and History* 27 (1985): 26–28, compares the positions of men and women and the resultant cultural patterns in fishing communities, primarily in Northern Europe and finds, as in the coffee districts on Colombia's western slope, that the absence of men from direct control over the household allowed for greater female autonomy and more equitable social arrangements in those communities. He argues that there is a "need to understand the changing dynamics of power between the sexes as part of a highly complex interaction, in which the economy, property, space, work, and the culture of the family, religion, and region can all play a vital part." For another examination of this question from a more anthropological perspective, see Susan Carol Rogers, "Female Forms of Power and the Myth of Male Dominance: Model of Female/Male Interaction in Peasant Society," *American Ethnologist* 2 (1975): 727–56.

6

Struggling over Land in China: Peasant Resistance after Collectivization, 1966–1986

David Zweig

When one thinks of monolithic states, few countries leap faster to mind than Maoist China. Since 1949, the Chinese Communist Party (CCP) and its state machine reached out to control more and more aspects of China's economy, polity, and society. At no time in the past 350 years has the state exercised as much power over the lives of its citizens.[1] Fortified by a loyal army of communist cadres, who, imbued with Marxist-Leninist ideology, terrorized society through incessant mass campaigns, the state appeared to have penetrated all aspects of Chinese society and to have maximized its control. In the rural areas, the state forced peasants into collectives and imposed a bureaucratic hierarchy on the countryside to control the means of production—land, labor, and capital—as well as the production and distribution of almost all rural produce. While terms such as "totalitarianism," "Oriental Despotism," or the "Asiatic Mode of Production" have flaws as analytic categories, they do impart the flavor of the statist world in which the Chinese peasant has lived for much of the past forty years.

Yet throughout the history of the People's Republic of China (PRC),

Research for this paper was funded by a research grant from the Social Sciences and Humanities Research Council of Canada, Ottawa, and was arranged by Nanjing University, Nanjing, China. I am grateful to Forrest Colburn, Morris Mottalle, Deborah Brautigam, and Donald Klein for helpful comments. Sonny Lo and Nancy Hearst provided documentary assistance.

peasants have successfully employed a variety of "weapons of the weak" to protect their interests against this oft-times oppressive state.[2] And, ironically, much of their success has been due to the same factors that increased state control. While ideology served as a powerful weapon for mobilizing local cadre support for tightened state controls, ideological battles among competing factions in Beijing engendered frequent policy shifts that weakened the state's authority and created local political and policy vacuums in which peasants advanced their own interests. Fearful that the state would label overt political action as ideologically unsound, peasants adopted less obvious forms of resistance.

The question of peasant resistance is entwined intimately with their relationships with local officials. In most instances, peasants relied on Janus-faced local cadres who determined the extent and success of those efforts. When cadre and peasant interests coincided, collusion was possible. When cadre-peasant interests collided, or state pressures intensified due to a mass campaign, many cadres ignored the peasants and responded to their own or to the state's demands. Also, while the state bureaucracy, running from the county to the village, controlled rural wealth and siphoned resources from the countryside, its weak monitoring mechanisms allowed for much formalistic or partial compliance.[3] Finally, although campaigns pressured cadres and peasants to comply with state, rather than local, interests, their limited duration afforded some leeway for local resistance. Thus the same factors with which the state expanded its control—ideology, personnel, bureaucratic structure, and campaigns—created "cracks in the monolith" and facilitated peasant resistance to this quite powerful state.

Dramatic post-Mao changes, however, have altered the nature of peasant resistance. First, the state is no longer the main target of resistance: local cadres and new entrepreneurs are. Under the *enrichez vous* brand of socialism introduced by Deng Xiaoping, the state ended political campaigns and withdrew some of its tentacles from society. The weakening of the collective system and the growth of markets meant that local officials could no longer rely totally on the rural bureaucratic structure to channel resources into their hands. Under the current mixed economy, they must aggressively pursue their own personal interests.[4] At the same time, a new class of rural entrepreneurs, many of whom are ex-cadres, have begun to increase their share of rural wealth.[5] Yet decollectivization, the end of campaigns, and the demise of Maoist ideology have significantly freed the peasants as well, making them more assertive in defense of their interests. Fear of cadre recriminations still suggest the judicious use of these "weapons of the weak." But confrontations between cadres, entrepreneurs, and peasants are more widespread as they now conflict directly for control of the means of production and prosperity.

Clearly, politically powerful cadres and wealthy peasants with economic contacts are dominating Deng's new order.[6] Nevertheless, common peasants have shown an ability to resist these new assaults by resorting to several strategies. First, to undermine the development of private wealth, peasants have resurrected Maoism's stress on an equitable distribution of income and have used slander and threats of social sanctions against those who would get rich. Second, peasants fight cadre corruption and other efforts to cheat them with the assistance of county cadres and county courts. These efforts often involve anonymous letters to higher-level officials or newspapers. And, third, when other localities, outside cadres or state officials, try to dictate peasant economic behavior, peasants rely on their own local officials to protect their individual and collective interests. These cadres often resort to foot dragging or false compliance. Thus, even as they defend their own rights, peasants remain highly dependent on officials at various levels.

To explain peasant resistance against cadres and the state during two eras—under Mao and under Deng—this chapter examines local conflicts in three Nanjing communes concerning five aspects of land policy: private plots, peasant homes, crop types in collective fields, expropriation of team land by brigades, communes and counties, and the constant battle over whether land should be farmed collectively or privately.[7] These local events are analyzed within the context of national trends. While more systematic nationwide data on local resistance might help convince readers that the local case studies can be generalized, one must recall that access to rural China remains limited. Moreover, reports of these events are rare precisely because peasants who employ "everyday forms of resistance" seek to avoid detection. This search for anonymity is inherent in Scott's very definition of the concept we are analyzing. Finally, the Chinese have not wanted to admit widescale resistance to national policies.[8]

Peasant Resistance in China:
A Framework for Analysis

Before looking at peasant resistance, one must understand the framework in which these local battles occur. As outlined above, peasant

efforts at resistance have been influenced by four major factors—
ideology, personnel, rural structure, and campaigns—each of which
has both constrained and facilitated peasant efforts to protect their own
interests.

Maoist ideology or "hegemony" glorified collective rather than
individual values and invalidated any political interests outside those
defined by the state.[9] Moreover, a constant emphasis on "class struggle" increased the probability that peasant efforts to defend their
economic and political interests would be labeled "counterrevolutionary." Yet shifting coalitions or factional alignments created fluc-
tuations in values emanating from Beijing.[10] These elite perspectives mixed with two dominant local values: a desire for prosperity
and a fear of expanding inequality, generating jealousy and egalitarianism.[11] Thus when Maoist egalitarianism ruled in Beijing, egalitarianism was the dominant local value; peasants who pursued private economic gain suffered opprobrium.[12] But under Deng's current line,
which advocates individual prosperity, peasants can expand and protect their own interests. Nevertheless, egalitarianism and jealousy
aimed at new rich peasants still strongly limit the pursuit of private
wealth.

The state's hegemonic values, and the policies emanating from
them, were introduced into rural China through a series of rural campaigns that forced peasants to demonstrate political support for CCP
policies and preempted peasant efforts to raise political issues. Inflammatory rhetoric about anti-party class enemies and symbolic beatings
of remnants of the old classes—common occurrences during such campaigns—sent a clear message to peasants not to fight back. Their
resistance became indirect and depended on presenting economic challenges to politically motivated policies aimed at limiting their control
over resources.[13] Political campaigns also taught rural cadres to be
circumspect in opposing state interests, which complicated their efforts
to help the peasants.[14] However, the use of campaigns, with pressures
for immediate compliance but weak monitoring mechanisms, meant
that cadres who dragged their feet until the campaign ended could avoid
implementation.

The local bureaucracy sharply curtailed resistance by placing peasants in a tightly controlled environment and taking all decisions out of
their hands. Each peasant lived in a production team, the basic unit of
labor and account,[15] comprised of about twenty to thirty households,
and each team had a team leader, who was usually chosen by brigade
officials, and a team management committee of three to five mem-

bers.[16] Each brigade had approximately seven teams (1,000 people), a management committee, and a party branch. This party branch, the lowest formal level of CCP penetration into the countryside, had a brigade party secretary, the most powerful local official, who was always from a village in the brigade. While these committees usually had three to five members, the number of brigade and commune cadres increased dramatically during the 1970s, increasing bureaucratic control. Above the brigade stood the People's Commune (approximately seven to ten thousand people), with a party and management committee, which could comprise two dozen or more cadres. Their leader, the commune party secretary, was a state cadre brought in from the outside by the county—the lowest level of the state bureaucracy directly above the commune—to support state interests.

This political organization, which combined economic and political organizations in one bureaucracy, maximized the power of the cadres who, after Land Reform (1947–52), replaced the old landlord class as the ruling strata in rural China. The cadres monitored local activities and used their party authority to dominate village politics. They were also the major agents of state interests in the countryside. However, team and brigade officials' positions in local society also forced them to consider the interests of their fellow villagers. Squeezed from above and below, the local cadres' behavior varied according to the pressures they confronted.[17] Particularly when elite pressures abated or peasant economic losses were great, peasants used personal relationships to compel cadres to negotiate with them, to tacitly approve their resistance by turning a blind eye to it, or to help them protect their interests.

Finally, the vastness of the Chinese bureaucracy and the distances county and commune officials covered to check on policy conformity helped cadres and peasants mask their opposition and feign compliance. These spatial factors also permitted cadres in the post-Mao era to ignore calls for more liberal land policies or to use this openness to their own advantage.

Thus peasant resistance in China has been no easy task. Prisoners of a bureaucratic structure that controlled its actions, buffeted by ideological and coercive campaigns decrying its self-protection, and dominated by rural officials who often pursue their own interests at the peasants' expense, China's peasantry, not surprisingly, has been rather passive since the mid-1950s. One need only recall that although 25 million peasants starved to death in 1960–62, due in part to government overrequisitions, we have no reports of major peasant collective action at this time.[18] Yet within the confines of this constrained environment, peasants employed various "weapons of the weak" to fight back. Moreover, as the shackles of the Maoist order were removed, they protected more assertively their expanded interests from ever more rapacious rural officials.

Pre-1966 Struggles over Land

While Land Reform divided the land among peasants and gave them contracts for it, the state reasserted its control over that land and its product through collectivization. Yet even after ownership was transferred nationwide to the cooperatives in 1956, the state controlled land use, leading one scholar to describe ownership rights as a "hybrid form of corporate and public land ownership."[19] Further complications in delineating de facto land ownership later arose into the 1960s and probably the 1970s from the peasantry's lingering memory of which land had been theirs. When the opportunity arose, peasants reasserted their property rights to the collectivized land.[20]

State management of land, however, turned into state ownership of land under the impetus of the radical ideology of the Great Leap Forward and the state's ability to manipulate ownership rights within the rural bureaucracy. During the Great Leap, when ownership of the means of production shifted to the commune level, state officials used their control over commune leaders to expropriate a great deal of collective land. They morally justified this "land grab" by announcing the imminent "advent of communism," under which land ownership would be transferred from small collectives to "ownership by all the people." Under this intense ideological pressure, peasant resistance was futile; in fact, many peasants accepted this chiliastic vision,[21] especially since in many localities food was given for free in the Autumn of 1958. With free food, who needed land? In any case, the locus of decision making on this issue was well out of the peasants' reach.

Local events around Nanjing reflect these national trends. In the Red Flag Commune, west of Nanjing, the state transferred hilly land belonging to several teams over to the state tree farm.[22] But after the dizziness of the Great Leap dissipated and land ownership reverted from the larger People's Communes to the much smaller production team, this land remained the state's. Although no one has researched this issue, China's historical lack of property rights, the dramatic growth of state agricultural farms in 1957–62, and the continuing state expropriation of land since collectivization suggests that similar land thefts by the state occurred throughout China.[23] Communes, too, stole land during the Great Leap. In 1957–58, while building a reservoir, leaders in the Red Flag Commune took half of one team's land. Thereafter, until the early 1980s, this village's disastrous land/labor ratio forced it to rely on state aid for food grain and made its per capita income one of the lowest among the villages in the commune.

Although peasants in this locality were totally unable to prevent this land transfer, they reacted to the expropriations in several ways. Peasants living around this commune's reservoir unsuccessfully petitioned commune leaders to give them commercial fishing rights in the reservoir, while peasants in villages near the hills who lost land to the state tree farm, frequently cut down state-owned trees.[24] This poaching mirrors what Scott's essay in this volume refers to as "state-created crime." With little land, these villages suffered from overemployment, so to prevent further theft the state tree farm employed their surplus laborers. Although peasants could not regain the land, by stealing trees they forced the state farm to repay them indirectly for the land it had stolen from them. This *de facto* property redistribution, which avoided the legal issue of ownership, fits Scott's definition of "weapons of the weak."

Struggles over Land
under the Collective System, 1966–78

The disastrous outcome of the Great Leap Forward set the stage for future battles over land. In response to the famine of the early 1960s, peasants in parts of China shifted to private farming.[25] Moreover, through a series of party documents, the CCP reintroduced a major role for the private sector and transferred decision-making authority down to the lower levels of the rural bureaucracy. In 1962, each team in China was allowed to divide 5 to 7 percent of its cultivated land into private plots, and peasants were allowed to open wasteland for private cultivation, as long as the total acreage of private plots did not exceed 15 percent of collective land.[26] In 1962, party documents admonished cadres not to compel peasants to move their homes without peasant agreement, while at the same time, the state insisted that the basic cooperative—the production team—be allowed to make its own decisions as to what crops it would grow without interference from commune and county officials. Finally, in the same 1962 document, the state criticized commune and county officials for expropriating team land, as well as labor and capital, during the Great Leap. These liberalizing trends were further compounded by the initial political vacuum brought on by the Cultural Revolution, which allowed peasants in many parts of China to further expand their private plots.

Events in Nanjing again show how peasants tried to advance their interests in the early stages of the Cultural Revolution. In this area, cadres were either too busy fending off political attacks or simply abrogated their leadership roles. According to an official in suburban Everbright Commune, in 1967–68, during the chaos of the Cultural Revolution, people opened up a lot of marginal land. While these suburban peasants opened up only small strips, peasants in Eternal Happiness Commune, thirty kilometers south of the city, cultivated as much as a fourth of a hectare.

In 1968, however, the state used ideology and terror to increase control over the private sector. At this time a "radical" Maoist elite, bent on saving China from the peasants' "petty bourgeois mentality," organized a series of political campaigns designed to bring the rural areas under its control. Indoctrination in the Maoist cult ensued under the guidance of People's Liberation Army "Mao Thought Propaganda Teams" who during the "Three Loyalties Campaign" descended on the rural areas. By beating "class enemies," or what the Chinese call "killing the chickens to teach the monkey," cadres used the threat of coercion to prevent public resistance. After all, who wanted to be accused of being anti-Mao? So, when radical leaders called for a major contraction, if not outright elimination, of private plots in 1968–69, labeling them the "tail of capitalism," local cadres in many parts of China responded.[27] In counties east of Nanjing, private plots were farmed collectively, while in Red Flag Commune outside Nanjing, peasants marched to party headquarters with a placard indicating the private plots they were "donating" to the collective.

However, even in the face of this intense pressure, peasant protests and cadre self-interest in maintaining their own access to private plots led local cadres to adjust these policies. In the near and distant suburbs of Nanjing, some officials only halved the private plots rather than collectivizing them. Similar collusion occurred in other parts of China. According to a Hong Kong informant, when peasants in a south China village complained directly to local cadres that without private plots they would be unable to grow tobacco, brigade officials allowed them to clear hilly land, but only for tobacco, and only if they promised not to tell outside officials. Many cadres in this locality smoked, so they also wanted land for tobacco. During this radical period, peasants were forced to rely on the good will of their local officials. One commune official claimed that he helped the peasants keep some of their private plots by "opening one eye and closing the other."

In response to peasants who built brick walls around their yards and cultivated the land within the yard, the radical faction tried to control the area and the crops within the yards. In 1975–76, national mobilization led a county party secretary in Nanjing Municipality to call on local officials to restrict these plots. Yet when local cadres in the Red Flag Commune tore up tomato patches, peasants beat them. This violence bore fruit as one team leader recalled that he had refused to tear up the plots precisely because he feared getting beaten. While beating cadres who implemented state policies was not common during the Cultural Revolution, this strong resistance was probably due to the fact that the cadres were destroying crops that were already in the ground.[28]

Some peasants also used the Cultural Revolution's chaos to surreptitiously divide land among households for independent farming. While such actions did not occur in Nanjing, an informant from Fujian Province reported that, in 1967, peasants in his village divided the land among themselves, and their income depended on the output of their specific plots. Also, their contacts at the county level warned them whenever higher level officials would visit; at these times they worked the fields in large groups, creating the appearance of collective agriculture. A novel about the Hunan countryside during the Cultural Revolution told how a similar strategy backfired. After the land was divided, the rapid rise in collective agricultural output made the village famous. Once the truth was uncovered, however, officials from the commune level down were purged for their procapitalist behavior.[29]

While peasants were actively involved in resisting the state's efforts to restrict their access to private land, they were much less successful in controlling the crops grown in the collective fields. After 1965, and especially after the 1969 Sino-Soviet border conflict, pressure to grow grain reached ludicrous proportions.[30] According to a Hong Kong informant, peasants in one locality in Guangdong Province were forced to level bamboo trees, terrace the hillsides, build irrigation canals, and lay pipe to a distant reservoir to make the hills ready for growing grain. Communes in parts of Nanjing were compelled to plant two crops of summer rice and one crop of winter wheat. Although local team cadres argued that three crops produced less grain at a higher price than two crops, fixed quotas made overt resistance impossible. However, some

localities found ways to resist these pressures. Teams in the Sputnick Brigade, Eternal Happiness Commune, did not report new land
brought under collective cultivation in the late 1960s, so they increased
total grain output without completely shifting to three crops. Keeping
20 percent of their land off the official records helped them meet state
quotas and apparently increase per hectare output without directly
confronting the state.

The state tried to introduce collectivist "residential planning" in the
Sputnick Brigade, but peasants and cadres resisted this effort.[31] As a
provincial model, that Sputnick Brigade always had to respond to
national trends. But, since relocating their homes in the hills and
making them into row houses left no land for growing trees or piling
straw, the peasants protested. So the brigade never forced anyone to
move, and only stipulated that people who built new homes had to
follow brigade rules. Nevertheless, some peasants manipulated this
situation by ignoring the plan and building bigger homes in the hills.
According to a brigade official, the rich families "moved early [and]
got the good locations."

But in other places cadres ignored peasant complaints. In a Red Flag
Commune village, a team leader forced everyone to move and, although many could ill-afford it, he gave financial assistance only to
families within his personal network. Several years later, when five
or six children of the peasants who had moved without assistance returned from school, they got revenge by forcing the team leader from
his post.

Finally, in the name of strengthening the collective and the state,
commune and county cadres nationwide transferred a great deal of
property, including land, from the teams and placed it under their own
control. They built collective factories and new office buildings with
which they dominated the local political economy. Various commune
organizations, such as supply and marketing coops, grain stations,
animal husbandry stations, schools, and hospitals, took land from the
peasants and their production teams.[32] In rural Nanjing, peasants tried
to prevent these attempts at land expropriation. In 1976, when the
Prosperity Commune needed team land to build a reservoir, several
families refused to move their homes. The commune secretary invoked
slogans from the ongoing campaign and piled dirt in front of their front
doors, closing off all access to their homes. They were forced to move
into sheds, where they lived for three years until the county built new
homes. This commune leader brooked no opposition, particularly

when national party leaders called for a massive mobilization for irrigation projects.

During these years the Friendship Brigade, Everbright Commune, in suburban Nanjing, lost land to the city for factories and new housing units. However, while peasants and local cadres could not resist most land transfers during the radical era, new policies begun in 1974 gave local leaders more bargaining power. For each fixed amount of expropriated land, the new plant had to hire one peasant permanently. Friendship Brigade's party secretary was an even better bargainer who persuaded a watch factory that took their land to help them build a watch parts factory. While he could not stop the land grab, he did improve the livelihood of his peasant constituents. This trend has persisted. Today that brigade has almost no land, and 85 percent of its peasants are now collective factory workers.

Similarly, anticipated peasant retribution over land expropriations helped peasants in Sichuan province increase the price they received for their land. One Hong Kong informant, who had managed a construction site in Sichuan province, admitted overpaying the peasants for the land taken by his project, arguing that if he had not increased the low state price for land, the peasants would have stolen his equipment nightly. Since he and his company were from outside this area, local officials would have ignored their complaints about peasant theft. This way he protected his property, but he could do so only by responding to this "weapon of the weak."

Although in 1962 state policy had returned control over the land to peasants and their production teams, from 1966 to 1978 the central government tried to reassert its control over the peasants' private land and decision-making authority on collective land. Ideological campaigns and threats of coercion dramatically increased the risk of resistance. Because many rural officials responded to these endeavors, the state was quite successful. Yet, particularly when state policies hurt local cadre interests, as well as those of the peasants, cadre-peasant collusion was most likely and peasants were better able to wield their weapons of the weak to get better deals for their lost land. But if cadre-peasant interests conflicted or external pressures were too great, many cadres chose the route of self-protection and forced state policies on the peasants. Without cadre support, peasants often quietly acquiesced. Clearly, peasant dissatisfaction with these and other radical policies was known to some national and provincial leaders who visited the countryside. But it was not until these people—the "reform faction"—

came to power and changed national ideology and policy that the peasants could more effectively control the land.

Post-1978 Struggles over Land in Rural China

In 1978, a new leadership group came to power in China determined to reinvigorate the moribund rural economy. To do this, they introduced a series of reforms aimed at increasing the peasants' individual incentives and decreasing state and collective cadres' abilities to interfere in local decisions. They liberalized and restructured the rural economy and created economic opportunities previously unavailable under the collectives.[33] These reforms significantly changed the nature of the struggle over resources and the weapons employed in that struggle. A concomitant shift in the distribution of power from cadres to peasants also altered the nature of peasant resistance and peasant-cadre relations, as cadres showed less concern for state interests and more openly pursued their own.

The demise of the radical line and its emphasis on strengthening the collective through class struggle and mass mobilization meant that cadres were no longer as free to use coercion against peasant resistance or to invoke collectivist values as a cover for their own expropriations. Moreover, the decollectivization that ended in 1983 represents a historic watershed in productive relations, as well as a shift in the ethos of the state's hegemonic values.[34] The cadres' mechanisms for controlling the peasants and their economic product were greatly weakened. Team funds reverted to the households, leaving little for cadres to expropriate. By developing sideline enterprises, some local peasants prospered and began to compete for control with local cadres. Reform leaders in Beijing even called for a split between the economic and political functions of local organizations, directly threatening the basis of cadre domination—the fusion of political and economic power; to signify this shift, communes were renamed ''townships'' and brigades were called ''villages.'' In the face of all these threats to their long-term supremacy over the rural political economy, cadre relations with peasants became more filled with conflict, making cadres less reliable as allies in the peasants' struggle with the state. Instead, cadres resorted to old and new strategems—their authority as members of the CCP, their influence through personal networks, and their access to and control over the bureaucratic allocation of the resources necessary for economic development—and tried more aggressively to expand their own economic power base and limit the burgeoning threat from emerging entrepreneurs. These actions often brought them into direct conflict with the peasants. As one of the primary sources of prosperity, land became a focus of conflict.

Yet while the rural reforms have made cadres more rapacious, they have also increased the peasants' willingness and ability to protect their land. First, the growth of inequality has made the gap between rich and poor, between winners and losers, more obvious. Since the benefits gained from exploiting them are greater and more obvious, peasants are more aware when they are being exploited. Second, the weakening of collective controls and the end of ideological campaigns have increased the peasants' freedom of expression. They use letters to newspapers, anonymous petitions to officials, and even the ballot box to express their dissatisfaction. And while cadre recriminations can be costly, economic sanctions are far less constraining than threats of political labels, which had been used so effectively in the previous era. Third, the institution of a new legal code, replete with contract law, has created a new sphere for peasant resistance. Although cadres may manipulate the law more effectively than illiterate peasants, the replacement of arbitrary cadre decisions by impartial rulings can only benefit the peasants.[35] Finally, even as the new hegemony has fostered the search for private wealth, peasants have maintained the local egalitarian ethos and the local prohibition against immoral behavior to undermine those who would grow wealthy or, at a minimum, to force the wealthy to share their money with the community.

All these national changes had ramifications for peasant resistance in areas around Nanjing and in other localities as well. The expansion of the private plots offered some peasants a chance to dramatically increase their incomes; at the same time cadres and peasants who opposed this increase generated some defensive actions. For example, the Sputnick Brigade, south of Nanjing, sold more grain to the state than any brigade in Jiangsu Province. To maintain this lead, peasant consumption of food and cooking oil had suffered since the mid-1960s. After Mao's death in 1976, commune and brigade officials decided that rather than decrease grain acreage, which would undermine their "model" status, they would resolve the peasants' food shortage by letting them open barren land. In 1978–79 national policy publicly supported this expansion of barren land, so by 1981 some peasants in this brigade privately farmed as much land as they had after the Land Reform. In one team, peasants spent more time during the busy summer season planting potatoes in their own fields than working on collective land. But the demise of radical ideology prevented the cadre from using coercion or threats to get the peasants into the fields. Instead, the team leader was forced to increase the financial rewards for peasants who participated in collective work, allowing peasants to extract more funds from the collective. He also relaxed labor obligations, giving peasants more time off from collective labor to work their own fields.[36] Expanding peasant private holdings had increased the peasants' leverage over the collective.

Yet, in 1981, powerful team leaders in several villages in the Sputnick Brigade insisted that all opened land be farmed collectively. According to one peasant, her team leader expressed concern that conflicts among peasant families would erupt if some peasants opened more land than others. More likely, this cadre simply wanted to keep all land under collective, i.e., his own, control. Although as in other villages many peasants favored privately opening land and told the leader so, "when we raise this to the team leader he says that we can go and live there, if we think that it is so much better. . . . People here do complain about the fact that we cannot have more private land, but he refuses to accept it." Since in the past he had beaten peasants who disagreed with him, peasants did not press the issue.

In part the team leader was correct, as a moral battle ensued within the brigade over the wealth this new land was creating. One old woman in another village criticized peasants who opened new land for being different. "These people have different thoughts. They don't think about resting or playing." Her sharpest criticism, evoking Maoist morality, was that "they sell on the private market," indirectly suggesting that they preferred the "capitalist" or individual, rather than the "socialist" or collective, path to development. But industrious peasants fought back against this effort to denigrate their efforts; they blamed poverty on laziness and saw nothing virtuous in it. According to a peasant who had opened land, "the strong people don't say anything [about opening land]. It is those who are lazy who complain."[37]

Even in 1985–86, social pressure based on egalitarian morality still prevented an entrepreneurial peasant in the Red Flag Township from getting very rich. Although he was extremely skilled at raising fruit trees, this peasant refused to subcontract more land for a big orchard because managing it would have entailed hiring labor. And while hiring labor was legal, he had been beaten in the past for his "capitalist tendencies," so he feared the peasants' wrath should Maoist policies return. As of 1986 he had still not expanded his land beyond the half hectare he and his immediate family could work.[38]

Also, the issue of hiring labor to work one's land is contentious in this locality. One peasant in Red Flag Township, who had been hired to tend another's tree seedlings, received a handsome yearly salary. However, when his employer made ten times as much from the sale of the trees, he took him to court. County court officials tried to dissuade him, since he had signed a contract; moreover, under the reforms this profit was legal. Yet this peasant wanted to make his own point—that this vast income discrepancy was immoral—and demanded that the courts legitimize his viewpoint. While court officials thought him foolish for pushing his case so far, it gained countywide attention for him and his cause.

Such moral issues forced other entrepreneurs in Red Flag Township to handle their new-found wealth cautiously. While many of the noveau riche built new homes, most also bought insurance against moral and political recriminations by giving some of their profits to relatives, friends, and their villages as loans that were unlikely to be repaid. Within this commune a ritual of redistribution had ensued.

New opportunities for profit making from commercial crops increased the value of land and cadre efforts to expropriate it from the peasants. In some cases, local cadres still protected the village's corporate interests when it was threatened by higher-level officials. For example, in Red Flag Commune in 1979–80, peasants who raised young trees doubled their funds in one year, triggering a local tree-growing mania. When a tree seedling shortage developed, some peasants clipped the ends off trees in Nanjing parks, plundered seedlings from the yards of suburban peasants, and bought seedlings through the "back door" from state companies. Criticized by the city government for permitting this outburst of pilfering, commune officials convened a very inflammatory meeting, reminiscent of the Cultural Revolution decade, and pressured officials to tear tree seedlings from peasants' private plots. As a result, some peasants approached local officials for help. According to one brigade official, peasants had entreated him to resist the policy. Given his own sizeable investment in trees, his personal political predilections which favored the private sector, and his awareness that current national policy opposed such expropriations, he dragged his feet until the affair passed and never pulled up the seedlings. Shared interests and a new hegemony prompted local cadres to protect the peasants' private land.

When commune cadres tried to increase their share of the tree-seedling business, peasants also resisted them vigorously. When the commune imposed a 10 percent tax on all tree sales, peasants wrote protest letters to the city party committee.[39] A city investigation team reduced the tax to 3 percent. A commune official, who was supervising repairs to the reservoir's dykes, cordoned off some land belonging to the team that had lost half its land to the reservoir in 1958, declaring it commune property. The team's leader argued heatedly and was supported by the brigade party secretary, who for a full six months thereafter publicly ignored this commune official. While public and private criticism did not lead to a formal recantation, local pressure prevented this commune official from planting any trees, and the land eventually reverted to the team.

In other cases, intravillage conflicts pitted peasants against their local officials, as in the case where peasants were forced to fend off a private land grab by a local cadre and his allies. A team leader, part of a subteam alliance of three families, cordoned off a small parcel of collective land and allocated it to his cousin. After commune officials criticized the cousin by name at the commune-wide meeting, peasants reportedly beat him and plundered seedlings from his yard. Other villagers refused to obey the team leader. This opposition forced the brigade leader to intervene and replace the team leader. This way peasants used local government efforts to restrict private activity to stop individuals from expropriating collective land.

As in Anhui and Sichuan provinces where decollectivization began in 1978, some peasants in the Red Flag Commune actively pushed decollectivization, believing it to be in their interest. In the fall of 1980, peasants in the two poorest teams asked commune leaders to let them decollectivize, and with the commune's approval the team cadres had to agree. Nevertheless, no one told city officials, who would have opposed this policy, about this experiment. On the other hand, not all peasants supported this decollectivization. In 1981, some peasants interviewed in the Red Flag Commune feared that they would be unable to meet the quotas imposed under complete decollectivization. Should they get ill, the collective would have no money to help them. Nevertheless, in many parts of Nanjing, the shift to household farming without any collective distribution was the result of government fiat, not the peasants' assertion of claims against the collective. In this instance, the reformers simply decided to enforce nationwide policy conformity.

Along with the division of collective fields, most localities also contracted collective property—factories, fishponds, and orchards—to individuals. This transfer of management rights over the means of production from collective to individual control led to many peasant protests.[40] The quotas—payable to collective accumulation funds— often underestimated the extent to which a motivated individual could outdo what the collective had produced when it had managed the business. Huge individual profits made from land into which they had sunk "economic rents" incensed most peasants. Some complained that since collective fields had been divided evenly, so should the orchards. Cadres often manipulated the peasants to demand that entrepreneurs renegotiate the contracts at a higher quota. If they refused, their or- chards could be pilfered, and they themselves beaten. However, when cadres contracted the collectively owned orchards, peasants sometimes took them to court, accusing them of using their power to get rich, even though in many cases only cadres dared take the economic risk involved in signing a contract. More and more of these cases are being decided by the courts, who seek both to uphold the law, which reflects the reigning hegemonic values, and to respond to the underlying morality of Chinese peasant society, which pressures them to protect collective property.

As peasants made money for the first time in two decades, they poured their funds into new housing. But with decollectivization blur- ring the line between collective and private land,[41] peasants and cadres began to buy and sell houses and land.[42] Nationwide private sales of collective land led the CCP's Central Discipline Inspection Committee in early 1981 to issue a circular criticizing cadres "mainly at the commune and county levels" who abuse their power.[43] Rural cadres in the southern Zhejiang district of Wenzhou, famous for its independent politics and entrepreneurial behavior, had sold one per- cent of all arable land in the county for housing in 1979 alone.[44] Since land in 1979 was still under collective control, only cadres could sell it.

While occupying collective land for house building was not a prob- lem around Nanjing in 1981, by 1985 it had become the major issue in Red Flag Township.[45] Red Flag Commune's former party secretary had always lived in the commune town, so he had prevented other cadres from moving into town. However, in 1985 the new township party secretary left his village several kilometers down the road and moved onto land owned by a village bordering the township town. This move cost him the moral authority to stop other cadres from moving. Within two years over 175 cadres and their relatives had moved into villages around the town. However, cadres building homes on collective land undermined each villager's income, as the collective had to redistribute and decrease the amount of land each household farmed to ensure a continuing even distribution. For example, when the township party secretary and another cadre moved into this village, each household's holdings shrunk by 20 percent.

How peasants resisted these expropriations varied. One team leader was so angry at the continuing loss of village land to outsiders that he refused to sign any more forms; in this case, brigade support strengthened his resolve. Since township leaders prefer to persuade team officials to "voluntarily" sign such documents, this foot dragging was showing results in 1986. A township cadre who wanted to move into this leader's team had been waiting for several months. His bricks were sitting there, but the signed form was not. On the other hand, peasants in the village into which the party secretary moved were so enraged that they sent photographs of the two homes to the county government.[46] They may have responded more forcefully because their loss had already occurred. Unfortunately, county cadres phoned the township and asked them to look into the problem, so of course nothing happened. And while city officials also knew of the problem, they too had taken no action.

Significant changes have transpired since the death of Mao. Although land issues were critical during the Maoist era, the press rarely reported them, and the courts ignored them. Few peasants dared confront state cadres who stole their land or rural officials who collectivized it. Mao's China was a frightening world for peasant resistors. In Deng's China, however, while myriad opportunities for prospering from the land have intensified the conflicts over it, political and legal reforms have brought more of those struggles into the open. The press regularly reports such stories, thereby indirectly telling peasants to resist and take cadres and peasants who act unethically to court. In this sense the role of the state and its institutions have changed, allowing peasants more freedom of action. Although decollectivization has forced rural cadres to seek aggressively a large share of the new rural wealth, peasants, often with state assistance, are more actively resisting attempts by cadres and wealthy peasants to exploit them or expropriate their rightful share of rural land.

Conclusion

The Chinese case offers an opportunity to witness peasant resistance under two different situations. The first involves the peasants' response to a powerful state that ruled firmly for most of two decades. Through ideological and political campaigns and the establishment of a collective bureaucracy, the CCP penetrated Chinese society and controlled most aspects of the peasants' political, economic, and social life. The collective structure also created a new class of rural bureaucrats who often surreptitiously used its power to extract wealth from the peasants to establish its own control. This search for resources brought collective cadres into direct confrontation with the state. Although cadres and the state both fought with the peasantry over ownership and control of its land, peasants could at times manipulate this state-collective conflict to their own advantage and gain support from local—team and brigade—cadres.

During the post-1978 era, the state progressively withdrew its controls, and, through decollectivization, the attempted separation of economic and political organizations, and the introduction of a new legal system, increased the peasants' ability to resist the cadres.[47] The state's withdrawal, however, and the shift in hegemonic values from Maoist moral egalitarianism to a more profit-oriented viewpoint has intensified the conflict between cadres and peasants and between richer and poorer peasants. In both cases, the former have become the major target of more vigorous peasant resistance.

While the mode of resistance varied across time periods, and also depended on which land issue was at hand, constraints imposed by the collective system from 1958 through 1978 made approaching cadres in informal settings and asking them to intervene the peasants' major weapon. Some cadres devised solutions amenable to both themselves and the peasants and, through foot dragging, false compliance, and other strategies, deflected the demands of the state. At other times they simply limited the harshness of state policy. Yet when political events weakened state controls, peasants could unilaterally advance their own interests—either by expanding private holdings or shifting to individual farming. They needed only the acquiescence of local cadres who, in any case, often abdicated decision-making authority during times of political unrest.

The critical role of cadres also meant that peasant resistance was most constrained when cadres acted in accordance with state policies. This coordination was often the result of intense mobilization, when cadres could invoke the heavily ideological hegemonic values of the regime—which from 1958 to 1978 involved building the state and the collective through "class struggle"—and utilize harsh techniques to suppress resistance. The coordination of state goals and cadre behavior placed peasant efforts to protect their rights from state or collective assaults beyond the pale of acceptable actions. The spectre of "class enemies" often melted peasant resistance. Yet even when radical influence persisted, cadre actions, such as pulling up crops, which violated local morality, led peasants to react violently and beat up officials.

But, after 1978, when cadres pursued their own interests or prevented the implementation of new state policies benefitting peasant interests, thereby making themselves the target of resistance, peasants responded in various ways. They circumvented the cadres and wrote letters to newspapers and state officials, an action most likely to succeed when cadre behavior conflicted with the formal values or laws of the current regime. Many letters to the editor in the national press criticized local opposition to the reforms. More assertive or better educated peasants have now turned to the developing legal system to seek redress from corrupt cadres or unjust decisions. One can only hope that the state will strengthen those aspects of the local environment that permit the peasant to protect his or her own interests. PRC history suggests, however, that even under Deng's regime the cadres will again come out on top.

Finally, the Chinese case offers an interesting perspective on the issue of hegemonic control and values, for the battle over land is tied to both policy and morality. Under the CCP, the hegemonic value system changed frequently, which allowed competing peasant value systems concerning the use of land and private property to emerge in the same locality. When state leaders invoked a Maoist morality, emphasizing collectivism and egalitarianism, state and collective cadres carried out their respective land grabs and easily established more effective control over land. In the post-Mao, post-radical era, however, the hegemonic values of the state have changed, while those of some peasants and many cadres remain unchanged. Maoist values have persisted locally, albeit perhaps as part of an opportunistic defense strategy against new entrepreneurs and the weakening of collective controls. In the face of, or behind the backs of, industrious neighbors, peasants have resorted to rumor mongering and criticizing the hiring of labor to hold entrepreneurs back from getting rich; they pressured the entrepreneurs to distribute some of their profits, or sometimes beat them. This local morality, which reflects the passing hegemonic Maoist values, has assisted the weaker peasants to battle the new entrepreneurial class. It also has helped collective cadres—the reigning, rural ruling class—to undermine the rise of this competing class of rural entrepreneurs, whose activities more closely reflect the new elite hegemony.

Notes

1. For a recent discussion of some of these issues, see Vivienne Shue, *The Reach of the State* (Stanford: Stanford University Press, 1988).

2. See James Scott, *Weapons of the Weak: Everyday Forms of Peasant Resistance* (New Haven: Yale University Press, 1985).

3. For a discussion of the issue of peasant-cadre relations and formalistic cadre compliance with state policies during the Cultural Revolution decade (1966–76), see David Zweig, *Agrarian Radicalism in China, 1968–1981* (Cambridge: Harvard University Press, 1989).

4. See Jean C. Oi, "Commercializing China's Rural Cadres," *Problems of Communism* 25 (September 1986): 1–15, and Jean C. Oi, "Peasant Households Between Plan and Market," *Modern China* 12 (April 1986): 230–51.

5. See *People's Daily*, 18 January 1984.

6. See Gordon White, "The Impact of Economic Reforms in the Chinese Countryside: Towards the Politics of Socialist Capitalism?" *Modern China* 13 (October 1987): 411–40.

7. In 1955–56, 2 to 5 percent of the collective's land was divided among peasants on a per capita basis as private plots. Peasants pay no tax on produce raised in these plots. See Kenneth R. Walker, *Planning in Chinese Agriculture: Socialization and the Private Sector, 1956–1962* (Chicago: Aldine Publishing Co., 1967), pp. 10–12. Their homes, however, are privately owned although the land on which they sit belongs to the collective. Nevertheless, while land was to be owned by the basic collective—the production team—cadres at higher levels of the rural bureaucratic structure often tried to take over that land for their own use.

8. See Scott's essay in this volume. In 1981, I spent three months living and researching in three communes in rural Nanjing and in the summer of 1986 returned for further field research. I also draw on press reports from 1968 to 1986, and interviews in Hong Kong in the fall of 1980 to supplement the argument and demonstrate that events described here are not unique to this area alone, all the while recognizing that regional variations are important in China.

9. For a discussion of hegemonic values see the concluding chapter of Scott's *Weapons of the Weak*.

10. At the elite level the values of various leaders include efficient economic development, political stability, equality, and high moral behavior. For the first three values, see Dorothy Solinger, *Chinese Business Under Socialism* (Berkeley: University of California Press, 1984).

11. For a discussion of the peasants' desire for wealth and fear of inequality see Zweig, *Agrarian Radicalism in China, 1968–1981*, ch. 4. Peasants also expect local officials to behave morally toward others and distribute fair justice. See Richard Madsen, *Morality and Power in a Chinese Village* (Berkeley: University of California Press, 1984).

12. For a story of how a bean-curd saleswoman who prospered in the early 1960s became the target of a political attack in 1964, see Gu Hua, *A Small Town Called Hibiscus* (Beijing: Panda Books, 1980).

13. See John P. Burns, *Political Participation in Rural China* (Berkeley: University of California Press, 1988).

14. For a discussion of the 1959 "Anti-Rightist Campaign," the "Four Cleans Campaign" of 1964–65, and the Cultural Revolution, see respectively, Liu Binyan, "Sound is Better than Silence," in Perry Link, ed., *People or Monsters* (Bloomington: Indiana University Press, 1983), pp. 98–137; Richard Buam, *Prelude to Revolution: Mao, the Party and the Peasant Question, 1962–1966* (New York: Columbia University Press, 1975); and Anita Chan, Richard Madsen, and Jonathan Unger, *Chen Village: The Recent History of a Peasant Community in Mao's China* (Berkeley: University of California Press, 1984).

15. Collectivization made land that had been owned privately into the corporate property of all team members. Thereafter, each peasant received "workpoints" for each day's labor based on task rates—each task had a particular value—or time rates—the value of a labor day depended on a peasant's personal workpoint value determined by the team leader and based on his or her skills or strength. At year's end, after the team deducted funds for taxes and reinvestment, it divided its net income by the number of workpoints it had distributed to determine the value of each workpoint. The total number of points a peasant earned times his or her team's workpoint value determined his income. See Fredrick W. Crook, "The Commune System in the People's Republic of China, 1963–1974," in Joint Economic Committee, U.S. Congress, *China: A Reassessment of the Economy* (Washington, D.C.: Government Printing Office, 1975), pp. 366–410.

16. In north China, each village was a team; in south China, where the villages are larger, each village could be divided into several production teams.

17. See Thomas P. Bernstein, "Problems of Village Leadership after Land Reform," *China Quarterly* 36 (October–December 1968).

18. See Thomas P. Bernstein, "Stalinism, Chinese Peasants and Famine: Grain Procurements During the Great Leap Forward," *Theory and Society* 13 (May 1984): 1–39, and Thomas P. Bernstein, introduction with an anonymous author, "Starving to Death in China," *New York Review of Books* 30 (16 June 1983): 36–38.

19. Fleming Christiansen, "Private Land in China? Some Aspects of the Development of Socialist Land Ownership in Post-Mao China," *The Journal of Communist Studies* 3 (March 1987): 57.

20. According to a May 1975 interview by Fred Crook with a mainland refugee in Hong Kong, some peasants in Shanxi Province collectively cultivated land outside their commune's borders because the land had been cultivated by their ancestors. See The China Group, Reports on Rural People's Communes, unpublished data set.

21. See Franz Schurmann, *Ideology and Organization in Communist China* (Berkeley: University of California Press, 1968), p. 49.

22. Although the names of the three communes, Red Flag, Everbright, and Eternal Happiness, and the brigades within them, are fictitious, they will be used consistently to protect my informants.

23. While 440,000 peasants ploughed 1 million hectares of land in 804 state farms in 1957, by 1962 the number of state farms had jumped to 2,123, with 2,168,400 peasants farming 2.74 million hectares of land. (Few major changes occurred in the next twenty years.) This growth in acreage was not due solely to the clearing of land. In 1957, at the peak of a nationwide irrigation campaign, state farms cleared only 0.20 million hectares for their own use; in 1962 they cleared only 0.1 million hectares. Thus the dramatic increase between 1957 and 1962 of 1.75 million hectares in the amount of

land under state farm control probably came during the 1958 Great Leap and at the expense of peasants and the people's communes. See *Zhongguo nongye nianjian, 1980* (Chinese Agricultural Yearbook) (Beijing: Nongye chubanshe, 1980), p. 5, which unfortunately gives data only in five-year intervals.

24. According to one team leader, peasants felt more secure stealing from the state's, rather than the commune's, tree farm because the commune would protect them if they got caught stealing from the state, but no one would protect them if they stole from the commune.

25. See Fredrick W. Crook, "Chinese Communist Agricultural Incentive Systems and the Labor Productive Contracts to Households: 1956-1965," *Asian Survey* 13 (May 1973): 470–481.

26. For this and the following points see "Regulations on the Work in the Rural People's Communes (Revised Draft)," *Issues and Studies* 15 (December 1979): 106–115.

27. See Han Ke-chuan, "Recent Development in Rural Communes on the Chinese Mainland," *Issues and Studies* 5 (May 1969): 4–11.

28. A *People's Daily* report (18 January 1979) also told how peasants in Jiangxi Province beat their cadres in April 1976, when they tried to uproot sugar cane from the peasants' plots.

29. See Gu Hua, *Pagoda Ridge and Other Stories* (Beijing: Panda Books, 1985). Although this is a novel, written to criticize the Cultural Revolution in the countryside, it reflects the tenor of the period. For similar events in Wenzhou District, Zhejiang Province, see *People's Daily*, 1 January 1978, p. 2.

30. See Nicholas P. Lardy, *Agriculture in China's Modern Economic Development* (Cambridge: Cambridge University Press, 1983).

31. Residential planning moved peasant homes into neat rows on nearby hills to increase the acreage of valley land and the state's control over the peasant's private domain. Such homes often had no front or behind yard for private economic activity.

32. A district in Inner Mongolia returned over 600 hectares of collective land that it had taken during the previous decade. See *People's Daily*, 9 July 1979, p. 3. In Yunnan Province, factories and mines in a commune in Kunming's suburbs had taken over 450 hectares of land from the peasants. See *People's Daily*, 15 August 1978. For similar reports see *People's Daily*, 28 July 1978, 19 August 1978, and 6 November 1978.

33. The acreage for cash crops, fish ponds, and orchards increased at the expense of grain acreage. The percentage of collective land allocated to private plots rose from 5 to 15 percent by 1980. From 1978 to 1983, decollectivization gave households more control over the land. The resultant leap in peasant per capita income—a four-fold increase between 1978 and 1986—precipitated a housing boom of worldwide historic proportions. For the best study of the early rural reforms see William L. Parish, ed., *China's Rural Development: The Great Transformation* (Armonk: M. E. Sharpe, 1985).

34. By 1983, over 98 percent of teams had divided all the land among households who—besides paying a state tax, making a small contribution (3–5 percent) to the team accumulation fund, and selling a significant amount of grain to the state at a fixed price—handle all the output on their own. Under a lesser degree of decollectivization prevalent in 1981–82, peasants gave the collective most of their output in return for workpoints and a year-end distribution based on the collective's net income. But they either kept any above-quota surplus or turned it over to the collective for extra workpoints. For the discussion of the importance of historic shifts in productive relations on the employment of everyday forms of resistance, see Scott, *Weapons of the Weak*, p. 49.

35. See David Zweig, Kathy Hartford, James Feinerman, and Deng Jianxu, "Law, Contracts, and Economic Modernization: Lessons from the Recent Chinese Rural Reforms," *Stanford Journal of International Law* 23 (Summer 1987).

36. Scott's essay in this volume discusses this reappropriation of time from the collective as a significant means of resistance to state socialism.

37. For a similar phenomenon where the wealthy assert that poverty is the result of peasants not being very industrious, see Scott, *Weapons of the Weak*, p. 146.

38. Similar problems have been reported in China since 1983. See the speech by Xu Jiatun, then first Party secretary of Jiangsu Province in *Jingji ribao (Economic Daily)*, 9 March 1983, p. 1. See also my own article, "Prosperity and Conflict in Post-Mao Rural China," *China Quarterly* 105 (March 1986).

39. Writing letters to party and government officials, as well as to newspapers, is common in China. See Hugh Thomas, ed., *Comrade Editor: Letters to the People's Daily* (Hong Kong: Joint Publishing Co., 1980), and Godwin and Leonard Chu, "Parties in Conflict: Letters to the Editor of the People's Daily," *Journal of Communication* 31 (Autumn 1981): 74–91.

40. For a more lengthy discussion of this and similar legal cases see Zweig et al., "Law, Contracts, and Economic Modernization," *Stanford Journal of International Law* 23 (Summer 1987): 319–364. The following references come from a case cited in this article.

41. See Christiansen, "Private Land in China?" in *The Journal of Communist Studies. Peasant Daily*, 28 June 1985 recognized that the responsibility system made land ownership unclear in some places.

42. See *Nanjing Daily*, 21 April 1981, p. 1, and *Foreign Broadcast Information Service*, 21 September 1981, p. 1.

43. *Foreign Broadcast Information Service*, 6 October 1981, p. K6.

44. See *People's Daily*, 17 March 1981.

45. For some national reports in 1985, see *Peasant Daily*, 30 August 1985, p. 1, and 26 October 1985, p. 1.

46. According to *Peasant Daily*, 26 October 1985, p. 1, peasants in another location wrote letters to the National People's Congress to protest against cadres buying and selling houses and collective land.

47. While peasants under the collective system relied almost entirely on interactions with their brigade secretary or team leader [Jean C. Oi, "Communism and Clientelism: Rural Politics in China," *World Politics* 37 (January 1985): 238–66] peasants under the reforms now interact with many more local officials and are less dependent on their team or brigade leader, generating a more pluralistic patronage system. See Jonathan Unger, "The Decollectivization of the Chinese Countryside: A Survey of Twenty-Eight Villages," *Pacific Affairs* 58 (Winter 1985–86): 585–606.

7

Foot Dragging and Other Peasant Responses to the Nicaraguan Revolution

Forrest D. Colburn

The Nicaraguan Revolution, which ousted the Somoza dictatorship in July of 1979, was a broad-based insurrection that enjoyed widespread popular support. The armed vanguard of the struggle was the Sandinista Front for National Liberation (FSLN), which had been formed in 1961 and tenaciously survived numerous setbacks. While the FSLN had worked for years building popular support in rural areas, the decisive battles of the insurrection were fought in cities. The instrumental support for the FSLN's final campaign came not from peasants, but from the urban proletariat and urban youth.[1]

The inequities and injustices of the Somoza regime made many, if not most, Nicaraguan peasants and rural laborers sympathetic to the FSLN's cause. However, while a few joined the FSLN's ranks, most poor rural Nicaraguans were withdrawn and reluctant to participate in politics.[2] Nicaraguan peasants and rural laborers displayed a similar caution toward radical political change that has been observed in other backward rural societies. For example, most peasants did not embrace the Spanish Republic, and acquiesced in the Loyalist's coup d'état.[3] Likewise, Allende's weakest base of electoral support in Chile was rural departments.[4] An old Central American peasant adage explains

An earlier version of this essay was published in *Peasant Studies* 13 (Winter, 1986). Helpful comments were provided by Lowell Gudmundson, James Scott, William Thiesenhusen, Crawford Young, and David Zweig.

the attitude of many poor rural dwellers: ''Better a familiar evil than an unfamiliar blessing.''

While Nicaraguan peasants and rural laborers participated only marginally in the insurrection, they have sought to exploit opportunities under the new regime for improving their welfare. Analyzing the behavior of the rural poor during three phases of post-revolutionary Nicaragua, when the state's economic and political resources have differed, illustrates the unique role played by the rural poor in this Central American country, and suggests propositions about peasant behavior during post-revolutionary rule in developing countries. The thesis advanced is that peasants and rural laborers have with self-interest, but also rationally, exploited opportunities presented by the threat to the erstwhile private sector, by the disorganization of the new regime and its sympathy for the poor, and even by the threat to the new regime from the counterrevolution. This opportunism has led to conflict with the state, conflict exacerbated by the financially weak state's need to impose ''austerity and efficiency.'' In the conflict, however, peasants are nearly defenseless: their lack of independent organization prevents them from confronting the monolithic state, and their poverty prevents them from withdrawing economically and politically. Peasants and rural laborers simply pursue wide-ranging individual strategies to maximize their welfare, regardless of the consequences to the state. In doing so they do not pose a political threat to the state. Still, through foot dragging and other responses they complicate the state's bid to control the economy, to promote state-directed development, and to defeat the ''enemies of the revolution.''

The argument and evidence presented here is often overlooked by scholars of the Nicaraguan Revolution and of other revolutions in small developing world countries. Most analyses of radical change in the developing world are state-centric, in part because of the greater difficulties in doing any other kind of research and also perhaps because of a common intellectual predilection for revolutionary change in the Third World.[5] State-centric research on such regimes, however, slights the conflicts of interest between the state and the rural poor, who are usually touted as the beneficiaries of the revolution. Equally important, this approach ignores the ways in which the rational but self-interested behavior of the rural poor can complicate a post-revolutionary regime's efforts at structural change.[6] More research is needed that looks at post-revolutionary change from the vantage point of the rural poor. Recent writing in the more mature corpus of literature on the Chinese Revolution suggests that such an approach buttresses the thesis advanced here—that peasants and rural laborers can undermine a post-revolutionary regime's efforts at radical change just as can remnants of the old elite, foreign capital, and other more obvious sources of opposition.[7]

From the perspective of the peasantry, revolutionary upheaval brings opportunities, benefits, costs, and risks. The behavior of the peasantry during the early tumultuous years of post-revolutionary Nicaragua suggests that the peasantry's allegiance is based on its perception of its well being, not on ideological grounds. Through all the upheaval the Nicaraguan peasantry's steadfast concern has been simply individual and household welfare. Behavior is shaped accordingly. The weapons of the weak are employed whenever and to the extent conditions permit the augmentation of meager earnings, the seizure of any possible windfall, and—most importantly—for deflating exactions. State strength, not regime position on the political perspective, best explains peasants' political behavior.

Misery in Rural Nicaragua

As in most developing countries, the most severe poverty in Nicaragua has always been in the rural areas. Somewhat paradoxically, the rural areas of the country are also the source of the nation's wealth; 80 percent of the foreign exchange, so necessary to a small state like Nicaragua, is derived from agriculture. Around 70 percent of the population earns its living from the land, though nearly half the population is considered urban.

A careful analysis by Philip Warnken demonstrates both the dominance of the export sector under the Somozas and the relative poverty of most rural Nicaraguans. Drawing upon data from the national census and the Central Bank of Nicaragua, he shows that although there were more than five times the number of farms producing basic grain crops in 1971 as produced export crops (coffee, cotton, and sugar), export crops accounted for 49 percent of the total value of production while food crops (maize, beans, and rice) contributed only 19 percent and livestock 32 percent.[8] Since most livestock was exported, the dominance of the export sector was very pronounced. Warnken characterizes the structure of Nicaraguan agricultural crop production as follows:

> On the one hand, a relatively small proportion of all producers are oriented to the export market, operate relatively large units and produce their product (with the exception of coffee) under relatively high technology levels. On the other hand, a very high proportion of all producers produce for the domestic market on very small units utilizing very low technology levels.[9]

Thus, there was a pronounced dual economy within the agricultural sector.

Although total agricultural production increased at a respectable annual rate of 6.7 percent between 1960–62 and 1969–71 and the average per capita value of agricultural production for the nation was quite high by the 1970s, the structure of the agricultural sector prevented a large part of the rural population from realizing this level of economic welfare.[10] Rural workers, who are generally landless, constituted over half of the economically active rural population but accounted for only 7.5 percent of the total gross value of output. The second largest group consisted of self-employed and family labor. In aggregate, they received 29 percent of the gross value of production. In contrast, employers accounted for only 3.5 percent of the economically active population yet received 63 percent of the gross income.[11] The dualistic structure of Nicaraguan agriculture that was begun under colonialism and perpetuated under the dynasty of the Somozas prevented sustained, broad-based economic growth and development and had abominable social consequences. Under the rule of the Somozas, between 50 and 75 percent of the rural population had a totally insufficient resource base for an adequate level of production and consequently lived at minimal subsistence levels.[12]

Nicaraguan peasant producers able to meet their household subsistence requirements entirely through their own agricultural production constituted a mere 12.7 percent of the agricultural economically active population.[13] Only 7.5 percent of the agricultural economically active population had stable employment, however. Landless workers without stable employment constituted 32 percent of the agricultural economically active population. Most peasants in need of wage labor only had access to seasonal labor, reflecting the almost complete dependence of the rural economy on agriculture. Seasonal labor primarily consisted of harvesting cotton, coffee, and sugar. Most rural Nicaraguans survived by patching together a number of income sources during any given year.[14]

The Aftermath of the Revolution

Though the FSLN had struggled to topple the Somoza dynasty for years, its activities were isolated incidents until the assassination on January 10, 1978, of Pedro Joaquín Chamorro, the popular director of the *La Prensa* newspaper. The assassination of Chamorro was the catalyst of the insurrection. The resulting outrage coalesced and emboldened all opposition to the regime. A little over seventeen months later, Somoza left Managua for Miami. The fighting to oust Somoza was bitter and bloody, but the Nicaraguan Revolution was not as protracted as, for example, the Chinese Revolution. The relative brevity of the insurrection, and the concentration of the fighting in urban areas, left many rural areas unscathed. Thus, while over 25 percent of Nicaragua's factories suffered serious damage to plant and inventory, the more important agricultural sector was only disrupted by the fighting.

The struggle to overthrow Somoza and the triumph of the revolution deepened a sense of deprivation among the rural poor and created a sense of hope for a better future. These sentiments were widespread, and not limited only to those who participated in the struggle to oust the dictator, or who were organized into the Sandinista rural organization, the Association of Farm Workers (ATC). The FSLN had labored for years to convince peasants that they were being exploited and that a better future awaited them upon the triumph of the Revolution.

In the words of many Nicaraguans, "Upon the triumph of the Revolution everyone thought that suddenly they would have everything they never had, and that it would no longer be necessary to work." The Sandinistas, upon seizing power, confiscated only the assets of Somoza and his cronies. Peasants and rural laborers acting on their own, though, seized many farms, particularly those of absentee landlords. However, it proved impossible for the rural poor "to suddenly have everything": there were few liquid assets to seize and redistribute. Rural Nicaragua is poor, and the productive infrastructure that exists cannot be turned quickly into household goods. Decapitalization and the practice of wealthy landlords to live in Managua removed whatever fungible wealth might have existed in rural areas.

Even the seizure of productive infrastructure, principally farms, proved unsatisfactory. The seizure of a farm, especially from a mean landlord, might bring emotional gratification, but it also brought a suspension of wage payments. Peasants and rural laborers did not have the organizational ability to run seized farms, and lacked capital, techni-

cal and managerial skills, and marketing information. In every principal case, peasant- and labor-initiated seizures of farms led to the state
assuming managerial responsibility and incorporating the land and
improvements into the state sector, the Area of the People (APP).
Workers resumed their role as wage laborers, albeit as employees of the
state.

The new regime sought to redistribute income to peasants and rural
laborers by raising wages for agricultural workers 48 percent in the
first post-revolutionary year.[15] Wages for harvesters of coffee and
cotton were raised similarly. The wage increases were offset by a 35
percent inflation rate, leaving a net gain in real income of 13 percent.
This gain was not insignificant, but hardly met the heightened expectations of the rural poor. Widespread shortages of consumer goods,
especially imported goods, added to difficulties engendered by inflation. The new regime had more success in its literacy campaign and in
the beginning of its efforts to expand public services, designed to
increase the "social income" of the poor. Still, while the new regime
made a commendable start in meeting the basic needs of rural Nicaraguans, the enormity of the challenge and the paucity of the state's
resources resulted in most rural Nicaraguans being as poor as ever.

While the rural poor were frustrated in their naive desire to suddenly
have everything, rural laborers proved more successful in achieving the
second part of their expectation, "that they no longer have to work."
Rural laborers throughout Nicaragua spontaneously took advantage of
the near anarchy in rural areas to reduce dramatically their labor obligations. Those employed for daily wages simply cut back on the length
of the workday. Those employed for piece-rate work insisted on switching to daily wages, and then followed their brethren in shortening their
workday.

Rural laborers working for the private sector were partly able to
reduce the hours they worked because economic activity slowed in the
final months of the insurrection. With the economy disrupted and
traumatized there simply was not much to do. Rural laborers were able
to adhere to shorter working hours and greater laxity when working
because of employers' trepidation. The insurrection had fostered worker militancy and weakened traditional authority structures. Employers
hesitated to challenge workers out of fear that workers would take over
their farms—as happened in many cases. Employers probably also
feared being bushwacked by machete-wielding peasants, though reported incidences of violence were rare. The fearful private sector

simply acquiesced to peasant demands that did not involve cash outlays and waited for a clarification of the "rules of the game."

The state was not immune from peasant pressure for immediate and radical changes. Indeed, the state was probably more affected than the private sector by the militancy the FSLN fostered. Hours worked per day on newly established state farms and enterprises fell nearly everywhere as did production. An administrator of a state rice farm recalled that upon assuming managerial responsibility for the confiscated estate his most difficult and intractable problem was labor indiscipline. Another government official recounted that immediately after the revolution, laborers in the state sugarcane farms of the department of Rivas worked only three hours a day, from six to nine in the morning.

Not surprisingly, in the aftermath of the revolution, state farms and enterprises pressured peasants into increasing employment beyond what was necessary, both by taking on additional laborers and by not discharging temporary laborers harvesting cotton, coffee, or sugar. The new regime was sympathetic to these demands; the insurrection and the contraction of activity in the private sector had exacerbated unemployment. One study suggested that employment on state rural enterprises (including farms) increased 25 percent within two years of their being confiscated.[16] In some cases the increased employment was due to an expansion in activities, but in most cases the increased employment was not absorbed productively.

The spontaneous pursuit of reduced labor obligations by Nicaraguans was rational from their class perspective. The corollary to the fundamental maxim of economic logic, that people desire more rather than less, is that people likewise seek to offer in exchange for what they desire less rather than more. Poor rural Nicaraguans, frustrated in their desire for an immediate improvement in their standard of living, simply took their "historical vacation." However, this rational strategy on the part of rural laborers exacerbated the new regime's financial difficulties and complicated its relations with labor.

Austerity and Efficiency

Despite the efforts of Sandinista labor organizations to restore order in the nation's centers of work, labor agitation and indiscipline continued to be a serious problem well into the second year of the revolution. Throughout rural areas, peasants seized land and farms they claimed were idle or abandoned. Strikes were a continuing problem. Although many of the workers' demands were undoubtedly justified, continued labor indiscipline was crippling the economy. Many owners of private farms and government officials administering state farms claimed that labor indiscipline was their most serious problem. Labor productivity was widely held to be down at least 25 percent.

In an effort to deal decisively with the problem, the government outlawed all work stoppages, strikes, and seizures of centers of production on July 27, 1981.[17] The justification for the order was to "avoid having labor indiscipline make the economic situation more critical."[18] The intention of the order was to "combat labor indiscipline and anarchy in production and centers of work."[19] The government proclaimed that the measure would be enforced rigorously. For the most part, the order was effective in halting strikes and seizures of factories and farms, but it did not address the more subtle difficulties of shorter workdays, the decline in the use of criteria for measuring work, and general labor laxity.

The outlawing of work stoppages and seizures exemplified a slow but unequivocal change in the position of the FSLN. The propaganda of the FSLN slowly switched from stressing the unnecessary poverty of most Nicaraguans, to arguing the need for austerity and efficiency. This change in orientation involved a shift from promoting labor militancy to stressing labor discipline. Conflict between workers seeking greater wages and power and the FSLN's politics of austerity and production led the FSLN to increase its control over labor organizations. Sandinista labor organizations have been used increasingly to build support for the state rather than articulating the perceived interests of workers. Independent trade unions have been pressured into affiliating with the Sandinista umbrella trade union, the Sandinista Workers Federation (CST).[20]

In concrete terms, this political line has resulted in a moratorium on salary increases. Salaries for general agricultural laborers were not raised at all for the 1981–82, 1982–83, and 1983–84 agricultural seasons.[21] Since inflation continued to be around 25–35 percent annually, laborers suffered a marked decline in their real income. As part of a broad effort to reduce price distortions, salaries in the 1984–85 agricultural season were raised appreciably, but so were many other formerly controlled prices. Since 1985 inflation has risen dramatically, reaching an estimated 1,000 percent by 1987. While adjustments in salaries have become frequent, the government openly acknowledges that it cannot protect real incomes. Declining real incomes have retarded state efforts to reverse the decline in labor productivity. An administrator of a state tobacco farm summarized the evolution in peasant response to exhortions to increase productivity: "After the revolution they said, 'No, we are free.' Now they say, 'You are too demanding; the salary is very low.'" Rural workers have been economically "squeezed," not because the Sandinista ruling elite wanted it, but rather because the exigencies of the national economy have made continued impoverishments of laborers a structural necessity. However, rural laborers have not been willing to increase their productivity in response only to appeals to their conscience and patriotism.

The difficulties rural laborers present to the revolutionary regime are openly acknowledged. The Minister of Agricultural Development and Agrarian Reform, Commander of the Revolution, Jaime Wheelock, summarized the problem:

> Since the triumph of the revolution we have observed in the countryside that contracts made by labor organizations with the Ministry of Labor, and in general with productive enterprises, have presented a tendency to set lower norms for work than existed previously. In sugar, the fall has equaled 40% of the historic norm, in rice 25%, in coffee 60%, this is to say, a very steep fall in the productivity of labor. What has happened as a consequence of this? Now we need two workers to do what before one did.[23]

In an effort to reverse the decline in labor productivity the Ministry began a campaign during the 1984–85 agricultural season to provide monetary incentives for laborers to work for piece-rate earnings instead of daily wages. Preliminary results suggest that laborers have responded favorably to opportunities for earning extra income by engaging in piece-rate work.[24] Otherwise rural laborers have few alternatives to ease the economic pressure that has confronted them.

Peasants—subsistence and small farmers—have also been economically "squeezed," but they have had greater opportunities open to them. Since its inception the new regime has been strongly committed to agrarian reform.[25] Agrarian reform is held to be desirable because it has the potential both for redressing rural inequalities and for improving food production. The paramount importance of generating foreign exchange, so crucial to a small developing country, has compelled the state to concentrate scarce resources (i.e., technicians and machinery) in the agro-export sector. However, peasants have received limited technical assistance and, above all, credit and access to land.

The Ministry of Agriculture and Agrarian Reform (MIDINRA) has centered its efforts to improve the welfare of peasant producers on three policies: (1) improved access to land at a lower cost, (2) the formation of cooperatives, and (3) improved credit. These three policies have often been tied together. In particular, access to credit and confiscated land has been linked to the formation of cooperatives. Cooperative members working confiscated land who demonstrate their organization's solvency can hope to have the land they work given to the cooperatives under the agrarian reform. Following the victory of the insurrection, a widespread effort was made to organize cooperatives, the most advanced form being the Sandinista Agriculture Cooperatives (CAS). They are based on the collective use of land, collective labor, and the collective distribution of any surplus produced. Credit and Service Cooperatives (CCS) have been much more common. The CCSs are based on the organization of small- and medium-property owners to receive credit and technical assistance and to purchase inputs collectively. Cultivation is usually based on individual land parcels. Similar in organization to the CCS are the Work Collectives, which differ in that they are temporary—usually just for an agricultural season.[26]

Since cooperatives differ in many ways from one another, only limited generalizations can be made about their functioning. It appears, though, that the more advanced the level of organization of the cooperative, the more likely it is to encounter problems. As is often the case with cooperatives, problems center on the division of work and the distribution of benefits.[27] Other problems cited by peasants interviewed are the politicizing of cooperatives and the amount of time taken up in political meetings. Peasants frequently desire to reduce the size of their cooperative and limit activities to nothing more than obtaining and distributing credit and agricultural inputs from the government. Unfortunately, cooperatives of this nature provide limited benefits.

The central incentive for peasants to join cooperatives has been the availability of credit. After the triumph of the revolution, peasants were strongly encouraged to join cooperatives so that they could receive government credit. In some cases they were told credit would not be available unless they joined a cooperative. Peasants in Nicaragua traditionally had little access to credit; despite their great numbers they received only about 7 percent of the agricultural credit dispensed in the previous regime. However, in 1980 the total amount of credit directed toward small and medium producers increased by over 600 percent.[28]

The massive infusion of credit into the countryside in 1980 did not have the intended consequence of increasing production and rural income. For the most part the credit was not accompanied by access to technology that would contribute to an increased yield. Most of the production costs incurred in peasants' cultivation of basic grains are labor costs; few commercialized inputs are used. Hence, for most small producers the credit received was just a windfall. There were few controls on the dispensation and recuperation of credit and less than 35 percent of the credit extended was repaid.[29] In the agricultural frontier a lack of roads greatly impeded the sale of peasants' crops of maize and beans. Elsewhere peasants spread rumors that there was no need to repay the loans. The government did little to persuade peasants to repay their loans, so the rumors proved to be true. Given the low repayment rate, the credit policy for small producers proved to be very expensive. Furthermore, the great inflow of cash into rural areas had the undesirable effect of stimulating inflation since, for the most part, it was not accompanied by increased agricultural output or an inflow of consumer goods. As a special report of the International Fund for Agricultural Development (IFAD) acknowledged, the experience of 1980 showed that the mere dispersion of credit to poor peasants is unlikely to result in either a redistribution of income or a greater production of basic grains in either the short or long term.[30]

In 1981, the government quietly scaled back its credit program, particularly for maize cultivation, but credit has continued to be a keystone of the government's efforts to increase production of basic grains. Since problems encountered in 1980 were never solved, credit has continued to be a largely ineffective policy instrument. By the fourth year of the revolution, the accumulated debt of peasants was so high that the government was forced to waive repayment. According to an official of the National Development Bank, the amount waived was 370 million córdobas (U.S. $37 million at the then prevailing official exchange rate). Unfortunately, canceling the debt of peasants and the acceleration of inflation have undermined efforts to improve peasants' credit repayment rate.

The central means of institutionalizing the government's policies toward peasants—increased access to land, formation of cooperatives, and credit—is the presentation of land titles to cooperatives. In the first two years, there was no legal distribution of land under the agrarian

reform. At the end of 1981, the government began awarding cooperatives that had demonstrated a certain solvency title to the land they were
working. Cooperatives usually have from twelve to twenty members. A
single land title is awarded the cooperative, giving the equivalent of
from five to twenty manzanas (1 manzana = 0.705 ha.) per member.
Under the terms of the agrarian reform, the land may not be sold or
distributed to heirs.[31] Most of the land distributions were in 1983 and
1984. By 1986 the agrarian reform was said to be nearly complete,
though confiscations and land grants have continued sporadically. The
extent and manner in which the government has altered the distribution
of land as of 1986 is displayed in Table 5.

For the most part, the government has not been able to provide
technological assistance to small producers that would enable them to
raise yields. Raising yields would contribute to increasing not only
income but also national production. There are many difficulties
though. Agricultural education in Nicaragua has traditionally focused
on the more remunerative export crops and concomitantly on modern
agricultural practices. Other problems are the sheer number of small
peasant producers and their concentration in isolated regions, the emi-
gration of many skilled agricultural experts, the low wages paid technicians in the public sector, inadequate supervision, the unwillingness of
many agricultural technicians to work in marginal rural areas, and
perhaps most importantly, the competing need of state farms for agricultural technicians.

Government policies seemingly have facilitated peasants' access to
factors of production for growing basic grains, rather than influencing
the cost of producing grains or the net income received from farming.
On the other hand, diverse changes have influenced the costs and
returns for basic grains, the principal crops of peasants. Inflation has
resulted in price instability. Also, the government now controls a large
share of the market for basic grains and therefore has a decisive impact
on prices paid to producers.

The day after the triumph of the revolution in Nicaragua, the National Enterprise for Basic Foodstuffs (ENABAS) was created to distribute
basic consumer goods at minimum prices as part of the new government's strategy to assist consumers. ENABAS is authorized to export
and import basic grains and other foodstuffs with the assistance of the
Foreign Trade Ministry. More importantly, ENABAS acts within the
country as the discretional state buyer and seller of these products,
which it distributes in a variety of ways.[32]

Table 5

Distribution of Agricultural Land

Property ownership	1978 Area (1,000s mz.)	In percentages	1986 Area (1,000s mz.)	In percentages
Individual producers				
Greater than 500 mz.	2,920	37%	796	10%
From 200 to 500 mz.	1,311	16	999	12
From 50 to 200 mz.	2,431	30	2,412	30
From 10 to 50 ms.	1,241	15	582	7
Less than 10 mz.	170	2	129	2
Cooperatives	—	—	1,703	21
State farms	—	—	1,452	18
Total	8,073	100	8,073	100

Source: Ministry of Agricultural Development and Agrarian Reform (MIDINRA).

The new government has resolved to maintain low prices in basic foodstuffs. It has followed the pattern documented in Africa of maintaining the allegiance of the politically important urban masses through low prices for food staples.[33] Since this policy is based in part on occasionally importing commodities, especially basic grains, that are sold at lower prices, and on the willingness of the state to absorb certain marketing costs instead of passing them on to consumers, the state has had to provide a large subsidy. In fact, the subsidy to ENABAS is the largest government expenditure after defense.

Although basic grains, particularly maize and beans, are produced by the most marginal sector of Nicaragua, the peasants, ENABAS's intent is to aid consumers and not producers. Producers feel that the government-controlled prices are too low and do not provide an adequate remuneration for their efforts or an incentive to increase production. Peasants who cultivate basic grains maintain that because of the low prices they are worse off than before the revolution. Furthermore, at least some peasants feel that setting prices for basic grains is the most consequential act of the new regime for producers of basic grains— more consequential than the land reform, the formation of cooperatives, the distribution of credit to small producers, or the provision of technical assistance.

Price incentives—or the lack of them—help explain the production of basic grains. On the whole, production has been lackluster, especially considering the quantity of land that has been turned over to peasants. Measuring the extent to which peasant dissatisfaction with government pricing policy has weakened production is difficult. The counterrevolution has disrupted basic grain production on the one hand, and on the other hand some slack in production has been picked up by the government, which has increased production by cultivating basic grains using modern technology on state farms and by coercing some large, private cotton growers to do the the same by threatening to withhold credit. However, it is obvious to the Nicaraguan regime that the production of foodstuffs has been severely disrupted by peasants unwittingly acting collectively. Commander Jaime Wheelock described the predicament with remarkable frankness:

> This policy of subsidies had been a disincentive for producers to produce. The day you give away water no one wants to buy it, the day you give away beans no one wants to produce them, this is logical. If you give me beans and I'm a bean producer, why am I going to grow beans, I prefer you to give them to me. That is why we have been taking to the countryside what we have never taken to the countryside and what in fact used to come from the countryside: we take beans to the countryside, we take maize to the countryside, we take powdered milk, and since the countryside receives this all so cheaply it stops producing, this is what has happened.[34]

Even meat has befallen the same result. The state is using its monopoly of slaughterhouses to provide consumers with subsidized prices. The result, however, is an explosion of what is referred to as "clandestine slaughters" throughout rural Nicaragua.[35]

Although peasants as of yet have not been able collectively to improve their welfare through prompting the government to pay higher prices, many peasants pursue individual strategies to improve their welfare. These individual solutions are both a result of the inability to reach a collective solution and a moderating influence on the pressures that might lead peasants to struggle for a collective solution. The different individual strategies adopted vary widely, but can be summarized as follows:

1. Increase production through use of their own resources.

2. Increase production through use of state resources, principally land and credit.

3. Use part of the credit or inputs as income.

4. Switch crops (especially to those without controlled prices).

5. Avoid selling to the government, and seek higher prices in the private market.

6. Produce only for consumption, and seek to earn needed cash elsewhere.

7. Switch occupations altogether.

Which of the above strategies is adopted depends on individual circumstances as well as individual preferences. It is impossible, though, to delineate even roughly which peasants opt for the varying strategies. The inability to predict who will do what aids peasants eager to escape confining government programs and regulations.

The government would obviously prefer peasants to adopt the first two strategies—increase production through their own resources, or with the help of the state. Some peasants are doing this—particularly those who have been heavily favored with government assistance. Many peasants, however, are resorting to the other five strategies, which have unplanned, or even adverse, consequences for the government. The most disruptive peasant strategy is to leave agriculture altogether—often to engage in petty commerce. A survey by the Secretariat for Planning and Budgeting (SPP) of rural areas not disturbed by the counterrevolution concluded that 15 percent of the rural labor force had in fact recently left agriculture, notwithstanding the country's agrarian reform.[36]

The Nicaraguan agrarian reform, which is attempting to improve the living standards of the rural poor, is being overwhelmed by broader economic policies, which act against the economic interests of rural producers, including the rural poor. Certainly technical and social factors are important in understanding this phenomenon. Nicaraguan peasants have attitudes that are encountered frequently elsewhere; for example, peasants prefer private ownership to cooperative ownership, and they resist efforts to create collective ownership. But the real problems stem from the political setting. The Sandinista movement derives its leadership and principal support from urban centers. This has led to misperceptions of the agrarian problem (for example, stressing too much the previous forms of land tenure and presumed forms of exploitation and looking for a quick solution through credit policies) to the neglect of more comprehensive and time-consuming strategies. More importantly, the urban base of the revolution has led the government to put more stress on subsidizing consumption to the relative penalizing of producers, especially food producers. The need for subsidies to urban consumers, and the concomitant pressure on producers' income, has been aggravated by the economic disruptions seemingly axiomatic to revolutionary change. Since Nicaragua is presently a mixed economy, peasants have responded rationally to price signals in a variety of ways: misusing subsidized credit, selling produce to private middlemen, withholding produce from the market, and even withdrawing from production.

Peasant dissatisfaction with certain facets of the agrarian reform, particularly the emphasis on cooperatives and government price controls, has not led to a challenge of government authority. Peasant organizations that do exist are controlled by the government (rhetoric to the contrary), and their primary purpose is to mobilize support for the government. However, peasants have unwittingly sabotaged the government's desire for Nicaragua to be self-sufficient in basic grains—a realizable goal. The decisions of individual basic grain producers have in the aggregate failed to produce a substantial increase in the production of maize and beans. Consequently, Nicaragua has had to use scarce foreign exchange to purchase maize, beans, and rice.

The Counterrevolution

From the onset the new Nicaraguan regime was confronted with armed resistance. Initially, however, resistance was isolated and poorly organized. U.S. assistance for the remnants of Somoza's National Guard, which fled to Honduras, and the concurrent cooperation of Honduras, resulted in a well-organized and financed counterrevolution. This locus of resistance was augmented by disgruntled Miskito Indians and by the opening of a second front along the Costa Rican border by the legendary Edén Pastora. Serious fighting began in December 1982. By 1985 the Sandinistas had largely beaten back the counterrevolutionaries, including the dismantling of Pastora's southern front. But in 1987 the Honduran-based counterrevolutionaries, aided by the United States, attacked anew.

The areas where the fighting has taken place are relatively marginal to the economy. The bulk of the GNP is generated in the Pacific region, which has been free from fighting. Indeed, the eastern Caribbean plain, which comprises 40 percent of Nicaragua's territory, has only 8 percent of the country's population. Fighting in marginal rural areas has disrupted local agricultural production—tobacco, some coffee, basic grains, and livestock. However, the most consequential material cost to the new regime of the counterrevolution has been the opportunity cost of devoting attention and resources to the struggle to defeat the counterrevolutionaries. This cost is incalculable but enormous.

Since fighting has taken place in rural areas the new regime has had to go to extra lengths to win and maintain the support of rural wage laborers and peasants. It is a truism of both revolutionary and counterrevolutionary insurgency that success depends on generating some popular support or, at least, the tacit support of those disaffected with the existing regime. As Commander Luis Carrión acknowledged in an illuminating speech, peasants are recruited by the counterrevolution, in part because of what Carrión termed "religious fanaticism," but also for economic reasons.[37] The economic constraints on the revolution and the resulting need to enforce a program of austerity and efficiency have resulted in both a decline in standards of living and cynicism toward the revolution. As Crane Brinton suggests in his seminal comparative study of revolutions, this is to be expected in the post-revolutionary era.[38]

The Sandinista leadership has responded to the counterrevolutionary threat with its own efforts to recruit the rural poor with moral suasion, an acceleration of the land reform in troubled regions, and, when necessary, subtle coercion. Sandinista propaganda equates counterrevolutionaries with Somoza's National Guard, using, in fact, the same nicknames (beasts, frogs) for the counterrevolutionaries that Nicaraguans traditionally used for Somoza's National Guard. This is a persuasive tactic since nearly all poor Nicaraguans have nothing but hatred for Somoza's National Guard. The government also appeals to nationalism by suggesting counterrevolutionaries are puppets of the United States, and by evoking the memory of Sandino's armed resistance to the U.S. occupying force. For example, one common slogan is, "After 50 years, the enemy is the same."

A more effective response to the counterrevolutionary threat has been to accelerate the land reform in areas threatened by fighting.[39] The intention is to give peasants a stake in the revolution. The economic and political cost of redistributing land is low; most of the land in question is already held by the government and is not used for the production of agro-exports. The government has also continued its credit program for peasants even though the program is acknowledged to contribute little to increasing production. The canceling of peasants' accumulated debt was also undoubtedly done to curry political support. Furthermore, the government appears to have quietly scaled down its drive to organize peasants in agricultural cooperatives. It is recognized in MIDINRA that cooperatives are for the most part unpopular with peasants (unless MIDINRA can heavily endow cooperatives with machinery and other resources). Land in border regions has even been distributed to individuals, breaking the practice of only distributing land to cooperatives. Thus, in this limited respect, peasants can be said to have profited from the pressure the counterrevolutionaries have exerted on the government in marginal rural areas.

The government, however, has not had the political and economic resources to favor peasants with what they would probably most like: higher prices for their crops. Paying higher prices for food crops would probably ultimately result in higher food prices for urban consumers. Urban areas continue to be the regime's strongest base of support, and higher food prices might weaken urban support, especially since consumers are already confronted with sharp price increases for goods not controlled by the government.

At times the government uses coercion to achieve compliance with its program and policies. For example, in some rural areas peasants caught selling their crops to private middlemen have their entire harvests seized without any compensation. The government is usually more subtle however. Benefits provided by the state are contingent on participating in state organizations, including the militia and the defense committees. Since the government is increasing its role in society, the favors it can award or withhold give it considerable power, especially over the poor. There is no doubt, though, that rural Nicaraguans feel pressured by the state. A common complaint is that, "If you don't do what they want, they say you are a counterrevolutionary." The government, in defense, argues that it is under serious threat and that extraordinary measures must be taken.

While some poor rural Nicaraguans have actually joined the counterrevolution, more have joined the government's bid to defeat decisively the counterrevolution. Most poor rural Nicaraguans, however, appear to have adopted a calculated air of indifference. Certainly, the economic difficulties in Nicaragua have led to cynicism about the FSLN. Still, the political apathy in rural Nicaragua seems largely a matter of selfish calculations about benefits and costs: the benefits are reckoned to be for "government" and the costs are personal. As one peasant exclaimed, "I don't get involved in politics unless I get something out of it." A bleaker view was provided by a young laborer on a cotton farm outside of León, "It is better not to get involved in politics because if there is another change those that are now in politics will be killed."

Peasants see their behavior as being eminently reasonable. It conforms to the traditional Nicaraguan proverb, "Flies do not enter a closed mouth." For the government, the apathy of many rural laborers and peasants must be seen as an annoying lack of political consciousness at best and of threatening ingratitude at worst. The government must expend considerable effort to mobilize political support among the declared benefactors and heirs of the revolution. Indeed, the coercion used by both the FSLN and the counterrevolutionaries seems to be carried out not as a response to the perceived success of the opposition, but rather as an antidote to peasants' proclivity to simply not get involved, or as said in the vernacular, "to take on color."

Conclusion

Post-revolutionary regimes in developing countries face numerous problems. First, there is the material and social damage from the insurrection itself. Second, fledgling regimes face opposition and subversion from defeated political forces and those social strata threatened by post-revolutionary redistribution. Small Third World revolutionary regimes also face the same constraints as many of their nonrevolutionary counterparts. Material scarcity limits the parameters of innovation. They often depend on exports of one or two primary products and are vulnerable to the structure and dynamics of international markets. Politically nascent regimes in countries where national traditions have been weak historically confront social conflict stemming from religious, cultural, tribal, or ethnic schisms. Where national traditions were strong, the heavy hand of a bureaucratic and authoritarian past weighs on those seeking revolutionary change.[40]

It is less readily acknowledged that the rural poor can also be an obstacle to radical structural change. Revolutions in this century have inevitably been made in the name of peasants, and many post-revolutionary regimes claim to base their popular support on an alliance of workers and peasants. Examining the attitude and behavior of rural Nicaraguans during three distinct stages of the country's post-revolutionary era suggests that, rhetoric notwithstanding, the rural poor often complicate state efforts at meeting basic needs while also instituting far-reaching reforms. Nicaraguan laborers seized the opportunity presented by the fall of the *ancien régime* to reduce their labor obligations.

Peasants abused the government's generous credit policy more consistently and blatantly than large landowners and have not matched the regime's distribution of land with increased production. When the counterrevolution, flush with U.S. funds, became a major threat, many peasants sat on their hands, forcing urban militias to do most of the fighting. The rural poor narrowly interpret their interests, at a cost to other strata of society.

The rational but self-interested maximization of welfare by the rural poor forces the new Nicaraguan regime into an awkward position. In an attempt to restore labor productivity it has to suppress the very labor militancy it fostered during the insurrection. It has been compelled to strip labor of its historical form of self-defense—the power to strike. The unwillingness of many peasants to produce food at government-set prices has forced the government to resort to subtle forms of coercion with peasants, and to allocate considerable foreign exchange for the purchase of food that is normally produced within the country. Throughout rural Nicaragua, the state has had to resort to manipulating access to state-controlled goods and services to win allegiance and support from the supposed constituency of the revolution. Resorting to cooptation and coercion has made it difficult for the revolutionary leadership to confront expectations it raised during the insurrection without losing its legitimacy.

Rural laborers and peasants have few defenses against the backlash of the state. They do not have the organization necessary to confront a strong monolithic state. Yet, they cannot just economically and politically withdraw. The expansion of the agro-export sector and the paramountcy of the state make that an untenable option except for the most isolated peasants. In complaining about the state-controlled price for coffee, a small coffee producer explained the dilemma most rural Nicaraguans confront: "If the price (of coffee) is not increased, coffee growers will lose the motivation they have to produce. The problem is that we have always supported ourselves from coffee cultivation, and if we do not work, we will not eat."[41] However, there appear to be some differences in the defense strategies of the rural poor: peasants with some resources, such as an agricultural enterprise, tend to rely on manipulation of the market. Laborers attempt to reduce the burden of employment through a number of evasive tactics or by switching occupations.[42]

In the post-revolutionary era the faltering cooperation of the rural poor is not likely to receive immediate attention. Once noticed, it is not likely to be publicly discussed. It is an embarrassment that the supposed benefactors of the revolution prove to be as selfish as the economic elite of the old order. Rural laborers and peasants are unlikely to ever pose a political threat to a post-revolutionary regime, but they are likely to complicate, if not derail, a regime's economic program. Ultimately the state must intercede with measures to control its stated constituency, though these measures are likely to be painted in a different light. Thus, for example, the collectivization of agriculture is touted as a means for increasing economies of scale when in reality it is a means for stopping peasants from slipping into subsistence farming or selling their crops on the "black" market.[43] Nonetheless, the state is likely to find that it is easier to control foreign capital and the national elite of the old order than to control its scattered rural poor.

Peasants, for their part, are likely to find the almost axiomatic post-revolutionary increase in state authority a source of vexatious problems, prompting them to rely on the cunning employment of everyday forms of resistance.

Notes

1. For accounts of the FSLN's struggle see, Humberto Ortega Saavedra, *50 Años de Lucha Sandinista* (México: Editorial Diogenes, 1979); Fernando Caromona, ed., *Nicaragua: La Estrategia de la Victoria* (México: Editorial Nuestro Tiempo, 1980).

2. Robert Dix, "The Varieties of Revolution," *Comparative Politics* 15 (April 1983): 281–84.

3. Hugh Thomas, *The Spanish Civil War* (New York: Harper & Brothers, 1961), pp. 205–206.

4. Arturo Valenzuela, *Chile* (Baltimore: Johns Hopkins University Press, 1978), pp. 42–43.

5. Paul Hollander, *Political Pilgrims* (New York: Oxford University Press, 1981), pp. xxi–xxvi, 3–39.

6. See, for example, a recent compilation of analyses of agrarian reform in developing countries: Ajit Kumar Ghose, ed., *Agrarian Reform in Contemporary Developing Countries* (London: Croom Helm, 1983).

7. Anita Chan and Jonathan Unger, "The Second Economy of Rural China," in Gregory Grossman, ed., *Studies in the Second Economy of the Communist Countries* (Berkeley: University of California Press, 1983); David Zweig, "Opposition to Change in Rural China," *Asian Survey* 23 (July 1983); John P. Burns, "Rural Guangdong's 'Second Economy,' 1962–1974," *The China Quarterly* 88 (December 1981).

8. Philip Warnken, *The Agricultural Development of Nicaragua* (Columbia, Missouri: University of Missouri, 1975), p. 16.

9. *Ibid.*, p. 27.

10. *Ibid.*, pp. 19, 44.

11. *Ibid.*, p. 44.

12. *Ibid.*

13. Figures are from Carmen Diana Deere and Peter Marchetti, "The Worker-Peasant Alliance in the First Year of the Nicaraguan Agrarian Reform," *Latin Ameri-*

can Perspectives 8 (Spring 1981). There is a dearth of analyses of the social differentiation in the rural population but see Central American Institute of Business Administration (INCAE), "Nicaragua: Estudio de la Situación del Empleo, la Absorción de la Mano de Obra y Otros Aspectos en Fincas y Productores de Café y Algodón" (Managua, 1982, mimeographed), and the ongoing work of the Center for the Study of Agrarian Reform (CIERA) in Nicaragua.

14. Rural subsistence strategies in Central America are outlined by J. Douglas Uzzell, "Mixed Strategies and the Informal Sector: Three Faces of Reserve Labor," *Human Organization* 39 (Spring 1980).

15. Figures are from Forrest Colburn, *Post-Revolutionary Nicaragua: State, Class, and the Dilemmas of Agrarian Policy* (Berkeley: University of California Press, 1986), p. 114.

16. International Fund for Agricultural Development (IFAD), "Informe de la Misión Especial de Programación a Nicaragua" (Rome, October 1980, mimeographed), p. 88.

17. *La Prensa*, 27 July 1981.

18. *La Prensa*, 29 July 1981.

19. *Ibid.*

20. *La Prensa*, 9 July 1981.

21. Rolando D. Lacayo and Martha Lacayo De Arauz, eds., *Decretos-Leyes Para Gobierno De Un País A Través De Una Junta De Gobierno De Reconstrucción Nacional*, Vols. 1–6 (Managua: Editorial Unión, 1979–1983).

22. Interview with an administrator of the state agricultural enterprise, Oscar Turcios, Estelí, February 21, 1985.

23. Jaime Wheelock, *Entre la Crisis y la Agresión* (Managua: Ministry of Agricultural Development and Agrarian Reform, 1984), p. 110.

24. *Barricada*, 29 July 1985, 18 April 1986; Nicaraguan Institute for Economic and Social Research (INIES), *Plan Económico 1987* (Managua: INIES, 1987), p. 23.

25. Discussions of the agrarian reform can be found in: Center for the Study of Agrarian Reform (CIERA), *El Hambre en los Países del Tercer Mundo* (Managua: CIERA, 1983), pp. 37–46; a bimonthly bulletin of the Ministry of Agricultural Development and Agrarian Reform (MIDINRA), *Informaciones Agropecuarias*; and a quarterly journal also published by MIDINRA, *Revolución y Desarrollo*.

26. Center for the Study of Agrarian Reform Agrarian (CIERA), *Producción y Organización en el Agro Nicaragüense* (Managua: CIERA, 1982), pp. 44–45.

27. Ministry of Agricultural Development and Agrarian Reform (MIDINRA), *Plan de Trabajo 1987: Balance y Perspectivas* (Managua: MIDINRA, 1987), pp. 17–19. For a more general discussion of the problems plaguing agricultural cooperatives see Cynthia McClintock, *Peasant Cooperatives and Political Change in Peru* (Princeton: Princeton University Press, 1981), pp. 259–315.

28. See Center for the Study of Agrarian Reform (CIERA), "Informe del Impacto del Crédito Rural Volumen 1" (Managua, 1982, mimeographed).

29. *Ibid.*, p. 253.

30. IFAD, "Informe," p. 124.

31. *Barricada*, 22 December 1981, 18 January 1982, 7 February 1982; *El Nuevo Diario*, 18 July 1983.

32. Ministry of Planning (MIPLAN), *Programa Económico de Austeridad y Eficiencia 81* (Managua: MIPLAN, 1981), p. 71.

33. Robert Bates, *Markets and States in Tropical Africa* (Berkeley: University of California Press, 1981), pp. 30–44.

34. Ministry of Agricultural Development and Agrarian Reform (MIDINRA), *Plan de Trabajo: Balance y Perspectivas 1985* (Managua: MIDINRA, 1985), p. 17.

35. *El Nuevo Diario*, 31 July 1985.

36. Secretariat for Planning and Budgeting (SPP), ''Empleo e Ingreso Rural y Agropecuario'' (Managua, 1985, mimeographed), p. 25.

37. *El Nuevo Diario*, 19 June 1983. In a more recent speech Carrión said, ''There are sectors that consciously or not contribute to the fulfillment of enemy plans.'' *Barricada*, 26 May 1987. Luis Carrión is the vice-minister of the Ministry of Interior.

38. Crane Brinton, *The Anatomy of Revolution* (New York: Vintage Books, 1965), p. 212.

39. *Latin America Weekly Report*, 22 June 1984, p. 10.

40. Gordon White et al., eds., *Revolutionary Socialist Development in the Third World* (Brighton: Wheatsheaf Books, 1983), pp. 6–7.

41. Forrest Colburn, *Post-Revolutionary Nicaragua*, p. 76.

42. This is likewise suggested to be the case in sub-Sahara Africa: Goran Hyden, *No Shortcuts to Progress* (Berkeley: University of California Press, 1983), pp. 24–25.

43. See Moshe Lewin, *Russian Peasants and Soviet Power* (New York: W. W. Norton, 1975).

8

How the Weak Succeed: Tactics, Political Goods, and Institutions in the Struggle over Land in Zimbabwe

Jeffrey Herbst

Land was the central issue during Zimbabwe's liberation struggle and continues to be the most important domestic issue in the post-independence period. The appropriation of African land by the European settlers guaranteed white economic dominance and black poverty during the colonial period. Today, the inequitable distribution of land in Zimbabwe is the most dramatic symbol of the enduring structures of an unequal society. Most of the attention devoted to studying the land question has centered on the government's attempts to redistribute land from large-scale white farmers to black peasants.[1] However, there is another ongoing conflict in the countryside that has received little attention: the battle between squatters and those peasants who have stayed in the old tribal reserves (now called communal lands) over access to land that the government has purchased from white farmers. The squatters are thought to be politically weak because of their lack of organization, their inability to influence the government formally on a national level, and because the government has repeatedly declared squatters' attempts to jump the resettlement queue and seize land to be illegitimate and illegal. In contrast, the communal farmers who have stayed on their land and waited for the government to redistribute land

I am grateful to Marcia Burdette, Forrest Colburn, Des Gasper, and James Scott for helpful comments. A Fulbright Scholarship funded my research in Zimbabwe.

to them are represented on a national level by a formal lobbying organization and are the intended beneficiaries of the resettlement program. Yet, in most places in Zimbabwe where there are squatters, these illegal settlers have managed, through subtle tactics and deception, to gain control over the resettlement plots.

A review of the tactics of the supposedly weak squatters leads to an understanding of how they repeatedly circumvented the resettlement bureaucracy and triumphed over those who waited in the overcrowded reserves. The squatters' success was due, in part, to their determination and innovative tactics when confronting the government. Though they are often pictured as isolated and powerless, the squatters repeatedly demonstrated a capability to develop powerful tactics that enabled them to win more land. However, the squatters' tactics cannot be considered in isolation because two other factors greatly aided their quest for land. First, the particular characteristics of land as a political good, especially in that it can be seized and immediately put to use without further state aid, was important to the illegal settler's success. Second, the initial weakness of the government bureaucracy charged with carrying out the resettlement program and the willingness of national politicians to circumvent that bureaucracy on the behalf of the illegal settlers was crucial to the squatters' ability to gain land at the expense of the intended beneficiaries of the resettlement program.

Understanding how the political good and the nature of state institutions allowed the weak squatters' tactics to be successful is especially important in any attempt to study everyday forms of resistance. In the rush to focus on "the weak" there is a danger that the opportunities and constraints posed by the larger political environment will be ignored. While examining the kind of tactics James Scott, Forrest Colburn, and others in this volume delineate is exceptionally important to understanding the actions of peasants and others without power, we cannot afford to lose sight of the fact that the weak still operate on terrain defined by the state and the nature of the political issue. In addition, there is the danger that if only the perspective of the powerless is taken into account the state will appear as it does to the weak: a forbidding monolith dedicated to exploiting the powerless. Instead, as this case study will make clear, certain state institutional arrangements and political goods may be particularly amenable to the type of political pressure that only weak, unorganized groups can bring to bear. Therefore, while the actions of the squatters in Zimbabwe are important to understand, they must be examined in conjunction with the operation of state institutions and the nature of the issue-area in order to fully appreciate a truly dynamic political process.

Colonial Land Policy 1894–1980

The history of land in Zimbabwe has been adequately chronicled so that a long review of the land question prior to 1980 is not necessary.[2] Instead, a simple historical outline, while ignoring the rich diversity of Zimbabwe's land history, provides the basic details essential for an understanding of post-1980 politics. Europeans began to alienate lands from Africans in Zimbabwe as early as 1894 in Matabeleland. In that year the first native reserves were created so that blacks who were moved off their own lands would have some place to go. After the 1896–1897 uprising was crushed, European encroachment onto African land continued and reserves were created throughout the country.[3] By 1910, 23.4 percent of the land had been appropriated by white settlers and 26 percent had been declared native reserves, later known as Tribal Trust Lands (TTLs).[4] The Land Apportionment Act (LAA) of 1930 formally enshrined the division of the country's land into law and prohibited members of either racial group from owning land in areas assigned to the other. By the time of the LAA, 50.8 percent of the total land had been declared "white" while 30 percent had been reserved for blacks.[5] At the same time, some land, eventually amounting to approximately 4 percent of the total land, was reserved for purchase by blacks, and these territories, usually located between native reserves and white lands, were called Native Purchase Areas.[6] Herding Africans onto overcrowded reserves containing poor land and blatantly discriminatory policies against African agriculture meant that "by the end of the 1930's, the agricultural economy of the Shona and the Ndebele [the two population groups in Zimbabwe], like that of the Kikuyu and most South African peoples, had been destroyed."[7] The LAA was superseded by the Land Tenure Act of 1969, which gave whites and blacks each 46.6 percent of the land. Colonial land policy was modified again in the late 1970s and the prohibition on Africans holding land in the white areas was abolished. Due to the high cost of farms in white areas, however, practically no blacks were able to own land in the previously white-only areas. By the late 1970s, 42 percent of the land was reserved for blacks while 51.2 percent was technically available to anyone but was de facto white land.[8] Eighty percent of the country's rural population and approximately 60 percent of Zimbabwe's total population live in the reserves.[9]

In addition to the sheer numerical inequality of approximately 4,000 white farmers holding roughly the same amount of land as 700,000 to 800,000 black families, there are significant inequalities in the quality of land held. Around the time of independence, 74 percent of all black peasant land was in areas where droughts are frequent and where even normal levels of rainfall are inadequate for intensive crop production.[10] Similarly, in the Native Purchase Areas (now known as the small-scale commercial sector), 75 percent of the land is located in regions where only extensive crop and livestock production, at best, is possible.[11] In contrast, white land is concentrated in good rainfall areas where intensive crop production is possible.[12] The communal lands have a population density of approximately twenty-eight people per square kilometer compared to nine people per square kilometer in white areas, even though the communal lands are least able to support intensive cultivation and large concentrations of people.[13]

The Importance of the Land Issue

Research on Zimbabwe has long emphasized the central role land plays in the politics of the country. One report concerning resettlement began by noting that:

> From the very onset of political armed struggle against colonialism, the key issue was land. It was the fight for land which led to the death of tens of thousands of Zimbabweans during the Armed Struggle: true Zimbabwean patriots saw there could be no freedom without the liberation of the land from the colonial settlers.[14]

Similarly, Prime Minister Robert Mugabe stated in his 1980 election manifesto: "It is not only anti-People but criminal for any government to ignore the acute land hunger in the country, especially when it is realized that 83% of our population live in the rural areas and depend on agriculture for their livelihood."[15] The prime minister has further stated that due to the importance of land to the lives of the people, "We can never have peace in this country unless the peasant population is satisfied in relation to the land issue."[16]

Land was such an important issue for both economic and cultural reasons. First, the inequitable distribution of land doomed most peas-

ants to ever-worsening poverty. Zimbabwe's major commission of
inquiry into incomes and prices, the Riddell Commission, bluntly summarized the economic problems caused by the inequitable distribution
of land: "The most fundamental constraint on raising the incomes of
families in the peasant sector to a level that will meet their minimum
needs is land shortage."[17] The carrying capacity of the land, already
stretched by overpopulation, is actually decreasing further now due to
severe erosion. One of the few microstudies of land quality in communal areas found in the mid-1970s in Victoria (now Masvingo) Province
that 59 percent of the peasant land was considered "average" with a
declining fertility and 26 percent was considered "poor" with "crops
that are not worth harvesting."[18]

It is not enough, however, to simply stress the economic and ecological effects of the settlers' appropriation of the land. The people of Zimbabwe, especially the Shona, who account for 80 percent
of the population, have a spiritual relationship with the land, which
was profoundly disrupted by settler colonialism. In a society where
land is held collectively and where it is a cardinal principle that no
member of the community should be landless, white appropriation of
the land was more than a severe economic handicap; it was a profound
challenge to the very foundation of African society.[19] David Lan,
in his excellent study of the Dande area on the Zambezi escarpment
during the liberation war, describes the importance of land to Shona
politics:

> The single most important duty of the spirit medium is to protect the
> land. From the grave, from the depths of the forests, from the body of
> the lion or of their mediums, the *mhondoro* control in perpetuity the
> land they conquered during their lives. Under the rule of the whites
> their land had lost its fertility. Sacred places had been fenced off and
> ruled out of bounds. The guerrillas offered land as renewed fertility
> and restored tradition. They offered a Zimbabwe returned to its
> original and rightful owners.[20]

The land grievances were the driving force behind the liberation struggle. As Lan notes: "The imagery of dispossession, of loss, of landlessness, of longing for the 'lost lands' to be restored was a constant pulse
in the literature, the oral tradition, and the rhetoric of the nationalist
movement."[21] The drive for land is therefore extraordinarily intense
and people in Zimbabwe will go to almost any length to gain more land.

Government Resettlement Policy

Upon gaining power in April 1980, the new government quickly tried to formulate a program that would meet and alleviate some of the land problems in the communal areas. The government initiated a program in 1980 to resettle 18,000 families on approximately 1.1 million hectares of land.[22] Given the clear inadequacy of this program in a country of 800,000 peasant families facing severe land pressure, the government soon decided on a much more ambitious program. In the three-year *Transitional National Development Plan* published in November, 1982, and covering the period 1982–84, the government stated its intention to resettle at least 162,000 peasant families, "subject to practical and economic constraints."[23] However, due to economic, logistical, and ecological problems, the government only managed to resettle 36,000 families on 2 million hectares of land in the first five years of independence.[24] The resettlement program is an ongoing exercise and the government's goal is to resettle 15,000 families a year between 1986 and 1990.[25]

Communal Farmers and Squatters

The distinction between communal farmers and squatters is by necessity somewhat artificial. Squatters are often former farmers from the communal lands and squatters will often bring their families from the communal lands once they have gained land. However, *politically* communal farmers and squatters are distinctly different groups and are perceived as such by the government. Communal farmers who have obeyed government dictates and waited for land to be distributed to them are the intended beneficiaries of the resettlement program. The former Deputy Minister of Lands, Mark Dube, noted that the government had a preference to resettle "people who had waited patiently than those who preferred to be squatters."[26] The communal farmers are also represented on a national level by the National Farmers Association of Zimbabwe (NFAZ), which is seen by the government as the legitimate lobbying organization representing peasant farmers and has received significant financial support from the government and foreign aid organizations. Finally, the government is seen by some as being obligated to the peasantry. Chiviya argues: "The peasants as an interest group are quite an important component of the government's land acquisition and redistribution program. It is the peasants who put political elites into

power and not the white commercial farmers or multinational enterprises.''[27]

In contrast, squatters are in a dramatically different political position. There are some government officials, notably some members of
the cabinet and elements of the ruling party, who are sympathetic to the
illegal settlers because squatting was encouraged by the liberation
armies during the war to disrupt white agriculture and because squatting is seen as a manifestation of the land problem in the communal
areas. However, squatting is now officially viewed as an illegitimate
activity. Squatters are viewed as illegitimate even though there is no
doubt that many squatters are poor enough to meet government criteria
for resettlement. However, many others are neither landless nor poor
and would not normally have qualified for resettlement.

Squatters are therefore viewed as politically weak by most observers. By their very nature, illegal settlers consist of small, uncoordi-
nated groups in widely separated rural areas with no contact with other
squatters. They have no national representation and, unlike the NFAZ,
cannot lobby the government. Chiviya therefore suggested: ''As a
group squatters are not formally organized. They do not have an identifiable leadership. This creates problems for the ruling political elites.
Because squatters are not formally organized and lack an identifiable
leadership they do not have a direct input into the policy-making
process.''[28] While it would be a mistake to argue that the communal
farmers as represented by the NFAZ are a particularly powerful group
in absolute terms, it is clear that in terms of traditional political analysis the squatters are the weak group.

Political Conflict in the Countryside

Zimbabwe has a relatively clear, if somewhat contradictory, process to
select settlers for newly acquired land. The formal process starts
by the Department of Rural Development sending out qualification
forms to the district council in each province (Zimbabwe has a total
of fifty-five districts in eight provinces). The councils then distribute
the forms to farmers in their areas and collect the completed forms
from farmers who want to be eligible for resettlement. When a new
area opens up for resettlement, the provincial resettlement officer and
the district council jointly review the returned eligibility forms and
select the farmers for the resettlement scheme. The selected farmers
then make their own way to the resettlement areas where they are

allocated plots that have been demarcated previously.

To be eligible for resettlement a peasant must:

1. be "effectively landless, i.e has no or too little land to support oneself and dependents" and

2. "is not employed (nor is spouse)" and

3. is poor. "The intention is to reach the rural poor; not, as many development programs have, the rural rich." And,

4. is "married or widowed with dependents" and

5. is aged 18 to 55 and able to "make productive use of the land allocated" and

6. be prepared to give up all rights to land in the communal areas or

7. returned Zimbabwean refugees are given special consideration or

8. is an experienced or a master farmer who is willing to give up land rights and wage employment elsewhere. [29]

The criteria are essentially the same as the ones first established in 1980 except for the provision for master farmers. The master farmer provision was added in 1982 in the hope that experienced farmers would have a "demonstration effect" in resettlement areas among other peasants who were not experienced in farming. This addition was a reaction by the government to the developing situation in the resettlement areas.

There is a significant disjuncture between the type of resettlement program the government was planning and the criteria it established for the selection of settlers. One of the most significant decisions made by the government regarding the land area, although one that is seldom discussed in Zimbabwe, was that the newly acquired land would not become simple extensions of the communal areas but would be developed separately by the Ministry of Lands. The holdings in the resettlement areas are significantly larger than in the communal lands and resettlement farming means a full-time commitment by all members of the family including the men who are supposed to give up employment. [30] This differs considerably from the type of farming presently done in the communal areas where most of the men are often missing because they are seeking wage employment to supplement family incomes. The decision not to simply append the resettlement areas to the communal areas was opposed by many chiefs who wanted larger communal areas (probably because land added to the communal areas would result in an extension of their authority) and by some peasants. [31]

The government rejected these pleas arguing that the communal areas were a product of colonialism and that proper agrarian development could only proceed if the resettlement areas were developed separately. However, the government then proceeded to establish criteria for resettlement plots that were in favor of those who were least able to put these large plots to use because the landless and refugees, by the very nature of their predicament, do not have significant farming experience and capital (especially in the form of draft power) to fully exploit the resettlement plots. One resettlement official in an interview estimated that perhaps only 15 percent of the people who actually resettled on what was sometimes prime commercial land were good farmers. This was more or less admitted by the government when it began to seek "demonstration effects" by placing master farmers into resettlement areas.[32] In the words of one provincial official, the government made a "political decision" to favor returning refugees and the landless because these people by squatting had significantly helped the liberation struggle and because they were able to exert significant political pressure on the government. The basic decision to settle people on the newly acquired lands who were least suited to them set the tone for the entire selection process, which has definitely not gone according to plan.

The truth about the resettlement process is that it has been, and to a considerable extent still is, overrun by squatters. Officials in interviews noted that in some provinces, notably Manicaland, Mashonaland West, and Matabeleland North, most to all of the resettlement plots have gone to squatters and that in other parts of the country entire resettlement areas have been largely controlled by squatters. Certainly, in Manicaland almost all those resettled have been squatters and this province accounts for approximately one-third of the total number of families resettled nationwide.[33] One resettlement official describing how squatters gain access to land planned for resettlement said that the formal process whereby district councils collect resettlement forms from qualified farmers and then choose the final group for the resettlement plots was so much "wishful thinking." He said that people in the rural areas often know that land will be sold before the government does (perhaps because the farm workers have spread the word) and illegal settlers then move onto the farm immediately or get close enough so they can claim occupancy once the land has been sold. In the words of one resettlement officer, "It is just a question of getting there first." It is important to note that this has not happened everywhere in the country. For instance, in Mashonaland Central, where there is not much of a squatter problem, the resettlement process has probably proceeded much more closely to the established regulations. However, where there are squatters, it is almost always the case that they are the ones who have been resettled.

While the government allowed the squatters to win the battle for the resettlement areas, it did not allow them to triumph throughout the countryside. In a number of instances the army has evicted squatters in search and evict operations and squatter settlements have been razed on more than one occasion.[34] The government was especially dedicated to ending the squatter menace when ongoing commercial activities were threatened. However, what has confused some people is that simply because the government dealt effectively with squatters who threatened working commercial areas does not mean that it was at all effective in preventing squatters from winning a large percentage of the resettlement plots wherever they were present.[35] Indeed, the government often moved squatters off commercial areas into resettlement plots. One department of rural development official estimated that, of the squatters forcibly evicted by the government, 50 percent were resettled. In contrast, only a small fraction of the 800,000 families in the communal areas have been resettled. It is therefore clear who proportionally benefited the most from resettlement.

Some would claim that resettlement-by-squatting would, in the end, accomplish the goals set out by the government because squatting is seen as a manifestation of land hunger in the communal areas.[36] However, studying the correlation between land pressure and squatting casts doubt on the assertion that squatting is solely the result of land hunger and, therefore, all illegal settlers who have made their way onto resettlement land are deserving according to the criteria set up by the government. Most of the squatting problem has been located in the eastern province of Manicaland. Between 1981 and 1982 it was estimated that 79 percent of the squatters were in this province.[37] However, when the Whitsun Foundation surveyed the communal areas under the most pressure it found that only two areas in Manicaland are among the thirty in the nation considered to be under the most pressure. Most of the districts under extreme pressure are in the two Matabeleland provinces and Masvingo where dry conditions allow for only very low densities on the land.[38] While there is certainly land pressure almost everywhere in the communal lands, there simply is not a clear correlation between squatting and extreme land pressure.

Instead, squatting seems to be caused, in part, by the availability of open land. The high percentage of open land in Manicaland, which was created by the fierce battles waged there during the liberation war, is probably what caused squatting to be so endemic in that province. It was, for instance, a Manicaland official's impression that the squatting there was "sheer opportunism" rather than a reflection of land pressure. Anecdotal evidence also supports this suggestion. One Ministry of Lands official said in an interview, "Sometimes these people [squatters] were just troublemakers but government was forced to give them land. Government had to be seen as doing something." Similarly, one investigation of squatting noted that some illegal settlers in the resettlement areas already have land and that others: "[Are] prosperous businessmen who simply takeover an area and divide it into plots, selling or renting them to people, frequently poorer relatives, they have trucked in from over-crowded areas."[39] Therefore, it would be impossible to claim that the de facto selection by squatting allows only those eligible to have plots. Many of the squatters are, like the farmers in the communal lands, desperately in need of land, but many clearly are not.

What explains the success of the supposedly weak squatters in circumventing government regulations and successfully competing against the communal farmers? First, the sheer determination of the squatters must be emphasized. Land in Zimbabwe is an extraordinarily emotional issue because it more or less directly determines the fortunes of those people in the countryside. Due to the poor conditions of the former tribal reserves and the dislocations caused by the war, some people had absolutely no alternative to squatting. Many others who might not have qualified under government regulations for land resettlement saw squatting as a once in a lifetime opportunity to improve the fortunes of themselves and their families. Thus, squatters in one area said that, "[Even] if they were convicted they would come back because they had not been given land and were hungry."[40] Some of the squatters, up to one-half in some areas, are also Malawian or Mozambican who formerly worked on white farms and who had no alternative to squatting. As one Malawian in Karoi (Mashonaland West Province) said: "I had to squat on this farm after my employer had fired me because he said he could not give me the minimum wage. Where would I have gone? Zimbabwe is my home and I cannot go back to Malawi."[41] One group of squatters summed up the determination of many who tried to seize land, "Now we have been ordered to be off by Monday but we are not leaving. We are staying and we are prepared to die and be buried here.''[42]

The squatters' determination was fueled by statements from the liberation forces and by certain politicians immediately after independence that created an atmosphere where squatting was seen as an important carryover from the nationalist struggle. For instance, Eddison Zvobgo (now the Minister for Justice, Legal and Parliamentary Affairs) said, in 1979, ''We intend to seize land and not pay a penny to anyone.''[43] While the Lancaster House Constitution prohibited land seizure and forced the government to purchase land on a willing seller-willing buyer basis, the attitude that land seizure was a part of the ongoing struggle continued for some time after independence in 1980. Moven Mahachi, when he was Deputy Minister of Lands, said of one area in the Eastern Highlands:

> What I like about the Makoni people is that they do not just sit idle saying, 'We have won the war, now we can rest.' They take action to solve the land problem for themselves. Makoni district is more infested with squatters than any other district in the country and this makes it easier for us: it puts pressure on the Ministry and pressure on the owners.[44]

This attitude trickled down to the squatters. One squatter in Manicaland said:

> I had only four acres of land in Tanda. The soil was always very poor. When I heard that I could have land here, I came. . . . A Deputy Minister, Mr. Mahachi, came and told us we would get twelve acres. We are waiting to be given land. . . . There is plenty of land, so why should we not have it?[45]

Government leaders quickly changed their views on squatting as they realized the implications for the agricultural industry, the backbone of the country, of a nationwide land grab. For instance, in 1982 the Deputy Minister of Lands, Mark Dube, declared an ''all-out war'' against squatters and said that they would have to vacate all land they were on by January 25, 1983.[46] Not surprisingly, the squatters were not receptive to this change in thinking and some squatters were still being encouraged to seize land by government and party officials long after all official deadlines had passed.

In the face of squatter determination and at least initial support by part of the national leadership, the bureaucracy that was supposed to institutionalize resettlement procedures was exceptionally weak. It must be remembered that the bureaucracy was assigned the task of resettling land and containing the squatters, which was an entirely new creation as the government before 1980 had not resettled anyone (except for moving people into the Tribal Trust Lands). The Ministry of Lands, Resettlement, and Rural Development that was established in 1980 had no established procedures or institutional memory. One official who was present at the creation of the Ministry of Lands said in an interview: "When the Ministry was established we had no files, no phones. Everything was new. . . . We had no idea what to do in the beginning. . . . Everyone asked, what are we supposed to do? It took us six months just to learn the issues." This institutional confusion was only natural for a new ministry assigned a complex task in the first chaotic months of independence.

Typical of the weakness and institutional confusion of the resettlement bureaucracy was the government's position on the deadline after which it would refuse to settle squatters. The government's first official position seems to have been that those squatting before November 1980 would be resettled but that no further squatting would be tolerated.[47] However, in the face of squatter pressure this deadline changed several times and there appears to have been considerable confusion within the government as to the exact cut-off date when squatters would no longer be accepted. For instance, in August of 1982 the Minister of Local Government and Town Planning stated that people squatting after June 1, 1982 would not be resettled while a Zimbabwe government press statement five months before had listed July 1981 as the squatter cut-off date.[48] Resettlement officers in the countryside point to the problems inherent to these deadlines as it is very difficult to determine just when a person started squatting, especially when the entire squatter community will vouch for him or her.

In practice, the deadlines at first did little to stop squatting. In December 1983, for instance, officials in the Department of Rural Development were complaining, in their words, that there was a "lack of political will to move back and/or halt the latest migration of squatters on the part of the government at large." As late as November 1986, the governor of the province hardest hit by squatting, Senator Dhube of Manicaland, was advocating, seemingly against government regulations, that resettlement be first for squatters. He said that more land had to be made available:

[Because] there has been talk of squatters—some 6,150 families which is about 37,000 people. These people are landless. They are in the wrong places—commercial farms, Forestry Commission land and even communal areas. We are asking Government to acquire land for resettlement as a priority. We can't move these people to nowhere.[49]

Yet, at the same time, the minister of local government, urban and rural development who actually supervises resettlement was stressing that land would only be bought for those who remained in the communal areas and that all squatters had to be returned to their own areas before they would be resettled.[50]

The institutional chaos present when the ministry was being formed often let squatters take over resettlement areas. As another official noted: "Our blunder was to buy land for squatters. But everything was being done without a plan. Our hands were being twisted by squatters." While procedures were being established, squatters were able to exert pressure on local officials and thereby ignore any regulations being set down by the Ministry's central office. One official recounted: "If a group identified itself as squatters, then they would be given a piece of land. . . . This was often done on an informal basis, often local resettlement officers would give them a piece of land." The pressure squatters placed on the weak government bureaucracy was incessant and often ingenious. Officials in Mashonaland recall that in one area the squatters were able to build a school and basic infrastructure and were even able to attract a foreign donor to aid them. Another squatter group in Mashonaland came to the Department of Rural Development and demanded, in the hope of legitimizing their claims, that the government's extension agency, AGRITEX, teach them contour plowing so they would not destroy the nation's resources.

Squatters also recognized that even when the situation in the resettlement bureaucracy became less confused they could still call on two sets of allies to strengthen their claims to land and thereby circumvent procedures established by the civil servants. First, many local branch chairmen of the ruling party, the Zimbabwe African National Union-Patriotic Front (ZANU-PF), provided significant encouragement to the squatters, and these officials often intimidated government officials. For instance, the ZANU-PF chairman of the Vumba region in the Eastern Highlands said while helping squatters to seize land:

We were waiting hungrily for this day. I am sure that when the farmers came to destroy our properties they had the backing of their government and I don't see why our Government should not back us. Now that we have come back to settle in our land they decide to call us squatters.[51]

Attempts to invoke the ruling party in order to give the squatters more leverage were common. A Manicaland resettlement officer recounted: "I am now used to meeting different delegations [of squatters] from different areas bringing in their grievances. Some even leave with me their donations for the new ZANU-PF headquarters."[52]

The alliance of squatters and local ZANU-PF officials created a powerful coalition that pressed squatter demands and intimidated the bureaucracy. For instance, a resettlement official in the Mashonaland region had to get the Zimbabwe Republic Police to arrest the local ZANU-PF leader and the local spirit medium for the day so the squatters in one area could be removed. Obviously, few government employees could be expected to face up to this combination of political forces.

The squatters were also, at first, able to call upon the national leadership in their effort to circumvent the bureaucracy. One resettlement official in an interview called the squatters "a force to be reckoned with" and said that they were quite articulate and skilled in gaining the support of the politicians. He described the typical pattern of politics in the countryside: "The politicians go to the squatters, hold rallies, call them the *povo* [the politically-charged Portuguese word used to describe the masses in Zimbabwe], and force government's hand to resettle them." For instance, when Senator Chief Kayisa Ndiweni instigated a group of his followers in Matabeleland South to squat, it was decided that the squatters would not be punished but, after screening, would be resettled. As one newspaper noted, "[Comrade] Mahachi could not punish the squatters by evicting them since it was Senator Ndiweni who instigated them into settling at the farms."[53] Resettlement officials across the country reported similar experiences.

The alliance of squatters and national leaders was possible, in part, because the government's own regulations gave the illegal settlers unusual direct access to the most powerful politicians in the country. According to the Ministry of Lands 1981 document, *Intensive Resettlement: Policies and Procedures*, when there is a squatter problem, "A meeting is held with the local people at which they are addressed by either the Minister or Deputy Minister of Lands, Resettlement and

Rural Development.''[54] In addition to the top leadership of the Lands Ministry, squatters often had access to other high ranking politicians. For instance, when Chief Chikwanda and 3,000 of his followers occupied farms in the Victoria East area of Victoria (now Masvingo) Province, they were addressed by Minister Mahachi (Lands) and Minister Zvobgo (then Local Government). The next day the deputy prime minister addressed the same group.[55]

An instructive example of squatter political pressure and the success it could bring with the help of national politicians occurred in what is known as the Angwa River Valley between Chinhoyi and Karoi in Mashonaland West. A 1983 report noted that the squatter problem was increasing there (though it was well past all government deadlines) and that the squatters were well organized:

> The leaders all appear to be self-proclaimed ZANU-PF local leaders. Many of them are said to be charging money for distributing the privately owned farmland among their followers. They also appear to see themselves as gaining political power and prestige through their action in encouraging the squatters to occupy farms. . . . Civil authorities refuse to even serve eviction warrants on the squatters for fear of violence.[56]

By 1985 the squatters were still occupying the area. The Deputy Minister of Lands, Mark Dube, had told the squatters they had to leave.[57] However, salvation in the form of another politician was soon to rescue the squatters and confirm that they had chosen the correct tactics. Zimbabwe's major newspaper, *The Herald*, in an article entitled, ''Mhangura Squatters Promised New Home,'' detailed the squatters' success:

> Squatters living along the Angwa River Valley near Mhangura are to be resettled before the onset of the rainy season. The Deputy Minister of Agriculture, Cde. [Comrade] S. Mombeshora, who is also the ZANU-PF candidate for Mahonde North . . . assured the squatters, estimated to be about 500 families, that the government had plans to resettle them, but there had to be adjustments to their settlements to accommodate development. . . . The squatters vowed to vote for ZANU-PF even if it meant travelling all the way to Harare to cast their vote. . . . Cde. Mombeshora said he was impressed by the squatters political consciousness and their desire to work with the ruling party.[58]

The article concluded by quoting the squatters to the effect that their talk with Deputy Minister Mombeshora was their "first amicable meeting with government."[59] Given the frequency of politicians aiding squatters to circumvent the bureaucracy, even the governor of Manicaland claimed that squatting occurs because people: "(listen) to the word of the politicians rather than the officials. The people hold to the politicians' promises, but there has been no coordination between this and the technical back-up of the officials."[60]

In contrast to the squatters who were repeatedly able to circumvent the young resettlement bureaucracy and who had access to influential politicians, the communal farmers who remained in their home areas had no effective way to pressure the government on the specific issue of gaining resettlement plots. The group representing the communal farmers, NFAZ, was and is ineffectual in pressuring the government because of its organizational problems, which make it difficult, if not impossible, for it to articulate local problems at the national level. A former permanent secretary in the ministry of Lands has noted that:

> probably one of the biggest problems of the NFAZ is poor communications within its structure. Within the districts there is lack of means of communication in the rural areas, lack of funds available to representatives to enable them to visit the clubs in their areas and some representatives are not very active.[61]

Even Robinson Gapare, president of the NFAZ, noted that "lack of communications between Government and communal farms is contributing to the squatter problem." He claimed that "in the absence of information about resettlement plans, rural farmers were beginning to think they were being neglected."[62] The squatters clearly saw the futility of waiting for the NFAZ to pressure the government so communal farmers might be aided and recognized the effectiveness of squatting as an alternative strategy. One newspaper article noted, "Squatters in the Karoi area have taken over an unoccupied farm because of growing impatience with government delays in resettling them."[63] The squatters described their move as "an act to draw the Government's attention to our plight."[64]

Another reason why communal farmers are unable to influence the government is because they face a very different institutional arrangement when trying to lobby the government. At the national level the problems of the NFAZ have already been discussed. Local action by communal farmers also does not seem to have the potential to be effective. The branch of the government that communal farmers have the most contact with is AGRITEX extension workers. However, as one AGRITEX official admitted in an interview, lobbying for farmers is not AGRITEX's job and "extension workers have no formal training in transmitting farmers' views." There is also still some suspicion of the extension workers on the part of some communal farmers because many of the government extension officials were also agents of agricultural policy under the white minority regime of Ian Smith. The only other government agency likely to be able to transmit communal farmers' concerns is the Department of Rural Development. However, it is clear from conversations with officials in that department that they do not respond to communal farmers' land demands. Provincial-level Department of Rural Development officials interviewed in all eight of Zimbabwe's provinces repeatedly said that they did not recommend that a certain piece of land be bought or that more land be acquired in a certain area because of communal farmer complaints. A typical attitude was expressed by one Mashonaland official who said that "we could possibly recommend which land should be bought but never have. I didn't want to take the initiative." The Ministry of Lands, which actually buys the land, does not have an institutional presence at the provincial level and, therefore, does not come into direct contact with communal farmers. Certainly at this point in time, Zimbabwe's institutional arrangements do not allow the communal farmers to have anywhere near the effective voice that the squatters have because the people remaining in the reserves are not provided with direct access to powerful politicians and are kept far from civil servants who make actual decisions concerning the purchase of land.

However, by 1986 the tide had probably turned against the squatters, not because of complaints by communal farmers, but because the resettlement bureaucracy had developed enough institutional resilience to resist squatters' political pressure. The government is now issuing even stronger warnings against squatters and seems more determined to stop illegal settlers. Provincial-level officials indicate now that the squatters are, in general, no longer able to jump the queue for resettlement plots. Of course, part of the reason squatters are no longer a major issue is because so many of them have been resettled. However, the Department of Rural Development's head office has also now had enough time to formulate concrete positions on resettlement, institutionalize procedures, and train personnel. As a result, it can now exert enough control over local operations so that formally stated practices can now be followed. Politicians also seem to be less successful in intervening for squatters as word filters through the government that circumvention of the bureaucracy will no longer be tolerated. Significantly, the 1985 second edition of *Intensive Resettlement: Policies and Procedures* no longer gives squatters automatic access to ministers.[65] In Manicaland, the government appears to be less successful in stemming the squatter problem but, in general, the squatters are not as powerful as before.

Why the Weak Succeeded:
Tactics, Political Goods, and Institutions

Three factors must be understood in order to explain the success of the supposedly weak squatters. First, as discussed above, the squatters' tactics of moving quickly against the resettlement bureaucracy and seeking allies in local ZANU-PF officials and some national politicians allowed them to circumvent effectively government procedures until the resettlement bureaucracy finally became strong enough to resist most squatter claims and limit bypasses to national politicians. The squatters' competitors, the communal farmers, in contrast, were unable to lobby successfully because the national organization that represents them could not successfully mobilize followers in the communal areas where its (potential) strength lies. Indeed, it is an interesting question if the NFAZ actually weakened the hand of communal farmers because the existence of a national organization might have discouraged communal farmers from taking local actions that might have made their claims more salient and drawn the attention of the national leadership.

However, it is important to note that two other factors were essential in allowing the squatters' tactics to succeed. First, the nature of land as a political good must be understood. Politics is often seen as the struggle for favor in the government's allocation of political goods. Unfortunately, too little attention is usually paid to the nature of the political good and how the characteristics of the political resource can affect the politics of state resource allocation. This is a particular problem when examining everyday forms of resistance because it is not necessarily the case that squatters and other weak groups are uniformly powerless across all issue-areas. Indeed, land in the political conflict examined here has important characteristics that actually aided the

nominally weak squatters. Specifically, the fact that physical possession of the land means, essentially, control over it, and that land can be
seized and put to use by individuals with few outside resources, is
exceptionally important in understanding the success of the squatters.
The squatters were able to win control of the resettlement plots because
when they moved in and were allowed to seize the plots they immediately had control over the land per se and the value that the land
produced.

Because land can simply be seized and thereby controlled, it is
dramatically different from other political goods that the government
allocates. For instance, health clinics need government expertise and
supplies to be productive and these requirements effectively prevent
local groups from playing a significant role in the siting of clinics.
Some groups in Zimbabwe have tried tactics much like the squatters
used to gain land to force the Ministry of Health into establishing
clinics in their part of the country. However, they have been unsuccess-
ful because gaining control over a resettlement plot gives a squatter
automatic victory in terms of control over the crop that the land pro-
duces; gaining control over another piece of land and declaring it a
clinic site means nothing unless the government agrees to provide the
equipment, staff, and supplies needed to make the clinic a reality. Thus,
it was reported that:

> . . . parents in the Mashyamombe area of Mhondoro communal
> lands, Chegutu district, have raised 7,000 dollars and molded 30,000
> bricks for building a clinic at Mutamba, but the project has hit a snag
> because the Ministry of Health has decided that the clinic should be
> built at Chanakira . . . the parents would have no choice but to
> withdraw the funds if the Ministry insisted that the clinic be built
> at Chanakira, a long distance from Mutamba. They would then use
> the bricks for building more classrooms at Govamombe Primary
> School.[66]

It is the nature of the political good that helps make the local groups
such as squatters so politically powerful on the land issue when other
groups have had very little influence in the determination of clinic
sites. During the dispute over land in Zimbabwe, possession essentially
meant victory while those who chose to stay in the communal areas lost
out in the political conflict for very understandable reasons. Given that
communal farmers lacked an effective national voice to convince the

government to stop the squatters, those who followed the law never had a chance.

Understanding the importance of the government's particular institutional structure is also essential to understanding why the tactics of the weak were successful. The squatters were more powerful than the communal farmers in this case because the institutional structure of the government was such that the type of political pressure they were able to exert was extraordinarily effective. The weak resettlement bureaucracy, the fact that government guidelines could be circumvented by top politicians, and the access to the national leadership that the institutionalized procedures gave to the squatters undermined the power of the civil servants who were trying to enforce the resettlement guidelines. The communal farmers, on the other hand, were faced with a government structure that did not allow them to effectively transmit their views. The central point is that political power cannot simply be judged in a vacuum by the organizational characteristics of the pressure group but must be assessed in light of the institutional arrangements on the part of the government that the pressure group is trying to influence. Different groups will have varying degrees of effectiveness in pressuring the government depending on how their organizational characteristics and tactics match up against the government's institutional framework. In the case examined here, the characteristics of the resettlement bureaucracy, especially poorly institutionalized procedures and the ability of national politicians to circumvent civil servants, allowed the squatters to be effective while preventing the communal farmers from exercising a significant political voice.

It would be a grave error to overestimate the political prospects of the weak simply because their tactics were successful for a period of time in this particular case. In Zimbabwe the squatters, assumed to be politically weak by their very nature, actually outperformed the communal farmers who were represented by the type of national organization normally associated with successful political influence. However, the squatters' tactics were only successful because of the nature of land as a political good and the particular institutional structure of Zimbabwe's resettlement bureaucracy. With a different type of political good and a stronger, more structured bureaucracy (such as the one that is beginning to emerge on the land issue) the weak would have done far less well on the land issue. Indeed, it is one of the stark realities of our time that the type of conditions that aided the weak in Zimbabwe are the exception rather than the rule.

Notes

1. A good review of the present program is program is provided by Sam Moyo, "The Land Question" in Ibbo Mandaza, ed., *The Political Economy of Transition* (Senegal: CONDESRIA, 1986).

2. The basic study remains Robin Palmer, *Land and Racial Domination in Rhodesia* (London: Heinemann, 1977). This study has been updated and sometimes challenged by, among others, John Godfrey Mutambara, "Africans and Land Policies: British Colonial Policy in Zimbabwe, 1890–1965," Ph.D. dissertation, University of Cincinnati, 1981; Malcolm L. Rifkind, "The Politics of Land in Rhodesia," M.Sc. thesis, University of Edinburgh, 1968; Henry V. Moyana, *The Political Economy of Land in Zimbabwe* (Gweru: Mambo Press, 1984); and Terrence Ranger, *Peasant Consciousness and Guerrilla War in Zimbabwe* (Harare: Zimbabwe Publishing House, 1985).

3. N. D. Mutizwa-Mangiza, *Community Development in Pre-Independence Zimbabwe* (Harare: University of Zimbabwe, 1985), p. 15.

4. John W. Harbeson, "Land and Rural Development in Independent Zimbabwe: A Preliminary Assessment" (Harare, 1981, mimeographed), p. 5.

5. *Ibid.*, p. 5.

6. Government of Zimbabwe, *Socio-Economic Review 1980–1985* (Harare: Government Printers, 1986), p. 210.

7. Robin Palmer, "The Agricultural History of Rhodesia" in Robin Palmer and Neil Parsons, eds., *The Roots of Rural Poverty in Central and Southern Africa* (London: Heinemann, 1977), p. 243.

8. All figures are from Harbeson, p. 5.

9. Roger Riddell, *The Land Question* (Gweru: Mambo Press, 1978), p. 7.

10. Central Statistical Office, *Statistical Yearbook 1985* (Harare: CSO, 1985), p. 132.

11. *Ibid.*, p. 132.

12. *Ibid.*, p. 132.

13. Whitsun Foundation, *Land Reform in Zimbabwe* (Harare: Whitsun Foundation, 1983), p. 26.

14. "Settling Debts before Peasants," *Moto*, September 1983, p. 17.

15. Robert Mugabe, *ZANU(PF) 1980 Election Manifesto* (Salisbury: ZANU[PF], 1979).

16. *Herald*, 29 October 1981.

17. Commission of Inquiry into Incomes, Prices and Conditions of Service (Riddell Commission), *Report of the Commission of Inquiry into Incomes, Prices and Conditions of Service* (Harare: Government Printers, 1981), p. 57.

18. Whitsun Foundation, p. 38.

19. Mutambara, pp. 107–108.

20. David Lan, *Guns and Rain: Guerrillas and Spirit Mediums in Zimbabwe* (Harare: Zimbabwe Publishing House, 1985), p. 148.

21. *Ibid.*, p. 121.

22. B. H. Kinsey, "Emerging Policy Issues in Zimbabwe's Land Resettlement Programmes," *Development Policy Review* 1 (November 1983), p. 170.

23. Government of Zimbabwe, *Transitional National Development Plan*, Vol. 1 (Harare: Government Printer, 1982), p. 66.

24. Government of Zimbabwe, 1986, p. 127.

25. Government of Zimbabwe, *First Five-Year National Development Programme* (Harare: Government Printers, 1986), p. 28.

26. Zimbabwe Information Service, "Press Statement," 10 February 1983.

27. E. M. Chiviya, "Land Reform in Zimbabwe: Policy and Implementation," Ph.D. dissertation, Indiana University, 1982, p. 165.

28. *Ibid.*, p. 218.

29. Department of Rural Development, *Intensive Resettlement: Policies and Procedures* (Harare: Department of Rural Development, 1985), pp. 23–24.

30. Bill Kinsey, "Resettlement: The Settlers' View," *Social Change and Development* 7 (1984): 2.

31. *Moto*, September 1983, p. 17.

32. *Herald*, 7 September 1982.

33. *Herald*, 8 August 1984.

34. See, for instance *Herald*, 2 July 1983.

35. See, for instance, Michael Bratton, "The Comrades in the Countryside: The Politics of Agricultural Policy in Zimbabwe," *World Politics* 49 (January 1987): 192.

36. See, for instance, Chiviya, p. 235.

37. *Herald*, 16 October 1981.

38. Whitsun Foundation, p. 153.

39. "Squatters: Our Land was Stolen from Us," *Moto*, July 1982: 7.

40. *Herald*, 8 May 1982.

41. *Zimbabwe Information Service*, 24 November 1981.

42. *Sunday Mail*, 8 November 1981.

43. *Herald*, 20 October 1979.

44. Ranger, p. 307.

45. *Sunday Mail*, 2 August 1981.

46. Ranger, p. 314.

47. *Herald*, 8 November 1980.

48. Compare *Chronicle*, 23 August 1982 and *Zimbabwe Government Press Statement*, 4 March 1982.

49. *Sunday Mail*, 30 November 1986.

50. *Herald*, 20 September 1986.

51. *Sunday Mail*, 3 January 1981.

52. *Herald*, 20 September 1982.

53. *Chronicle*, 10 September 1982.

54. Ministry of Lands, Resettlement and Rural Development, *Intensive Resettlement: Policies and Procedures* (Salisbury: Ministry of Lands, Resettlement and Rural Development, 1981), p. 10.

55. *Sunday Mail*, 30 August 1981.

56. *Financial Gazette*, 22 December 1983.

57. *Herald*, 25 June 1985.

58. *Ibid.*

59. *Ibid.*

60. *Herald*, 1 December 1986.

61. L. T. Chitsike, "Agricultural Cooperative Development in Zimbabwe" (Harare, 1986, mimeographed), p. 182.

62. *Herald*, 22 April 1981.

63. *Sunday Mail*, 30 August 1981.

64. *Ibid.*

65. Department of Rural Development, p. 25.

66. *Herald*, 26 November 1986.

Commentary

Milton J. Esman

In *Weapons of the Weak* James Scott has exposed and highlighted for further analysis and evaluation an important dimension of peasant politics. But, as Scott himself suggests in his chapter in this volume, the tactics of nonconfrontational resistance are not limited to peasants. There is extensive reporting of methods historically employed by American slaves, from feigned ignorance and stupidity to malingering, foot dragging *à la* "step'n fetchit," extravagant deference and flattery, and cutting humor by which they attempted to mitigate the harsh material and psychological realities of their subordinate and powerless status.[1] Two generations ago industrial sociologists discovered what every worker on the factory floor had long understood—the methods by which workers informally resist the industrial speedup by establishing and enforcing among their fellows work rates that they consider "reasonable."[2] The "good soldier Schweik" exemplifies the elegant and cunning way that a private soldier can devise to comply with the literal requirements of military discipline, while preserving his own skin and protecting his own interests.[3] The dismal performance of Soviet collective agriculture over a half-century attests to the stubborn foot dragging skills of Russian peasants, in contrast to the remarkable productivity they have achieved on their small private plots.[4]

There is no need to multiply examples. The phenomenon is so pervasive that it can be posited as a universal tendency. There are common methods by which weaker groups in any society attempt to protect themselves against the exactions, material and psychological, of those who are institutionally more powerful than they, to lighten the material toll of exploitation and the symbolic burdens of subordination, to achieve some minimal autonomy and control over their lives where the main rules that govern their everyday existence are made and enforced by others. These weapons of the weak and the methods by which they are employed appear to have the following common properties wherever they are employed:

1. These weapons can be material or ideological. If material, they attempt to reduce the labor required or increase the share of the product available to workers, their families, and kinfolk. If ideological, they seek to shame and thereby deter the exploiter, to justify infractions of the rules, or to sustain the morale of the subordinate group.

2. The tactics employed tend to be individual and unorganized, but they depend for their effectiveness on silent complicity and support. This informal group solidarity serves as a substitute for formal organization, but the common understandings that underlie this behavior can be and indeed are enforced against potential violators from within the community by social sanctions that can be extremely harsh and do not exclude intimidation and violence against persons or property.

3. These weapons are deliberately nonconfrontational in style and nonrevolutionary in their goals. Instead of challenging existing structures and rules, they seek to mitigate their impact and improve the terms of exchange for the weaker party within prevailing institutional arrangements.

Specific tactics depend on the context, but the methods can be sufficiently identified and generalized to qualify as significant expressions of nonformal, unorganized politics. These are not merely random assertions of individual interests or individual defenses against unfair and unequal treatment. What make this behavior a form of politics are tacit understandings within the community of the disadvantaged that sanction, protect, and, where necessary, enforce these patterns of resistance. It is this solidarity that confounds and frequently compels more powerful individuals and groups to acquiesce in these tactics because they have no means to combat them directly and the costs of attempting to defeat them would be too high. The collective character of this behavior qualifies it as a form of politics, real though nonformal, and makes it interesting to political scientists and political sociologists.

It is no small achievement to have identified and elaborated these methods of resistance as patterned expressions of politics. They are certainly worth examining for their intrinsic interest. In this respect they are similar to tactics employed in other political contexts, for example, election campaigns or interest group lobbying. How politically useful instruments are mobilized and deployed is an important and legitimate subject of inquiry, as they vary from the crude to the subtle and the effective to the futile. But eventually the focus must move beyond description to evaluation and explanation. Broader and deeper questions must be asked about the significance of this style of nonformal politics for the weaker parties who employ these methods, for the elites who are their targets, and for the polities in which these conflicts unfold. What can be hypothesized about the potentials and the limitations, about the effectiveness and the consequences of this style of politics? Some of these questions are raised and addressed by the contributors to this volume. They need to be further developed conceptually and empirically. To facilitate this task several questions are suggested here that attempt to extend this inquiry more systematically beyond the tactics themselves.

The first question is this: what is the threshold beyond which avoidance tactics, such as foot dragging, pilfering, and rumor mongering become confrontational and represent a direct challenge to established authority? Nathan Brown's essay in this volume reports an epidemic of assassinations in Egypt of local officials and agents of the state by seemingly unorganized laborers. And Scott points to desertion from the military as an example of nonconfrontational defiance of authority. Yet, no government that intends to maintain its authority could afford to ignore or countenance such challenges as the assassination of its officials or desertion from its armed services. Those who commit these offenses surely recognize the differences between these acts of challenge and the defiance and behavior of the peasants Scott describes in northwest Malaysia or the tactics of Schweik who never contemplated desertion.

Between tactics of more or less passive, defensive, nonviolent resistance and revolutionary violence there are several stages of disobedience, protest, and guerrilla activity. Those acts that are organized and represent direct and explicit challenges to political authority have been treated extensively in the literature.[5] The quieter and subtler forms of resistance are the focus of Scott's attention and the original contribution of this volume. If this is, indeed, a distinctive style of resistance, then for analytical purposes this category must have a boundary. Variables that might be useful in drawing that boundary could include the degree of formal organization, the incidence of physical violence, and the level of confrontational rhetoric. Some behavior, such as the assassination of officials discussed by Brown or the large-scale burning of state forests described by Ramachandra Guha, raises questions about that boundary. Beyond some as yet undefined line lies the realm of antiregime activity that directly challenges the authority of the state.

The second question that extends this analysis beyond mere tactics focuses on the targets of these weapons: does it matter whose authority they are attempting to disarm or resist? In some cases the targets are economic powerholders—landlords or factory owners; in others they are the state and its agents. Normally, as among the peasants Scott studied, the poor and the weak understand all too well that local economic elites can call upon the repressive apparatus of the state for support when they feel challenged. Therefore tactics of resistance must be calibrated, fine-tuned, to neutralize or avert this threat. But there are reports in this volume of local elites protecting the peasantry against the exactions of the state, for local elites may harbor their own grievances against the state and they must live their everyday lives in close proximity to the poor who greatly outnumber them. And there are cases where governments or national politicians are available, for a limited time at least, to vindicate the rights of the poor against abuses by local economic elites. Such shifting alliances in post-revolutionary Zimbabwe are outlined by Jeffrey Herbst in this volume. How are these different dispositions of forces likely to affect the choice of tactics by the weak and their effectiveness? These possibilities need to be sorted out.

A third question: under what circumstances can nonformal, defensive tactics be escalated or transformed into revolutionary challenges, into efforts not merely to make the prevailing dispensation more tolerable at the margins, but to change basic structures and rules? Given the vulnerabilities they encounter whenever they directly challenge the "system," the weak can be expected to choose tactics that minimize their risk and that avoid overt protest and collective action such as land seizures, factory sit-ins, or public demonstrations. They will rely on more cautious tactics until (1) a force emerges, usually from outside the community, that is able to help them articulate their common grievances and organize them for collective defense, *and* (2) the state loses the capacity, as in Russia in 1917, or the nerve, as in France in 1789, to turn aside these challenges.[6] At times the machinery of the state may fall into the hands of politicians who are willing to support the weak in some of their demands or are unprepared to turn the repressive organs of the state against them. Institutional reforms and revolutionary changes may produce significant gains, such as land redistribution or civil rights, for subordinate groups. Sooner or later, however, emergent elites consolidate state power in a new or reformed social order where some will be politically and economically strong and the majority relatively weak; rules will be established and enforced, and the cycle of everyday resistance will be renewed in a different context. In the meantime, however, revolutionary action is not impossible, and historically it has produced fundamental improvements. Under what conditions can the everyday tactics of defensive resistance be converted into more positive assertions of group interest?

The final question goes to the bottom line: how effective are the tactics of avoidance and defense that are elaborated in this volume? Within limits they may ease the burdens of the weak and the disadvantaged, achieving thereby a more tolerable accommodation to harsh realities than would be possible in default of these tactics. And where organized methods of protest and bargaining through unions, associations, or political movements are denied them, nonformal tactics of resistance that evade the control of their superiors are the only resources reasonably available to prudent people who are disinclined to risk martyrdom or suicide. But having "discovered" these weapons, should there be any illusions about what they can accomplish? Do they significantly reduce the vulnerability of the weak or improve the terms of their struggle?

Peasants, most of whom are located today in Third World countries, are highly vulnerable to two sets of forces identified by Jacek Kochanowicz in his essay: technological change and population growth. The effect of much modern technology is to reduce the demand for labor; the effect of rapid population growth is to increase its supply. As the availability of labor increases in relation to land and as capital substitutes for labor in the production and processing of agricultural commodities, the bargaining power of the poor and the weak is eroded. As more and more of them become economically redundant in agriculture, their ability to defend their interests by nonformal tactics correspondingly declines. This reality is not lost on landowners and employers. Indeed they often mechanize, substituting capital for labor, even when this achieves no cost advantages, in order to reduce their dependency on tenants or workers and thereby dispense with troublesome and annoying demands from subordinates and clients.[7] How effective can malingering, petty pilfering, character assassination, even Luddite tactics be under these conditions?

The historical evidence is not reassuring. When determined elites with the support or acquiescence of the state undertake a course of action in their own interest, they are usually able to nullify the nonconfrontational tactics of the weak and reduce them to futility or irrelevance. The weapons of the weak that had long been known to and applied by British peasants proved utterly useless against the enclosure movement in eighteenth-century England and against the brutal Highlands Clearances and the displacement of the Irish peasantry in nineteenth-century Scotland and Ireland, respectively.[8] Nor could similar tactics, including those discovered by twentieth-century industrial sociologists, prevent or even delay the current epidemic of factory closings in the United States by multinational firms transferring their operations to low-wage countries, though these closings devastate the lives of hundreds of thousands of factory workers and reduce their communities to ghost towns.[9]

The informal, unorganized, nonconfrontational weapons of the weak can be effective as long as their services are required and cannot be dispensed with. The economic indispensability of the poor appears to constitute their real, though unequal, bargaining strength, thus the necessary condition for the effectiveness of nonconfrontational methods of resistance. These are gradually less useful as competition for tenancies and employment becomes more intense. As landowners in Malaysia became less dependent on Scott's hosts and neighbors, traditional tactics of defense and resistance became increasingly irrelevant. These peasants were indeed compensated, but only in part, because another sector of the elites, the ruling political party, continued to need their votes. This, however, had little to do with the utility of their defensive tactics. These forms of minor civil disobedience may be useful where a weak state, such as the embattled regime in Nicaragua, as described by Forrest Colburn, is unable to compel compliance or unwilling directly to confront groups that it counts among its constituents. Under normal conditions an effective state, supporting determined economic elites, can override such tactics at minor cost.

It is an axiom of contemporary political thought that the weak can be empowered only when they succeed in capitalizing on their superior numbers by organization—cultural, economic, or political.[10] But effective organization is likely, sooner or later, to produce confrontational tactics. Such tactics are inherently risky and dangerous even when they are nonviolent, but they have nevertheless been attempted by many subordinated and disadvantaged groups historically and in our time. These methods are, however, excluded by definition from the everyday, but inherently defensive armory that is the distinctive focus of this book.

Without confrontational choices, the weak seem to be left with two options. The first is the possibility of exit, to depart the scene as thousands of peasants have done every day during the past few decades, in search of better opportunities.[11] This is the optimistic expectation of growth economics: by individual initiative and enterprise that avoids the need for collective action or for confrontation, those who are displaced by advancing technology or demographic growth can find employment in the expanding modern economy. Thus economic growth can create employment faster than the expansion of the labor force, improve the market situation for job seekers, and thus yield higher material rewards than were available in the areas from which they migrated. Everybody benefits. This pattern of economic growth has indeed created millions of jobs in Third World countries; it has transformed the material lives of whole societies in such countries as South Korea, Taiwan, and Singapore and has benefited large numbers on all continents. But the hard truth is that in most Third World societies the growth of job opportunities in the modern sectors is running behind the expansion of the labor force, especially where technological change simultaneously reduces employment in primary production and processing. Despite continuing migration to urban centers and indeed across international borders, the rural areas of most Third World countries will have to accommodate still larger populations during the next several decades at least. As opportunities for exit become realistically available only to the most enterprising minority, the majority who remain are left with only one nonconfrontational option: continued reliance on the weapons of the weak to eke out marginally better accommodations to harsh realities under increasingly unfavorable conditions entirely beyond their control.

This is the tragedy of Third World peasantry in our era, and of their sons and daughters in urban shantytowns, as economic growth stagnates and populations continue to increase, while at the same time governments strengthen their capacity to control protest. This harsh reality leaves the sympathetic reader with a nagging question: under these conditions, and in the absence of organization or violent confrontation, how effective are the weapons of the weak and the powerless?

Identifying these weapons, detailing how they are activated and deployed is an interesting, sophisticated, and hitherto understudied aspect of lower-class politics, a universal phenomenon which Scott's work and this volume have done much to remedy. The evidence reported in this book demonstrates that under some conditions such unorthodox tactics of struggle can make a difference, can successfully defend peasants and other subordinate groups from exactions by the more powerful and cause the latter to back off. But no set of tactics, however imaginative and cunning, can be effective under all conditions. What remains to be clarified are the circumstances under which these low-risk tactics are likely to yield positive benefits for those who employ them. Where these favorable conditions do not prevail, subordinates may nevertheless have collective options other than submission. They may resort to the more conventional, confrontational, higher risk tactics and weapons that have enabled some subordinate groups, as Forrest Colburn observes in the introduction to this volume, to become agents of historical change.

Notes

1. Robert Fogel and Stanley Engerman, *Time on the Cross: The Economics of Negro Slavery* (Lanham, Md.: University Press of America, 1985).

2. F. J. Roethlisberger and W. J. Dickson, *Management and the Worker: Technical vs. Social Organization in an Industrial Plant* (Cambridge, Mass.: Harvard University Graduate School of Business Administration, 1939). See also William F. Whyte et al., *Money and Motivation* (New York: Harper and Brothers, 1955).

3. Jaroslav Hafsek, *The Good Soldier, Schweik* (New York: The New American Library, 1963).

4. Stefan Hedland, *Crisis in Soviet Agriculture* (New York: St. Martins Press, 1984).

5. Mostafa Rajai, *The Comparative Study of Revolutionary Strategy* (New York: David McKay, 1977). Also the classics on revolution, Crane Brinton, *The Anatomy of Revolution* (New York: Vintage Books, 1965) and Hannah Arendt, *On Revolution* (New York: Viking, 1963).

6. On Russia, Leonard Schapiro, *The Russian Revolution of 1917: The Origins of Modern Communism* (New York: Basic Books, 1984). On France, Alexis de Tocqueville, *The Old Regime and the French Revolution* (New York: Doubleday-Anchor books, 1955).

7. Milton J. Esman, *Landlessness and Near-Landlessness in Developing Countries* (Ithaca, N.Y.: Cornell University, Rural Development Committee, 1978).

8. On the English enclosures, W. H. R. Curtler, *Enclosure and Redistribution of Our Land* (Oxford: The Clarendon Press, 1920). Also Royal Commission on Common Land, *Report* (London: HMSO Cmnd 462, 1958). On the Scottish Highland Clearances, I. F. Grant, *The Economic History of Scotland* (New York, Longmans Green and Co., 1934). Also, John Prebble, *The Highland Clearances* (London: Sekler and Warburg, 1963). On the Irish famine and its aftermath, C. B. Woodham Smith, *The Great Hunger, Ireland 1845-49* (New York: Harper & Row, 1962). Also William Dudley Edwards and T. Desmond Williams, eds., *The Great Famine: Studies in Irish History, 1845-52* (Dublin: Browne and Nolan, 1956).

9. Barry Bluestone and Bennett Harrison, *The Deindustrialization of America* (New York: Basic Books, 1982). Also John Zysman and Stephen Cohen, *Manufacturing Matters: The Myth of the Post-industrial Economy* (New York: Basic Books, 1987).

10. See Milton J. Esman and Norman T. Uphoff, *Local Organizations: Intermediaries in Rural Development* (Ithaca: Cornell University Press, 1984).

11. Albert Hirschman, *Exit, Voice, and Loyalty* (Cambridge, Mass.: Harvard University Press, 1970).

INDEX

Acuña, Cosme R., 139
Adas, Michael, 107–108
Aesopian language, 29
Agrarian resistance to state socialism, 15–20
AGRITEX (Zimbabwe), 211, 215
Aguilar, Federico, 124
Al-Ahram (newspaper), 96, 101, 102n, 104
Al-Babli, Muhammad, 96, 101–104
Allende Gossens, Salvador, 175
Almora and Almora district (India), 71, 76, 77, 79–82
Al-Mugattam (newspaper), 102n
Ambiguous messages, 25–26
Angwa River Valley, 213
Anhui Province (China), 166
Arson
    euphemisms for, 26
    in Himalayan forests, 65, 75–76, 81–85
Association of Farm Workers (ATC; Nicaragua), 179
Asyut province (Egypt), 116
Atomistic activity, definition of, 94–95
Avoidance protest, 67, 86, 223. *See also* Everyday forms of resistance
Ayrout, Henry, 93

Babli. *See* Al-Babli, Muhammad
Bageshwar (India), 79–81
Balzac, Honoré de, 29–30
Bandits, 23, 108
Bareilly (India), 70
Bhotiya herdsmen, 67
"Black" Act, 9

Bloch, Marc, 13
Bourgeoisie, in 18th-century Eastern Europe, 58
Brazil, 125
"Brer Rabbit," 25–26
Brinton, Crane, 191
Brown, Nathan, xi, 93–121, 223
Buhayra province (Egypt), 116

Captain Swing, 24, 25
Carrión, Luis, 191
Catholic Church, in Colombia, 131, 132, 135–37
Chamorro, Pedro Joaquín, 179
Chayanov, A. V., 36, 40
Chikwanda, Chief, 213
Chile, Allende's rural support in, 175
China
    Cultural Revolution in, 158–59
    decollectivization in, 152–53, 162–70
    everyday forms of resistance in, 153, 154, 157, 159–61, 169
    gender relations in, 143
    Great Leap Forward in, 4, 16, 156–58
    local rural bureaucracy in, 154–55, 162
    new legal code in, 163
    1960–62 famine in, 155
    peasant resistance to collectivization in, xii, 16–17, 154–56, 157–62, 177
    poaching in, 157
    pre-1966 struggles over land in, 156–57
Chipko movement (Tree Hugging movement), 64, 78
Chiviya, E. M., 203, 204

Civil War, U.S., 13–14
Class struggle
  Chinese emphasis on, 154
  everyday forms of resistance in, ix–x, 5, 7–8, 21–23
  in Polish peasant studies, 36–37, 57
Cobb, R. C., 14
Coffee plantations. *See* Colombia
Cohen, Sandy, 99
Colburn, Forrest D., ix–xv, 175–97, 199, 226, 228
Collective public action, 28
Colombia
  Communist-led movement in, 141, 142
  contraband economy in, 139
  everyday forms of resistance in, 127–29
  "hot country" of, 124, 125
  paternalism in, 126, 129–30, 133, 136, 140, 142
  plantation tenancy in, 125–30, 140
  sex and family life in, xi–xii, xiv, 123–24, 130–44
  traditional native gender relationships in, 131
  workers' leagues and unions in, 126, 130, 138, 141, 143
Commercial logging. *See* Forest management
Confederate Army, desertions from, 14
Confrontation
  in Colombian coffee plantations, 127
  danger of tactics of, 226
  everyday resistance contrasted to, 28, 109, 222
  state generally favored by, 19
  when avoidance protest becomes, 67
Conspiracy of silence, x, 222
  of Egyptian peasantry, xi, 93, 98–99, 109–15, 117, 119
Corvée. *See* Forced labor (corvée)
Cossack uprisings, 55
Credit and Service Cooperatives (CCS; Nicaragua), 184
Cromer, Lord (Evelyn Baring), 95–96
Cundinamarca department (Colombia), 123, 132

Decentralization, 3
Dehradun (India), 71
del Corral, Jesús, 122–23, 126, 132, 134, 137
"Democratic patriarchy," 143
Deng Xiaoping, 16, 152–54, 168, 170
Desertion from the army, 13–14, 223
Development, use of term, 3–4
Dhube, Senator, 210
Dible, W. C., 79–81
Diggers, 28
Disguises, 25–26, 27
Divisional Forest Officer (DFO), 69, 75
Dube, Mark, 203, 209, 213
DuBois, W. E. B., 21
Duchy of Warsaw, 54, 63

Egypt
  alienation of peasants in, 112–15
  attacks on railroads in, 104–105
  conspiracy of silence in, xi, 93, 98–99, 109–15, 117, 119
  crop destruction and vandalism by peasants in, 104
  everyday forms of resistance in, 105–107
  expansion of state in, 97–98
  newspaper reports of crime in, 100
  peasant atomistic action in, xi, 93–104, 107–109, 114–19
  peasant attacks on officials' reputations in, 104
  peasants' rejection of the state in, 117–18
  reports of atomistic action in, by year, 102–103
England
  enclosure movement in, 226
  poaching in, 9
English Revolution, 28
Esman, Milton J., 221–28
Everbright Commune (China), 158, 161
Everyday forms of resistance, ix–x, 3–30, 94–95
  agrarian resistance to state socialism, 15–20
  in Colombia, 127–29

in Communist China, 153, 154, 157, 159–61, 169
cumulative effects of, 118
definition of, 7–8, 23–24, 223–24
desertion from the army, 13–14, 223
effectiveness of, 225–26
of Egyptian peasants, 105–107
of Himalayan peasants, 66, 70–71, 75–77, 81–84
after Nicaraguan Revolution, 176, 188
poaching, 9–10, 22, 26, 29–30, 157
of Polish peasants, 37, 45, 48–55
possible escalation of, 224–25
tacit cooperation needed for, 108
tax resistance, 10–13
three common properties of, 222
written record evaded by, 20–21

Fayyum province (Egypt), 116–17
Forced labor (corvée)
in Colombia, 128–29, 141
of Himalayan peasants, 70–73, 80
Forest management
basic requirements of, 73–74
establishment of, in Kumaun, 69–70
Himalayan peasant resistance to, 64, 65, 74–87
Foucault, Michel, 9
France
desertions after Revolution in, 14
peasant resistance to Catholic tithe in, 13
poaching in, 9–10
French Revolution, prehistory of, 29
FSLN (Sandinista Front for National Liberation), 175, 179, 181, 182, 192–93
Fujian Province (China), 159

Gairola, Taradutt, 73
Gandhi, Mohandas K. ("Mahatma"), 79–81
Gapare, Robinson, 214
Garhwal district (India), 71, 75, 80, 81, 84, 85
Garhwali regiments, 68, 73, 76, 84

Gender
in China, 143
in Colombia, 123–24, 130–44
Genovese, Eugene, 21
Gestures, political, 26, 30
Gorbachev, Mikhail S., 19
Gramsci, Antonio, 36
Grass-roots initiatives, 3
Guangdong Province (China), 159
Guatemala, 125
Guha, Ramachandra, xi, 64–92, 223
Gutiérrez de Pineda, Virginia, 136

Hapsburg Empire, Polish peasant compared to that of, 44, 57
Herbst, Jeffrey, xiii, 198–220, 224
Hettner, Alfred, 124–25
Himalayan, peasant resistance. *See* Kumaun Division
Hirschman, Albert, 26
Hobsbawm, Eric, 21, 82, 108
Honduras, 190
Hunan Province (China), 159
Hungary, peasant resistance in, 17–18
Husayn Kamil, Prince (*later* Sultan), 96
"Hush arbors," 27

India
Himalayan peasant resistance in. *See* Kumaun Division (Himalaya)
right of revolt in, 78
Indian National Congress, 66, 80
International Fund for Agricultural Development (IFAD), 185
Ireland, 19th-century, 226
Islamic tithe, Malaysian peasant resistance to, 10–12

Jiménez, Michael F., xi–xii, 122–50

Kamshush (Egypt), 113
Kerkvliet, Benedict J. Tria, 118
Kersten (writer), 56
Khalifa, Ahmad Muhammad, 114
Kochanowicz, Jacek, x–xi, 34–59, 225
Kollataj, Hugo, 48
Kula, Witold, 48, 51
Kumaun Division (Himalaya)

ecological zones of, 67
forced labor in, 70–73
peasant resistance in, xi, 64, 65, 70–87
sociology of peasants of, 68, 85–87
traditional administration of, 67–68
Kumaun Forest Grievances Committee, 72, 84
Kumaun Parishad, 71, 78–79, 81, 86

Ladurie, Emmanuel LeRoy, 13
Lam, David, 202
Land Apportionment Act of 1930 (LAA; Zimbabwe), 200
Land Tenure Act of 1969 (Zimbabwe), 200
La Prensa (Nicaraguan newspaper), 179
Les Demoiselles, 24
Logging, commercial. *See* Forest management
Luddite tactics, 225

Mahachi, Moven, 209, 213
Malaysia, 226
Islamic tax resistance in, 10–12
Mao Zedong, 153, 158, 168
Marxism, Polish, peasant studies in, 35–37
Masked men, 24, 25
MIDINRA (Nicaragua), 192
Minufiyya province (Egypt), 106, 110
Miskito Indians, 190
Mit Tamama (Egypt), 113
Modernization, meaning of, xv
Mombeshora, S., 213–14
Moore, Barrington, Jr., xv
Mouse-deer (Malaysian culture), 26
Mugabe, Robert, 201
Murder
by Egyptian peasantry, xi, 93, 96, 99–104, 110–12, 116–17
revenge for, in Egypt, 114

Nahhas, Yusif, 105
Naini Tal (India), 71, 75, 76, 82
Nanjing (China), 156, 158–60, 163–67
National Enterprise for Basic Foodstuffs (ENABAS; Nicaragua), 186–87

National Farmers Association of Zimbabwe (NFAZ), 203, 204, 214
Native Purchase Areas (Zimbabwe), 200, 201
Ndebele people, 200
Ndiweni, Chief Kayisa, 212
New Economic Policy (USSR), 18
Nicaraguan Revolution
agricultural self-sufficiency and, 190
brevity of fighting in, 179
cooperatives after, 184–86, 189–90, 192
counterrevolution against, 190–93
everyday forms of resistance after, 176, 188
inflation after, 180, 182–83
labor problems after, 181–83, 194
land reform after, 191–92
peasant misery before, 177–78
peasant responses to, xii, xiv, 175–77, 193–95
rural Nicaragua immediately after, 179–81
urban base of, 189–90

Pande, Badridutt, 79, 81, 82, 84
Pant, Hargovind, 80
Participatory development, 3
Pastora, Eden, 190
Patnak, Shekhar, 79, 80
Peasant heroes, 23, 27
Peasant rebellions
infrequency of, 66
romanticization of, xiv
Peasants. *See also* specific countries; topics
as change agents, xv
definition of, ix
population growth and, 225
subculture of, 22–24, 27
technological change and, 225
People's Communes (China), 155, 156–57
Poaching, 9–10, 22, 26, 29–30, 157
Poland
absence of absolutist state in, 34, 44, 57
18th-century peasant resistance in,

x–xi, 34–35, 42, 44–59
estate farming in, 38–39
lords' monopolies in, 50–51
Marxist studies of peasantry of, 35–37
peasant economy in, 40–42
peasant emancipation in, 58–59
Referendary Court in, 43, 46, 49, 52, 54, 56
"second serfdom" in, 38
village government in, 42–43
Political action. *See also* Everyday forms of resistance
changes in forms of, 28–29
hidden realm of, 4–8
Poniatowski, Primate, 52
Prosperity Commune (China), 160
Prussia, Polish peasantry compared to that of, 44

Qina province (Egypt), 109

Railway sleepers, 69, 70, 81
Ramsay, Henry, 67, 68, 71, 86
Rebecca Riots, 24
Red Flag Commune (*later* Red Flag Township, China), 156–60, 164–67
Red Flower of Tequendama, 141
Religious myths, 23
Resin tapping, 69, 70, 81, 82, 84
Resistance. *See also* Everyday forms of resistance
paired forms of, 5–6
symbolic (or ideological), 8
tax, 10–13
Rev, Istvan, 18
Revolutions
failure of, 3–4
prehistory of, 29
Riaño, Leonilde, 141
Riddell Commission (Zimbabwe), 202
Robinson, Armstead, 13–14
Rural poor. *See* Peasants
Russell Pasha, Sir Thomas, 96, 110, 116
Russia. *See also* USSR
Cossack uprisings in, 55
Polish peasantry compared to that of, 44
Russian Revolution, Czarist desertions in, 14

Safay (Egypt), 104–105
Sandinista Agriculture Cooperative (CAS; Nicaragua), 184
Sandinista Workers Federation (CST; Nicaragua), 182
Sarofeen, Chalaby, 106
Schweikian forms of resistance, 5, 221, 223
Scotland, 19th-century, 226
Scott, James C., ix–x, 3–33, 37–38, 66–67, 94–95, 108, 112, 123, 142, 153, 157, 199, 221, 223, 226
Scott, Joan, 124
Sennett, Richard, 129
Shakti (weekly paper), 79
Sharqiyya province (Egypt), 106
Sholokhov, Mikhail, 18
Shona people, 200, 202
Sichuan Province (China), 161, 166
Silence. *See* Conspiracy of silence
Smith, Ian, 215
Spanish Civil War, 175
revolutionary exhumations in, 27–28
Spirituals, 26
Sputnik Brigade, Eternal Happiness Commune (China), 158, 160, 163–64
Squatters, 6, 25
in Zimbabwe, 6, 198–99, 203–204, 206–18
Stacey, Judith, 143
Stalin, Joseph, 18
State socialism, agrarian resistance to, 15–20
Subaltern Studies school, 66
Subordinate groups, politics of, 24–26
Suez Canal Zone, 105–106

Tax resistance, 10–13
Third World (developing countries)
massive peasant noncompliance in, 14
peasants in anti-colonial movements of, 65–66
population growth in, 227
post-revolutionary regimes in, 193
state-centric research on, 176
Thompson, E. P., 10
Thompson, Paul, 144

"Til Eulenspiegel," 25
Totashiling (India), 81
Traill, G. W., 68
Tree Hugging movement (Chipko movement), 64, 78
  Gandhian ethic in, 64
Trelawny, Bishop Jonathan, 3
Tribal Trust Lands (TTLs; Zimbabwe), 200, 210
Tricksters, 25–26

United Provinces (*later* Uttar Pradesh; UP), 80
United States
  Civil War desertions in, 13–14
  contemporary factory closings in, 226
  slave uprisings vs. everyday resistance in, 7
USSR (Soviet Union). *See also* Russia
  collectivization in, 4
  peasant resistance in, 18–19, 221
Uttaraini fair, 79–81, 83

Vasquez, Waldimira, 143
Vergara y Velasco, José, 125
Viotá coffee plantations (Colombia), 123, 124, 126, 130–31, 134, 139, 141–44

Warnken, Philip, 177

Weapons of the weak. *See* Everyday forms of resistance
Weber, Max, 78
Wheelock, Jaime, 183, 188
Whitsun Foundation, 207
Workers' resistance to speed-up, 221
"World Upside Down" broadsheets, 26
World War I
  in Egypt, 106
  Kumaun in, 70, 73, 76
Wyndham, Percy, 73, 76, 82

Zakat, Malaysian peasant resistance to, 10–12
Zamindars, 85
ZANU-PF (Zimbabwe), 211–12, 216
Zhejiang Province (China), 167
Zimbabwe
  colonial land policy in, 200
  government resettlement policy in, 203–207, 210–11, 215–16
  Lancaster House Constitution for, 209
  native reserves (communal lands) in, 198, 200, 206
  squatters in, 6, 198–99, 203–204, 206–18
  state weakness as peasant strength in, xii–xiii
  white- vs. black-held land in, 201
Zvobgo, Eddison, 209, 213
Zweig, David, xii, 151–74